THE YOUNGER SELF LETTERS

HOW SUCCESSFUL LEADERS & ENTREPRENEURS TURNED TRIALS INTO TRIUMPH

MONARCH
CROWN PUBLISHING   PUBLISHING

ISBN: 978-1-7373222-1-4

CONTENTS

INTRODUCTION

Do you ever hear yourself saying... '*I wish I knew then, what I know now*'?

Imagine if you had the wisdom you have now, 10, 20, 30 or 40 years ago? How could that have changed your life?

In *The Younger Self Letters* you'll hear from an incredible group of leaders, visionaries, CEO's and entrepreneurs who have transformed obstacles into opportunities. Who used the fuel of the obstacles they faced to burn brighter, get stronger, tougher, clearer, fiercer, sharper, and more determined than ever to achieve their dreams and goals.

You'll hear from successful 6 and 7 figure entrepreneurs who have achieved incredible success such as:

- A Licensed Clinical Social Worker turned Life Coach who unleashed her as*-kicker attitude and who advises her younger self not to believe everything she thinks.
- An international intimacy expert who transformed her childhood trauma into the anointing of her feminine divinity, and transformed her marriage, with four children in tow.
- An attorney who made a huge mistake that almost prevented

her from graduating law school and the lessons she learned from that experience.

- A top tier Corporate Communication professional hears a voice that she will become a "corporate dance therapist"! and it all magically unfolds over 7 years, with her global coaching clients learning potent movement in their lives and careers!
- An executive coach, TED speaker, and bestselling author who sends a message in a bottle to her younger self about the six most important principles that will guide her throughout her life.
- A leading master success coach who gave it all up and was forced to confront the spiritual crisis of her life and business on her walk of 1000kms, and the subsequent wisdom that she gains on a life-changing journey that gives her the codes to success and wealth.
- Two entrepreneurs who used *energy* as their superpower to start a 7-figure innovation agency while on maternity leave— and then during a pandemic—founded a second company while running their first business, all while home schooling their children.
- An internationally acclaimed energy healer, spiritual coach, and bestselling author who founded the world's biggest spiritual multiplex enterprise, who teaches her younger self how past pain can be turned into fierce inner strength.
- A fearless mom to four children (including triplets), founder of 3 successful businesses, and wife of a career military officer, who knows how it feels to parent while submerged in stress, how to overcome and how to get the job done with humor and wisdom; who now teaches other parents how to do the same.
- A physical therapist-turned intuitive reader who discovers the true life-saving power of medical intuition in an acute hospital setting.
- A successful attorney turned full-time fiction writer who travels back in time to have a conversation with his younger

self through incredible and vivid stories of his childhood in Austria during the Hungarian Revolution.

- A survivor of childhood domestic violence – turned to drugs and alcohol to find reprieve from her trauma, thanks her younger self for all of the dysfunctional decisions she made that ultimately led her to a successful 6 figure business – supporting leaders, coaches and practitioners to clear their own addictions and learn how to hold space for themselves and their clients.
- An engineer turned Yoga Instructor who ignored her intuition for years and finally found the courage to follow it and create new adventures in her life as she learned to listen to her soul.
- A third generation entrepreneur who raised millions of dollars for nonprofits around the world, obtained her pilot's license, devoted her life to competing in marathons, overcame an eating disorder, and now coaches people around the globe in health and fitness.
- One of the Top 50 most influential men on LinkedIn and Top 50 most globally admired Indians, who overcame a difficult childhood, many life challenges and became an incredible leader.
- An entrepreneur who was bedridden and bankrupt from Lyme disease, that went on to build a 7-figure online company and became a minister teaching others how to prosper and create a life they love.

So, what are you waiting for? Turn the page and dig in!

CHAPTER 1

MICHELLE KULP

ear younger self,

You don't know it now, but you will become a prolific and successful writer and entrepreneur one day. The road to get there will be filled with numerous twists, turns, bends, barriers and roadblocks designed to create the character and characteristics you need to survive and thrive in this world.

The culture you were born into doesn't encourage listening to your intuition and embracing your soul voice. It aggressively ambushes a woman's connection to her insights, inspirations, and intuition.

And so, you will go on many detours that will take you far from your soul voice and light-years away from your authentic path.

You see, my dear, the deepest work is always the darkest.

Don't be afraid to look at the betrayals, wounds, pain, and disloyalties because once you can see them clearly, you can find true answers to your deepest questions. Once you see the truth, you will no longer be naïve.

Consciousness is the way out of the darkness and into the light.

You will have to fight persistently for your voice to be heard, decisions to be honored, truth to be revered, and intuitive powers to be unleashed and respected.

You will also discover the high price of being nice.

You have a *too-nice complex,* and you respond sweetly no matter who assails you. This complex results from your upbringing, but it is a dangerous game for sundry predators searching for women who are asleep and unaware of their true value.

Another struggle you will have to face is setting boundaries with others in your personal life and your business—as a woman without value, who has no boundaries, tends to over-give to the point of complete and utter exhaustion.

Those times of exhaustion, however, are turning points in your life and the places where you learn to say, *"Enough is enough."* There is power in those words.

You will learn to set boundaries, and they will set you free—it will free up more of your time since you won't be doing for others what they can do for themselves, and you will be free to speak your truth because your fear of abandonment no longer controls you.

You will arrive at a place where you don't care what others think, not in a callous or cold-hearted way, but in a way that honors your knowing, instinct, and intuition above everyone else's.

A Course in Miracles says, "You do not ask too much of life, but far too little."

You were taught that it was selfish to dream big and to *want what you want.* "Just settle for crumbs," they will tell you. And even if others don't say those words openly, that is what they mean.

Don't listen to those negative voices, whether they come from family, friends, or complete strangers.

Crumbs will never sustain you or fill you up, and eventually, the lack of sustenance will cause you to die.

You must keep expanding, evolving and growing; part of that process is having bigger dreams and being unapologetic for having them.

As an older and wiser you, I want to remind you that we see it like this...

10% of the world's population are quitters who don't even try—they've completely checked out. 80% of the world are campers who find a comfortable spot and camp out for life—they are neither too happy nor too miserable, but they only live at 50% of their potential. The remaining 10% are climbers and ascenders, and you are an ascender. You are always reaching for the next level in your personal life and your business; you will never be a camper.

Do not apologize for your ambition, drive, and big dreams.

The following quote by Theodore Roosevelt will inspire, motivate, and remind you of this:

"It is not the critic who counts; not the man who points out how the strong man stumbles, or where the doer of deeds could have done them better. The credit belongs to the man who is actually in the arena, whose face is marred by dust and sweat and blood; who strives valiantly; who errs, who comes short again and again, because there is no effort without error and shortcoming; but who does actually strive to do the deeds; who knows great enthusiasms, the great devotions; who spends himself in a worthy cause; who at the best knows in the end the triumph of high achievement, and who at the worst, if he fails, at least fails while daring greatly, so that his place shall never be with those cold and timid souls who neither know victory nor defeat."

Those who criticize and tell you they know best are the ones who are *not* in the arena, and their faces are *not* marred by dust, sweat and blood.

Yes, you will make mistakes and experience failures. Your sheer determination to learn, grow, and evolve will allow you to no longer see "failures as failures" but rather as *experiments* that move you closer and closer to your success.

As you learn to shed the voices of others and start tuning in to your intuition and instincts, some big shifts will happen in your life. You will:

- Leave a 17-year career in the legal field to follow your dreams of writing, teaching and speaking.
- Leave an unhealthy relationship and learn to be happily single and take care of your own needs.
- Shift from law to sales and double your income and your free time.
- Start your first online business and wonder why you didn't do it sooner.
- Become a newspaper reporter and learn the art and rhythm of writing through an amazing editor.
- Hire a transformational business coach who will help you triple your income in 90 days.
- Help hundreds of entrepreneurs and experts write their books and become bestselling authors.
- Write a book a month for an entire year as an experiment and then write a bestselling book about that experiment, *28 Books to $100K,* which will develop into a successful online program.
- Inspire others to write a book a month and reclaim their creativity and voices.
- Start doing interviews to share your wisdom with the world.
- Grow your business to multiple six figures and eventually to seven figures on your own terms.
- Become a Wall Street Journal bestselling author.
- Inspire others to believe in themselves and to find their true purpose in life.
- Honor your deep knowing.

Remember, do not consult your intuition only once; you MUST consult it every step along the way. Do not forget your intuition because it is not disposable.

Your intuition is the wand of knowing and will always guide you to the light of truth. Trust it.

Continually ask these questions to yourself:

- What do I want more of?
- What do I want less of?
- What must die so _____ can live?

Your intuition is the direct messenger of the soul, and you must communicate with it *daily* until it becomes second nature.

When you honor your deep desires, others may shun you because the idea is to force you to conform, and if you won't, they want you to perish.

An oppressed woman is a dead woman. You cannot fit into what others want you to be without dying.

Over the years, you will try to conform like a pretzel tied in multiple knots, but one day you will wake up and learn to stop tying yourself up in knots and you will follow your heart instead.

Remember, you must constantly fight for your freedom; it is not a "one-and-done" event.

Being 'good,' 'orderly,' or 'compliant' will cut you off from your intuition and knowing.

Defend your soul life with everything you have. It is your life, and it can be whatever you want it to be. Never give up your quest for an authentic life.

Live by the water because the water reminds you to be fluid, to move gracefully and assertively when needed. The water has a beautiful and natural rhythm that will sustain you in good times and in bad.

Covet your solitude and protect it against interruptions, intrusions, and invitations of others who want to derail and distract you from your dreams.

Now, dear one, I want to talk to you about something that you will struggle with repeatedly over the years: addiction.

You will be on what I am calling the *Addiction Merry-Go-Round*. As you overcome one addiction, another will covertly take its place.

Some of the addictions you will overcome are:

- Smoking
- Alcohol
- Toxic/Narcissistic men
- Underearning
- External Validation
- Fantasy thinking
- Technology

Many great artistic women including Janis Joplin, Marilyn Monroe, Billie Holiday, Judy Garland, Anne Sexton, Frida Kahlo, and Cheryl Strayed have struggled with addiction.

Sarah Hepola, a successful author with an alcohol addiction, talks about remembering 'the things she drank to forget' and described alcohol as the 'gasoline of all adventure.'

As you grow in consciousness, you will begin to realize that it is not about the 'substance' you choose, but this *pattern of addiction* and why you overindulge.

People typically think of alcohol or drugs when they hear the word *addiction*. But *work* can be an addiction, *shopping* can be an addiction, *negative thinking* can be an addiction, and *bad relationships* can be an addiction. An addiction is anything we do *unconsciously* to combat our soul's emptiness and starvation mode.

Time spent in captivity dulls your senses and confidence, causing you to lose your intuitive powers.

The good news is that you have fierce survival instincts, and you will always recognize when *"enough is enough"* as you battle one addiction after another.

Then begins the deep excavation work as you try to untangle the mysteries of why you are numbing yourself with alcohol, toxic relationships, and all your substances of choice.

The too-nice syndrome kicks in as you find yourself staying in bad relationships waiting for the good while overlooking the bad.

Being caged, trapped, and having to conform to a life you don't want and didn't choose causes you to escape into addiction. Trying to numb yourself and distract yourself never works long-term.

You will constantly try to prove your worth to others through over-giving and over-doing. Your worth is in your *being*, not your *doing*.

You will sever these addictions one by one and as you do, you will create a joyful, handmade life that no one can take away from you.

There are many cages and traps in the world. You will learn through hard work and determination to identify these traps and escape from the cages as you finally return to your wild nature—to the wild woman within.

You lost your instincts at a young age, as many women do. However, you must do the critical work of finding and reclaiming your lost instincts to survive and thrive in this world. Once you reconnect with your instincts, hold on to them with everything you have or you will once again be struggling with addiction.

When you leave the legal field after 17 years, you will be completely drained mentally, spiritually, and physically.

Part of your journey is learning to nurture yourself and fill yourself back up with things that matter.

Writing saves your life.

You discover that writing is your dream through a series of serendipitous events and go after it with everything you have.

Your writing is not an escape, but a way in which you can process life and understand yourself deeply while expressing yourself.

Journaling every day will reconnect you to your source of wisdom.

You will teach classes from Julia Cameron's book, *The Artists Way*, helping you reclaim your lost creativity and find the deep wounds that need healing.

You will learn to play like a child because creativity is play and because your lost artist is a child.

You will grow, and you will reclaim the magic of spontaneous expression.

Remember that growth is not a straight line; it is two steps forward and one step back. You may be capable of great things today, and tomorrow, you may slide backward a bit. It's okay.

Give yourself permission to be human and let go of the great lie of perfection.

As Julia Cameron reminds you: "*Perfectionism has nothing to do with getting it right. It has nothing to do with fixing things. It has nothing to do with standards. Perfectionism is a refusal to let yourself move ahead. It is a loop—an obsessive, debilitating closed system that causes you to get stuck in the details of what you are writing or painting or making and to lose sight of the whole.*"

You will, as many do, struggle with perfectionism and tell yourself it is just having "high standards" when the reality is that perfectionism is self-sabotage and just a sneaky way of staying stuck.

Through your writing, creative expression, and self-awareness, you will create a joyful, handmade-life you treasure.

To hold on to your joy and happiness, you may sometimes have to fight for it and do battle with anything or anyone that tries to take that away from you—even your own demons and self-sabotaging patterns.

You must remain vigilant. However, I want to remind you NOT to get stuck in that "fighter" identity you built in your time in the legal field. You have to learn that not everything means WAR, and sometimes you must know when to walk away.

Sun Tzu reminds you, "*He will win who knows when to fight and when not to fight.*"

Your knee-jerk reaction is to fight, but as you grow in consciousness and awareness, you will learn how *not to fight*; how to retain your energy instead.

Speaking of energy, young Michelle, it is paramount to have a morning routine that will nurture you in all of your days.

Begin your days with prayer, meditation, journaling, spiritual reading, yoga, and healthy green smoothies. Make sure to go out in nature and do not stay in front of the computer all day.

Technology, as you will learn, is a double-edged sword, and what it *giveth* to you in some respects, it *taketh away* in others.

Like many others, you have been seduced and are chained to your cell phone 24/7. It is critical for your sanity and creativity that you maintain technology-free days and blocks of time, or you will find yourself escaping from life by mindlessly scrolling on your phone.

You can write books or you can write emails and texts, the choice is yours.

Once you realize the insidious nature of technology, you will protect your writing time and creativity at all costs. You must train others not to expect you to be available 24/7.

Many great writers like Carl Jung and Mark Twain had their writing time and their writing space.

Carl Jung had a two-story stone house he named "The Tower," and no one was allowed in there without his permission. There was no electricity or heat in the Tower. Jung was not escaping from his family or his life in The Tower, but he retreated there to advance his professional career and do his *deep work*.

You must create a 'Tower' of your own, dear one—a place where technology is not allowed and not welcome, a place of solitude with no interruptions from the outside world.

You must also learn to take time off from client projects, and this will be hard for you, but you will make the transition in new and inventive ways. Doing this will give you your creative time back.

In elementary school, all of your teachers write on your report cards, "*Michelle daydreams too much.*"

Daydreaming is a great talent required to create and write books, so never think of it negatively as your school teachers mistakenly had you believe. You must prioritize your daydreaming and *deep work time*.

Mark Twain, a great writer, would write in a shed on his New York property so that he was isolated from the main house. Even in that era, great thinkers and writers knew they could not do their best work with fragmented time. They needed long blocks of solitude and uninterrupted time.

You do as well.

Be aware of the pattern of addiction that runs throughout your life. An addiction to technology and distraction is one that you will have to overcome again and again. It won't be easy since most others around you are addicted to their phones, television sets, and computers.

Remember, there is high value in people who can do deep work, so protect your time at all costs.

Life is about creating.

Many people who suffer from depression are not expressing themselves. You have found writing to be the best way to express yourself, so you must cherish your writing time and honor your creativity.

Creativity is about the unknown and moving into the mystery of yourself.

The creative process is about coming back to yourself and who you really are.

Always write, speak and honor your truth, and you will have a good long life that you will cherish.

Love always,
Your older and wiser self
Michelle Kulp

ABOUT THE AUTHOR

Michelle Kulp helps leaders, visionaries, CEOs, and entrepreneurs write Wall Street Journal bestsellers they can use to build their businesses and attract highly-aligned dream clients.

Michelle is the CEO and founder of the *Bestselling Author Program* and has written and published more than 20 bestselling books. She has also helped over 300 authors write, publish, and launch books that grow their business.

You can connect with Michelle at:

> *Website: www.bestsellingauthorprogram.com*
> *Facebook: www.facebook.com/michelle.bachteler.kulp and*
> *www.facebook.com/groups/28BooksTo100K*
> *LinkedIn: www.linkedin.com/in/michelle-kulp-732b8615*
> *Twitter: www.twitter.com/6figurewoman*
> *Instagram: www.instagram.com/michelle.kulp*

CHAPTER 2

ADRIANA MONIQUE ALVAREZ

ear younger self,

After years of studying every edition of National Geographic and International Living, your time to travel has come. Once you get on that plane to Tirana, Albania, nothing will ever be the same. You are 21 years old and this is when you decide who you wish to be and how you desire to move through your life.

YOU ARE ON A SPIRITUAL PATH

You will, for the first time, have space between who they expect you to be and who you really are. You will be on a wonderfully exciting journey of unlearning the behavior that earns you gold stars and what you would enjoy doing in the moment. Everyone you know is thousands of miles away and while this will create homesickness, it is also what provides you with the opportunity to get to know yourself.

You are about to experience the most wonderful years of your life, but

ow it. You will by and large experience it alone, and even
n home and tell your tales, no one will understand.
.....c is for you, not for them.

You do not actually enjoy religion and all that it includes. You neither appreciate the people that it attracts nor believe that you are in this awful world awaiting heaven one day. You are seeing that you create heaven on earth minute by minute. You will feel twinges of guilt as you realize this, but the joy that comes as a result will far out weight it.

Your deep and real connection to God will not diminish. Your heart and mind will finally open to what is possible once you let all the rules go.

Your inner knowing and premonitions will increase and you'll be shown snippets of what is to come. You will know when to go and come and when not to. You will know who to trust and who to avoid.

Trust this always.

You can also ask for miracles and they will happen.

YOU HAVE A PURPOSE FOR BEING HERE

No one will tell you this, but for being so young, you have a very good grasp of your true identity, your desire, and why your soul chose this life. You will not be good at articulating this in a way that makes sense to the average person though.

Part of you thinks you are here to take care of children in an orphanage. What you are figuring out is that loving people right where they are and simply being a strong and loving presence in their life is all you're being asked to do. You do not need to rescue them or attempt to alter the past.

Your light will illuminate the way enough for them to remember who they are and what they came here for.

Your love is enough.

You will see the transformations this creates, and the children around you will benefit, but most will never value this.

Make note of this, people will not understand you. They will never understand the idea of moving far from home to a place where you do not speak the language. They do not see this as exciting or fun. They will fear for your life even though you are safer than they are.

And remember this: people will try to control what they do not understand.

They will question your motives and wonder if you have anything in your head. They will criticize you for not going to college, getting a good job, and living the American dream.

You will be called irresponsible and you will lose your confidence in your gifts after some years and question your life purpose, but do not fear, you will find your way.

Yes, you will dedicate many years to proving yourself and showing you can make it in the real world. You will tick off all the boxes in your own way. You will be respected by many. You will then, from the position of "success," choose yourself because truthfully, the following and admiration do not fill the hole inside of you.

You will want nothing more than to be true to yourself.

You will listen to the words your ancestors and guides give you. You will return to the place of holding up your lantern and loving people back to themselves.

The good news is you will take the wisdom of this success journey with you back to your soul's work and no one will ever sway you again.

No one will ever knock you off your throne.

Your roots will grow deep into the heart of Mother Earth.

You will know how to live in this world you can see, taste, and touch, and you will have a more real and intimate connection to the unseen world than you can imagine.

YOU ARE MORE THAN ANYONE HAS EVER SEEN IN YOU

You will find that you are not nearly as helpless and frail as anyone has lead you to believe. You are incredibly capable and resourceful. You have a knack for always figuring it out. Your inner strength will stretch out and flex her muscles. Soon, people will begin to realize the soft exterior is paired with a steel determination that a thousand warriors could not deter.

It will feel like you spend a good chunk of your life begging people to take you seriously; to acknowledge you, see you, and listen to you.

The day will come when you let it all go and you will learn how to tap into your power.

Your power will fuel you. Most people fear power—or misunderstand it at best—but you will become very comfortable with yours. Once you are in your power, every word will be heard, and the world will respond to you differently.

The life you will lead is one that no one ever saw for you. You will defy the limits that were unknowingly set on you from a young age.

YOU ARE A TRAVELER

You do not travel; you are a traveler. Even though you come from a small town in the middle of nowhere and do not have anyone in your life that has decided to travel, you will find you are a natural at it. Exploring and going on adventures will unlock who you really are. It will inspire your best ideas and lead to your most meaningful relationships.

You will travel even after you have responsibilities: a husband, children, and a business. Once again, it will not make sense to those around it. It will feel absurd and they will say you are selfish and ruining your children, but trust me when I say you will look back with nothing but joy on those memories you created.

Whenever you feel as if life has become groundhog day or feel dull, get lost in an adventure. Go on a road trip. Visit somewhere new. Talk to strangers. Allow your inner compass to emerge. Feel the wind in your hair and the fire in your bones.

YOU CAME TO EXPERIENCE THE FULL SPECTRUM

You were raised in a culture that values positive emotions and experiences over negative ones. Even the names we give them convey some are good and others are bad. You will maintain this belief and will do your best to avoid frustration, impatience, worry, doubt, anger, sadness, loneliness, rage, guilt, and grief. This will work out well for you for a season and then three important people will enter your life and bring you face to face with each of these. The third will bring you to your absolute edge. Complete and utter despair will consume you like a raging fire.

You will question if you deserve to be here. You will lose all confidence. You will doubt everything you have ever done. You will sit in the darkness and there will be nothing anyone can do to save you from this experience because you chose it.

You came to experience the full buffet of life: the sweet, salty, bitter, and sour.

The minute you remember this, you will find your way through the long dark hallway that holds you captive. You will find a new perspective and by doing that, everything will shift.

When you cannot imagine that any good can come out of something, stand in a new place. Zoom out so you can see from a broader perspective, but most of all, immerse yourself in the emotion you are feeling. The more you attempt to escape it, the more aggressively it will hunt you down.

Be mad; be sad; be disappointed. Explore every nook and cranny of how it feels and communicate it and express it as thoroughly as you can. In doing this, you will become one with it. Instead of being in an opposing position, you will be on the same side and together you will move forward.

In the end, you will discover that your children—that you wanted more than anything—came to fiercely guide you to your soul's true calling.

YOU WILL BE VERY LUCKY IN LOVE

An aspect of your life that you are most curious about right now is if you will find the one and I have good news for you: you will. You intuitively know that you must be very careful about who you give your heart to.

Anyone who feels controlling, limiting, or confining, is not right for you. You will forever be a free bird and if someone wishes to cage you, it will not be good for either of you.

The best way to know if someone is worth your time and energy is to see what their initial reaction to your dreams is. If they discount them, discourage them, or attempt to distract you, they are not right for you in any capacity. On the other hand, if they love your dreams and never stand in your way, they could be a very good companion.

The one you ultimately give your heart to will not look good on paper. He will not make sense as a right fit to those around you, but you will know beyond any doubt that he is the one who will allow you to be wild at heart forever. He takes no pleasure in control. He has no desire to change you. He loves and accepts you exactly the way you are.

He will make you laugh and will show you how to tap into a deeper side; the strength you carry but have not fully acknowledged. He will have your back and can easily spot when someone is trying to take advantage of you. He will also teach you this skill so you can be street smart in all you do.

You will share many adventures all over the world and every day together will be good. Living with him will be easy and joy-filled, he will truly be your Sweetie.

YOU WILL DO EVERYTHING IN A UNIQUE WAY

You can already sense that you will not follow the path that most do. By getting on this plane, you are rejecting the notion that every straight-A student goes to college, gets a corporate job, and lives inside the white picket fence.

You will never get a degree and you will not need one. You will never hold a job for more than a few weeks, and you will not need one. You will create a sense of home and security in a very different way than most, but even in the path you choose, you will not do things like most.

For starters, you will start a business with your husband, work side by side every single day, and it will be a great experience. Most cannot imagine spending all day with their spouse, and it probably feels like a nightmare to imagine working with them.

You will also travel full time while running a business. You will arrange your work in such a way that you can do the things you enjoy all the time, not in a few vacation weeks a year.

You will also become a mother and work around your children. They will inspire you to work most efficiently and effectively. They will continuously remind you of what is most important and you will give them the gift of travel early.

In your business, you will not follow the gurus, although you will learn key lessons from a handful of teachers. You will be given two main guides along with your ancestors, Mother Mary and Nina. These two will give you clear guidance each morning and you will act in complete faith. They will share business ideas with you and will show you how to call in your absolute dream clients. They will teach you rituals that make your work feel effortless.

You have a knack for creating solutions and opportunities that people around you eagerly want.

It might sound silly but when you are excited, it is contagious and it will not matter what you are desiring at any moment, your passion and optimism will deliver everything to you on a silver platter.

Your word is truly your wand and you will learn how to spin stories and communicate daily with the Universe. This connection and communion trumps all.

YOU ARE A BRIDGE BETWEEN THE SEEN AND UNSEEN

Through a very unusual series of events, you will remember you are here to be a bridge between heaven and earth. Your words will serve as a reminder that the other side is not separate but deeply desires to co-create with humanity. The veil is thin and all you need is to ask for support from the unseen.

This honor and duty will be the biggest challenge for you because it could sound bizarre, but in the exact season that you are asked to step up, the world will be ready to listen.

The greatest unknown for humans is death and the other side.

Nothing is cause for more fear than these. When you show people how to communicate with those they love on the other side, it will change their perspective, and this can begin to dissolve.

By opening the dialogue and allowing the world to see how you communicate with your daughter Nina, you will help many to see it is safe to do the same.

The other side is more real than the one you can see and the support you have is vast.

When you stand as the bridge between heaven and earth, you create the way for many to experience heaven on earth.

No one is here to struggle, pay bills, and die in hopes of heaven.

Every soul is here to experience how sweet life can be; to know they are never alone; and that they contribute something of great value to the collective. Every soul is here to thrive, expand, and grow daily. Every soul is here to love and be loved. Every soul chose to be here and the only thing that matters is that we remember why we came.

The greatest work you will ever do is remind others of this.

Your path to do this work is through stories. Open your mouth and speak. The words will be given to you in the perfect way and timing.

You must shine your light. Do not dim it for anyone. Do not hide it under a bush. Do not play small.

When you speak, you will radiate pure light into the ethers and it will illuminate the path for those who are open to it.

Oracle SPEAK!

Sacred storyteller ARISE!

Beloved, break free. Be who you came to be!

ABOUT THE AUTHOR

Adriana Monique Alvarez is the CEO and founder of AMA Publishing. She's an international bestselling author and has appeared in Forbes, Huffington Post, International Living, Addicted2Success, Elephant Journal, FOX, ABC, and NBC.

She mentors high-level coaches, consultants, and service providers to start their own high-earning, global-impact publishing houses. She currently lives in the middle of nowhere in Colorado where she is renovating her grandparents´ home and learning to homestead with her husband Derek, and two sons, Sam and Grant.

Website: www.adrianamoniquealvarez.com
Freebie: www.adrianamoniquealvarez.com/how-to-start-your-own-publishing-company

CHAPTER 3

ANANDI SANO

ear younger self,

Little One, breathe. Allow the breath to flow deep within you. Do not be afraid. It is often in your sleep and in the moments of stillness that you will feel him around you. Feel the quietness that opens your heart and stops you from being afraid. Little One, I see you. I see you when you cry out in the night. I feel your loss, your pain, your hurt, your confusion in understanding your life—why you are here and why you have returned because it does not feel right. It feels as if being in this world makes no sense.

There are memories of where you have been, but there is confusion about where you are now. There are feelings of being lost; of searching for something else that you cannot quite grasp. And yet, when you walk into that temple in Japan at six years old, that moment of recognition will flow through you: a recognition of the energy, the peace, the stillness; a sense of being whole. That is what you feel and that is what you will seek all your life—not that you will grasp or comprehend this or put it into words.

Life will never feel quite right. Perhaps the hazy memories of where you have been before keep you from accepting this world. A yearning for that time you were a monk, and your daily practice was deepening peace. To then appear in this world that seems so busy, disconnected, and full of anger causes so much confusion. As you hit your teens, you will become even more fractured and there will never be a place of quiet within you, and you will start to fear life.

It will feel like everything around you is there to harm you, and so you will withdraw from experiencing life to keep yourself safe. Those years of traveling, moving every 18 months or less with the family, will deeply affect you. Moving to new countries, learning new languages, and trying to fit in will amplify the feelings of not being good or smart enough, and feeling like you do not belong.

Little One, I need you to know it is going to be okay, and in those moments of sadness when the endless tears flow, when fear feels like your only friend, know that you are held. Underneath it all, there will always be the presence of Source. When you fall, he will pick you up. When you cry, he will gently hold your tears. When you feel like you cannot go any further, he will gently push you forward. Know that everything is seen and heard, known, and understood.

I need you to remember this, Little One, and I need you to trust and accept. A lot will happen in your life; a lot of good things and a lot of not so good things. You will face fear and bullying and anger and violence but know that you rise beyond this. I am not going to say it will be easy, and most of the time you will have no sense of worth; like there is no reason for you to be in this world. And there will come times when it all feels like it is too much to bear.

But it is in those moments you must become aware that you are being held, being asked to move forward, and cradled in an energy that you do not yet recognize. You will move through life within different careers, and some will not align with who you are, but know that everything that is given, everything you will undertake has been given so that you can stand in a space beyond comprehension.

You will have brief moments in your life where you will feel the essence of Source and you will feel peace deep within you. There will be four specific periods in your life when you will enter a deep state of bliss, but they will not last, and you will shift back to a place that feels so dark, where all those feelings of not being good enough, the anxiety and depression, where images of past jobs as a paramedic and the trauma of life will flood you. Even when you feel alone or cry out in the night when that sense of loss and disconnect from self just feels like it is too much to endure, know that you are being held.

But I want you to always reflect on and carry with you how caring and compassionate, smart, gentle, creative, kind, and funny you are. Do not let anybody tell you otherwise. You will weave through life with careers in music, design, EMS, health and safety, management, consulting and building your own businesses and you will excel at everything you set your mind to. Do not be discouraged by those that say that you lack focus because the truth is: you are driven and guided. Every step filled with uncertainty has also been guided.

However, you will still struggle during all those years. There will be prolonged periods of ill health, but a wonderful by-product of one of those periods is that you will recognize that your life needs to change. Before this happens, earlier in the same year in 2012, you will be notified that your father is dying, and at this point, you will not have had contact with him in over 20 years. Do not be angry at him, Little One. He was so lost, and he was seeking a way to flee from who he was and the hurt and the anger that was within him. Allow that compassion within you to extend to him.

It will be difficult initially but allow that compassion and forgiveness to flow. You will need to resonate with compassion when you call him on his deathbed but be prepared to not understand what he is saying. He is so weak, and it will deeply affect you that you cannot be by his side. But you will connect with him one final time in the form of offering him an energy healing, because by now you have explored that part of yourself. Little One, in the moment you connect with Papa, something incredible is going to happen. You are going to feel a completely different energy, and that connection between you and Papa will open, but there will also be a connection between you and Source.

It will be like nothing I can even describe, and it will completely fill you. It will fill every corner that holds the hurt, the fear, the pain, the less than, the anxiety and the sadness and it will take it all away. And in that moment, there will only be this beauty and silence. Little One, I want you to know that this is the beginning of something bigger than you could have ever imagined. After this experience, you will feel things shifting around you and within your body that you will not understand, and these experiences will intensify, and you will feel a presence and an energy around constantly.

The strength of the energy will scare you at times, and it will turn your world upside down. You will try to figure out what these experiences are and try to understand what you feel and see, and eventually you will learn you are in a midst of a very intense spiritual awakening, and this will continue for approximately four years when your body, mind and spirit evolve. And then in 2016, when you think that life was already difficult enough, your world will come crashing down.

I need you to know that during this time, this next period, you will not realize that this is, in fact, the richest and most profound gift you will ever receive. You will try to fight it and to push everything away, and you will not understand it. In late 2016, you will start receiving guided messages from Source. They will be written and verbal but will make no sense whatsoever. And these guided messages will keep coming and will be accompanied by the most intense energy that will wrack your body with pain.

I know it sounds awful and painful, but you will get through this. At the end of 2016, whilst working with a client, you will suddenly see these expansive energetic vibrating layers that affect all human beings, animals, and our environment and you will also see that vibrating energetic components lie within these vibrating layers. These energetic components affect how we experience and react to life. They hold our memories, words, events—virtually everything—and when filled with low vibrating negative energetic components, they attribute to the appearance of disease, anxiety, pain, and other negative physical and mental reactions within our body and mind. Little One, I need you to listen to what Source tells you. I need you not to push away the information given.

You will not understand, but I need you to keep re-reading the guided messages, and I need you to allow those words to absorb into you and into that energetic part of yourself.

Listen to Source when he tells you to stop and work within your energetic layers. Do not push the moment away, because it is then that the energy becomes too strong, resulting in you being curled up into a ball in overwhelm and pain. And you will want to fight it, and you will scream for it to leave, but I need you to accept what is being given. The more that you are shown, and the quicker you can accept with calm acceptance, the deeper you can heal.

It will be a battle where you will choose to reject yourself and what is being offered. At times, you will think you are going mad, and there will be such low moments when you will think about leaving this world. But you will realize much later that Source was pushing you forward, because your purpose in life is to bring healing and a fast track to enlightenment and inner peace for others. It is that profound inner peace that you have always been searching for.

As you heal, and as Source guides you, the process accelerates and your PTSD disappears within three months with what is taught, and you start feeling less pain, anxiety, fear, and overwhelm. Just accept what is being given and do not fight any of it.

The more you focus on releasing those energetic life moments, those negative things that have bound you not only in this lifetime, but in other lifetimes, the more peaceful you become. The more your body heals, the more you will smile again, and the more you will have moments of peace within your life. You will stop fearing life. Approximately eight months after the guided messages have begun, Source will ask you to teach what you have been given and shown. And again, you will fight it, because you do not understand what you have been given, and you will feel like you are not worthy. And with that comes the thought: how can I teach this? I do not want to be someone that is seen as woo-woo. The fear of putting yourself out there and speaking the truth as it has been given is constantly in the forefront of your mind. You will not want to reveal who you are becoming or what has been happening to you. But it is your destiny. It is your purpose. It is why you are here; why you have been placed on this earth.

And it will not be easy. But as you heal, as everything becomes deeper, you will step into that space that you have been asked to stand, and you will teach others what you are shown. They will find a peace within themselves that they would never have thought possible. They will find healing that they have never experienced. You will continue your healing and your peace will deepen. The healing within your physical vessel will become deeper. Yet, the energy that flows through and around you will become stronger and more powerful. Little One, you will need to look after your physical vessel to carry this flow.

You will be affected by the strength of the energy deeply and there will come a point when you readily study the guided messages again and begin to understand them because now they have become a part of you. They will guide you in what is to come, where you will need to stand, what you will be capable of doing. And on your journey, you will be given unceasing information about healing, and you will teach and guide more people so that they too are able to heal themselves and others and step into peace.

Little One, there will come a moment when all you will feel is profound inner peace. You will become aware that everything else has ceased and this stillness and peace will be present from that time on. It will be like the stillness of a deep blue lake that becomes deeper and deeper. That inner peace that you were looking for becomes a reality, but it does not end there; it becomes even richer, more expansive, and deeper. And it is from that space that you will heal and awaken others in a profound way with your state of presence, the teachings given, and the energy that flows constantly through and around you.

It is the most beautiful and divine space to live, to feel the universe flow within you and through you, and know that everything that you have felt that has brought you pain, fear, anxiety, and such tremendous feelings of inadequacy will cease to exist. And as you step into that space, you will continue to be guided by Source and your life and a business will flow with abundance. The abundance has always been held for you and once you tap into it, the growth will be rapid and you will stand in that state of presence in every moment, guided every step of the way.

What I also need you to understand, Little One, is that everything you have done in your life, every single job has brought you to this moment of standing in the space with Source. All your skills matter. Do not listen to those who say you have not focused on one career. Do not listen to the people who try to pull you down. Do not listen to those who do not believe. Do not listen to those who say that you cannot sit in this continual flow. That it cannot be done.

When you first hear these words, I want you to read the guided messages again, because they will speak the truth and assist you to refocus. Everything has been given for a reason, but you will believe that things are progressing too slowly. In hindsight, this is far from the truth. One of the main reasons you believe this is the constant adjustments that your body needs to make to integrate the energy that flows through you as it intensifies.

It will become increasingly powerful, and it will need to take its time because your physical vessel must be able to withstand and integrate the energy that flows. With the intensity of the flow, as it is now, I would not have coped with it two years ago. You will need to follow what Source shows you because everything has happened for a reason. Source says, "Build the roots deep and then the branches will bear the fruit, and then the harvest will come."

Little One, I know how you always want to be invisible—you do not want to be seen—because being seen means that you could get hurt. Know all of this must change and within what has been given and what has been asked of you, there is peace and success. Allow the peace and the success to grow, hand in hand, it is all very real. It is a divine gift that anyone can have; it is our birthright.

When I see photos of you now and I look back to that time when you were around six, I see something in your eyes; like depth, wisdom, understanding, joy... That knowing or joy was not present in my eyes for so many years, but it has now returned. That peace, wisdom and that joy is back, and I want to thank you for everything you have done; for the strength that you have shown, the willpower and the stubbornness, and for the compassion and gentleness that carried you through all those years. I am so very proud of you, Little One. There is so much more to come. The guided messages speak of so much more. Many blessings to you.

ABOUT THE AUTHOR

Anandi Sano is the CEO of Peiec International and the founder of Peiec Energy Medicine and Peiec Approach for Business. She has been named the inner stillness specialist and is a speaker, author, master healer, inspiring teacher of spiritual transformation and sacred musician who offers others the opportunity to experience both high levels of success and profound inner stillness. Her profound yet simple teachings, programs and retreats have helped countless people throughout the world find inner stillness, self-healing, awakened states of consciousness, greater fulfillment, and abundance within their lives and business.

Anandi also works with conscious entrepreneurs, professionals, CEOs and athletes who have achieved high levels of success and find that they struggle to break the cycle of their fast-paced life and need assistance to move from a hyperdrive, high results state into other states that are more productive and sustainable to prevent burnout and chronic illness. As a result, her clients rediscover their inner stillness and brilliance and can recalibrate their nervous system so they can experience calm, clarity and the power to align their inner self with the practical steps to create sustainable high results with ease.

Website: www.anandisano.com
Email: info@peiecinternational.com
Facebook: www.facebook.com/anandisano
Instagram: www.instagram.com/anandi_sano

CHAPTER 4

ELEONOR AMORA MARKLUND

ear younger self,

It may feel as if you are standing in the middle of a tornado right now, but just remember, this too shall pass. You may think you are worthless and that the pain within your soul is so excruciating you must do anything to stop it, and I know that you did what you thought was right when you swallowed the sleeping pills to end your life. Right now, you are lying in the hospital bed, crying, because all that you want is to go back to the void where your soul rested the moment you stopped breathing. You don't understand the magnitude of this moment yet, but you will.

The floor is moving, and sometimes a clear thought is processed in your mind as the toxins get cleansed out of your system. You think you are experiencing delirium, but in reality, you are seeing the building blocks of the Universe shifting, and when the time comes, you will harness this power and use this gift to create miracles. You are now, and have always been, a miracle. Not only because you came back from the dead but also because you were born.

If I could, I would wrap my arms around you and carry you out of the hospital, away to some far-off island where you could rest and heal. But I know that the coming year is something you must endure, even if it happens to be the worst year of your life.

Just one year from now, you will be free from the hell you are living in. Even though he tries to scare you and make you think he will find you and kill you, he won't. He doesn't hold that kind of power. A truly strong man will never try to break a free-spirit like you, and deep down you believe this. When you feel the strength and will to keep going, this, my love, is your soul, your inner self speaking, which can never be bent or broken. The anxiety that is eating you up inside right now will ultimately be the catalyst to your freedom. I want you to realize that you have an inner core frequency that is always unaffected by the events surrounding your reality because you are whole at your center and nothing—*nobody* —can take that from you.

No matter what society may lead you to believe, you matter, you belong, you are enough, and you are capable of achieving your wildest dreams.

When he said you could not survive without him, he was wrong, and you will prove him wrong thousands of times over, in thousands of different ways.

I know it feels like you will never find yourself again.
That you are broken and lost.

But I promise you this: you will sing on big stages again and you will empower millions of people. All of this will be made possible because of your commitment to being true to yourself, sharing your life experiences and owning your voice unapologetically with courage, strength, and authentic expression. Don't ever let your voice be silenced again. It is necessary for the evolution of humanity, and the lives you will touch in the process of coming home to yourself.

As you move through life, you will inevitably be faced with obstacles, some which may feel monumental, especially as you navigate the unknown world around you. But don't let others' opinions or expectations keep you small. You have a fire burning within yourself for a reason, and it is up to you to stoke it, feed the flames, and use the heat to catapult you forward into the life you're destined to lead.

You may have times when you feel lost, alone, like a square peg trying to fit into a round hole. But keep the faith.

There is a reason your soul yearns for more.

And it's not a coincidence that you're feeling the growing pains of being human—because you are so much more than that. And most of all, I want you to know you were never alone. I am always with you – holding your hand, in the dimension where time and space do not exist. The chorus of the Angel's will be heard once more, and they will guide your inner voice during times of hardship and beyond.

Growing up in a small Scandinavian community, you will be surrounded by people who love the simplicity of small-town living. This will only further prove that you are 'different'- own it!

There is freedom in expressing your truth.

In telling your story. Never feel that you are not worthy because of your past. Your past helped you get here and will guide you to where you want to go. I am always right here supporting you, cheering you on, and loving you forward!

When I close my eyes, I can vividly remember the feelings that consumed me for years; something that is now a memory that you will experience firsthand as you navigate the world around you. Even as I write this letter to you now, I feel a lump forming in my throat as I reflect on the loneliness and sadness that once held me back and made me a victim of a narcissist. All the stress of trying to fit in, to be perfect for others, working to conform to be what 'they' wanted... all of that energy will leave you feeling like a shell of a woman, unrecognizable and anxious to the point that you won't know where your anxiety begins and where you end. But when you take charge of your life, all of that anxiety will stop and you will see and feel like yourself *fully* for the first time.

You will finally feel free in your mind, body, and soul.
Welcome home!

You are not the labels others give you or labels you choose to wear based on others' opinions of you. Freedom comes when you release the grip of what you think you should do, who you think you should be, how you think you're supposed to act—all based on outside influences—*and learn to harness your sovereignty and reclaim the power that's always been within.*

It's said that we are often born into the environment that will best support the path meant for our highest growth, unveiling our biggest lessons and often some pretty hard-to-swallow heartache in the process. Even though you are in the process, don't allow it to dim your spark, for you are the light the world needs. And whether or not you see it now, the magic you've kept hidden behind your silence, sadness and confusion is the very thing that will allow you to lead others back home to themselves and make the difference you came here to make.

*You will not only survive but also thrive, as your light will manifest into the success you've always dreamed of, **so keep going!***

As you manage out of your marriage, you are going to realize that this experience was just part of a deeper wound, originating from the patterns in your upbringing. You may feel like the black sheep of the family— embrace this! Being born into a prominent family comes with its set of obstacles, but *you are strong* and will navigate it beautifully, although you may feel messy at times. It's okay! You may feel like the expectations of your parents and society are too much but trust me when I say it's all perfect. As you evolve into the woman you are meant to be in the world, you will realize that you have the power to release anything not serving you (including any perceived expectations from the outside world) and instead, shift your mindset to align with your purpose and mission. This is your superpower—use it!

She is fierce and perfectly flawed. She is enough. She is worthy. She is you. And you, my indigo girl, are beautiful, whole, and capable of all that your heart desires simply because you exist.

I tried to be perfect. God, did I try. Repeatedly, you will twist and bend your truth, doing whatever you think you need to do to fit into the box society has built for you. But it will only get you a front-row seat to the 'People Pleasers Hall of Fame'! No matter what you do, you will never feel capable of reaching the standards others have set for you and you will feel the lingering, often unspoken, disappointment of your family in the process of your own becoming. Whether or not the disappointment is real, it is the story you've come to believe and with that, the additional weight of your own disappointment in yourself will be unbearable.

But here's the deal. You will go through different experiences in your life. Some will feel magical, while others will leave you gasping for air. I know because I have experienced those very emotions myself, along with many others. And you know what? Every time, I have made it out stronger and better. I've proven to myself (most importantly) that I am far more capable than I credit myself for. Please don't confuse any of what I am telling you here to mean that life should (or will) be easy. It won't!

But the work you put in, always and forevermore, is worth it because you are worth fighting for!

I would be lying if I said the path to discovering and coming home to yourself isn't scary; it absolutely is!

It's about the commitment to self and providing your soul the love you give so freely to others so that you trust yourself enough to leap, even when it's scary, and continue choosing yourself in every situation.

You have been involved in relationships that leave you empty and insecure, and yes, there will be a few more relationships before you find your harbor—but this last one was the worst. They will get better and better. Every relationship will show you how far you've come in healing old subconscious beliefs. Eventually, all the stagnant mental blocks that you are carrying around in your backpack will fall away, and you will see yourself just as I do.

You will finally see that you are destined for more and you will refuse to settle any longer. "Enough is enough!" will become your mantra, and for the first time, maybe ever, you will say, "fuck it!" to outside influences and become an entrepreneur at 32 and you will never look back! You won't care what your family thinks or what society thinks... you will just know it's your time to shine and you will be ready to be ridiculously happy! Because of this decision that will feel so aligned to your heart, and because you were brave enough to take wild and messy action, regardless of how it might look to others, your life will be nothing like how it had been for the three decades prior... and you won't be either.

Ultimately, it's about being your own best friend, finding the center within yourself, learning to love and accept yourself as you are and trusting in your ability to make it all happen. Thinking that we need validation and approval from anyone other than ourselves keeps us stuck in a box of mediocrity. Indecision and fear lead to inaction and clip our wings as our soul begs to soar above the clouds and experience all that life offers.

Your dreams, voice, and purpose are just as important as everyone else's.

Tune in, listen closely, and become a master at honoring your soul's whispers. They will never lead you astray.

For the empaths, we have so many inputs from the outside world that we often confuse our own internal thoughts and beliefs for that of others. Entanglement is a slippery slope, which makes it that much more important to know yourself at the deepest level, and learn to trust your soul, even when you can't fully explain it. When you aren't free in your energy field, it's hard to remove yourself from others' opinions. When you honor yourself and release the myriad of energies begging for your attention, your internal environment will soften and become quieter, giving you room to hear your truth and feel into your personal power. Harnessing this skill will help you see that all the years of telling yourself the story that you were a disappointment wasn't accurate. In fact, this belief will no longer exist within, and because of this, it will no longer exist externally either. Your new, more empowering story will become of triumph, possibility, resilience, and success. And your courage will make it so.

I want you to close your eyes and think of your internal power like a satellite tower. All day long, you're getting pings from all over the place and it can be downright exhausting! But what if you could be your own source of energy, thus creating your own reality instead of relying on others to fuel you and dictate what's possible for you?

The good news is you can!

Your internal compass is not by mistake. Trust yourself, for you know more than you may realize. The more you lean on your understanding and knowing, the easier it will become to follow your 'pings' and in doing so, pave the path necessary to achieve your wildest dreams. You are limitless, we all are! Don't worry about trying to fit in. Maybe you don't, because you were born to stand out and lead others with your divine purpose and magic. Trust yourself, and your ability to fly, my indigo girl. I promise you, you can have, be, and do it all.

You want more out of life, so grab a hold, enjoy the ride, and make it happen! If you don't allow yourself to try because of a limiting mindset and false beliefs that say, "if I fail, it will be the worst thing in the world," you will never reach your pinnacle of influence. Success is your birthright! Somewhere inside of yourself, you already know that although you're surrounded by simplicity, it isn't the life that's meant for you. You may feel suffocated by this environment, and your 'differences' may make you feel isolated. It will take you a long time to understand that being different is a gift. And the uniqueness that *is you* is what will continue to set you apart from others—and this is a good thing!

Successful leaders must be willing to be different, to take a stand for what they believe in, and to show up even when they're afraid.

Embrace your unique self. This level of happiness is available, and I want you to experience it all!

Had you not allowed your mindset to shift and jumped into the fear that had once felt paralyzing, you would not have been able to create the life you are living now; one that feels so cosmically aligned. Everything you have been through is going to be worth it. You may wonder, how can being beaten and having your soul crushed repeatedly be worth it? It will be those moments that allow you the compassion and capacity to help others heal their wounds and live freely. What you recall as sudden flashes or words from voiceless energies is really just your destiny unwinding. The pieces of your soul that you thought were broken for good will heal. You will see that all of this had to happen for what remained to come together with other incarnations to create a new form, so that you could become more you than you have ever been. There will come a time soon when the void will speak directly to you and show you how to use the energy of this new creation that is you, to harness your power from within. You will learn how to use your gifts as the light that they are, shining brightly to be seen even from eons away.

I believe in you, and I know that even though the road may look far and winding, your journey as your *true self* has just begun. In your future and my present time, you have incredible clients from all over the world. You have saved so many lives by teaching people about the illusion of the matrix and the core frequencies you are going through right now. You will have it all; a devoted and loving husband and beautiful children. But best of all, YOU made this happen through learning to tap into your intuition and trust your inner guidance to lead you towards your truth. You are finally living life on your terms because *you opened yourself up to the fear, leaned into courage, and chose more for yourself.*

You will thrive and become the hero of your own life—all because you chose the path less traveled and tapped into the gifts that have always been inside, the ones you are questioning at this exact moment in time.

The Universe has a plan for you, my beloved Indigo girl...trust it and watch the magic unfold.

ABOUT THE AUTHOR

Eleonor Amora Marklund is an internationally acclaimed expert in energy healing, highly esteemed as the forefront coach for spiritual warriors known as Indigos. Renowned for her groundbreaking work in esotericism, Eleonor is an award-winning international best-selling author who has published over ten bestsellers.

With over 25 years of experience as a therapist, Eleonor has been featured for her authority on energy work and the Indigo awakening on television, podcasts, radio, and in magazines. Her award-winning publications on the intersection of womanhood, entrepreneurship, and metaphysics have achieved critical acclaim.

As a spiritual philanthropist and innovator, Eleonor founded the House of Sovereignty multiplex enterprise where she is committed to changing lives through exponentially expanding and strengthening her community of spiritual rebels. Her publishing and media arms help readers connect to the Universe and their consciousness on a deeper level.

Website: www.houseofsovereignty.com
Instagram: www.instagram.com/eleonor_amora
Clubhouse: www.clubhousedb.com/user/eleonoramora

CHAPTER 5

EMMA TURTON

ear younger self,

You're 42 right now, sitting in the hospital waiting room with your family. You feel like your still-beating heart has been ripped out of your chest and held up for the world to see. Only a few hours ago, you answered questions fired at you by a young doctor as you watched the medical team desperately resuscitate your dad who lay broken and intubated on a narrow hospital bed in the emergency department. Trying to make sense of what's happening, you wish your ears weren't still ringing from last night's Prodigy concert.

I know it's hard to believe that his fall off a children's scooter while playing with your son at the park could have done this much damage to your irrepressible dad. Only a week ago, he was climbing Bluff Knoll in the mountains with your mom—mountains that you would find hard to climb. He's unstoppable. He's a legend on the scooter. He taught both of your other boys to do tricks on theirs. But this time, he wasn't wearing his helmet. And for reasons you'll never know, he fell and hit his head.

As you sit there shell-shocked, waiting for news about the brain surgery to save his life, I want you to know you are not alone. Your mother and your brother are with you, yes, but more than that; your ancestors are with you. Your guides are with you. Your whole energetic support team is with you.

EVEN IN THIS, YOU ARE SUPPORTED

This moment is activating you beyond what you could possibly imagine. If you knew what I know now, you wouldn't feel so afraid.

Up until now, you felt like you were expanding your work as a medical intuitive. Having left your career as a university lecturer and conventional health professional to answer your soul's calling, you've been stepping up year after year to grow and expand in new ways; serving clients, creating courses, and becoming more visible. Only this week, you started teaching your first medical intuition training course to an excited group of students.

A long time coming, this course barely scratches the surface of what you will create because of what will unfold over the next few weeks.

Only yesterday you delivered your first masterclass for this course before you went to the concert with your friends. And today you sit here in the special hospital room where families wait for hours on end to find out if their loved ones have survived surgery, holding your breath.

I see you, my dear. I feel your heart hurting.

You are wondering what it's all for, aren't you? If life is in such a finite balance and can be taken away at any time then what's the point? You are doubting life. Doubting yourself. Doubting the relevance of your work. You work in health, and yet it all feels frivolous and meaningless in this context. Fluffy spiritual stuff that's only good for minor health issues.

But I want you to hear me when I tell you that it's not.

I will share with you what will unfold over the next few days, weeks, months, and years that will reinforce to you the importance of this one phrase:

TRUST YOUR INTUITION, NO MATTER WHAT

Not only when it's easy. Not only when it makes sense. Not only for the minor, frivolous, almost meaningless things.

Trust your intuition at all times.

In all contexts and settings. No matter what.

You've honed your intuition like muscles you exercise daily in a strength training program, just as you teach it to your students. Your intuition is strong. It guides you true. It has led you through some of the toughest times in your life; from health crisis through to divorce. It has also guided you to some of the most exquisite events of your life; from reconnecting with your childhood sweetheart to building the business of your dreams. And it has served your clients incredibly well to identify and heal the parts of them that were crying out for healing and to change their lives as a result.

Your intuition will continue to guide you, even though today has shaken you to your core. Even though it has you questioning everything you stand for. Even though, right now in the hospital, you aren't even sure if you can still hear your intuitive guidance or if it's even a real thing.

My dear, this is just the beginning. In the next few days, your intuition and your willingness to believe and to allow it to guide you will be tested to the extreme. And your dad's life will depend on it.

You will feel helpless and alone.

But, in truth, you will be powerful and supported. You just don't know it yet.

You will be the one who will save your dad's life, more than once. Guided only by your intuition.

The skilled neurosurgeons will do their best to save your dad. They will stop the bleeding and piece his poor broken head back together. Twice.

They will ask you questions that a daughter should never be asked about her dad: about whether to end his life right now by deliberate starvation, dehydration, or suffocation or to try and salvage some of it, not knowing what that salvaged part might look like. This will be the hardest decision you'll have ever made in your life and it will break your heart in two.

The medical team will speak to you about logic. About statistics. About his age. About expectations and being realistic... They will tell you, after seven days, that it is 'very, very unlikely he will EVER wake up from his coma,' and if he does, that there is a 'very, very high likelihood of him having moderate to severe disability.' They will ask you to make a decision—one that will tear your grieving family apart as you all argue your case on behalf of your unconscious dad.

You'll wish you could ask him what he wanted. His end-of-life plan didn't account for this situation; it didn't say how much disability he'd be happy to live with. Only if there was a chance for survival, to give him that chance. If only he could let you know if he was still there, inside his comatose body.

You make a discovery that changes everything while sitting by his bedside in the intensive care unit. You learn that you can use your intuition to connect with your dad.

You can use your intuition To guide your decisions.

You intuitively connect with him like you do with your clients and you feel him still in there, despite the EEG findings. He is just deep, deep down in the murky pool of his coma, unresponsive and hard to reach but he's still there and you can see it.

On that most difficult of days on Day Seven, you and your family will share your fears and heartbreak over what has happened and what horrors might still be coming, and you decide to keep the ventilator on. You begin to learn to advocate for your dad, not just as a family member should.

You learn to advocate, guided by your intuition.

Far from being irrelevant in that acute healthcare setting, you'll learn the hard way that following your intuition in the hospital is the most relevant it has ever been in your life.

Two days after deciding—as a family—to keep the ventilator on, your dad wakes up from his coma. He won't wake from the sharp pain of objects regularly pressed into his fingers and shins by doctors looking for a response. He will wake because he hears your mother's voice pleading quietly in his ear, asking him to open his eyes if he can hear her. Against all odds, he will claw his way back up from the dark recesses of his consciousness and open his eyes to her familiar, loving voice, surprising every single member of his medical team.

You will be right. He WAS there the whole time.

But he's most certainly not out of the woods yet. At that point, you will push your intuitive guidance aside as irrelevant once more and focus on what the medical team tell you about his prognosis and rehabilitation. You still haven't learned your lesson about how important following your intuition is in an acute health setting.

Dad's observations will begin to change. He won't respond and recover as quickly as they expect, now that he's awake and becoming alert. You'll wake up one morning, before going to the hospital, with a pain in your lower belly. It will feel uncomfortable when you go to the bathroom but you'll dismiss it as a sign you're not drinking enough water while you spend every waking hour at your dad's bedside. You'll hope it isn't a urinary tract infection brewing, and resolve to drink more water.

But you're missing the signs that usually tell you when your physical symptoms aren't yours. Intuition can be received in many forms. Your intuition sometimes comes in the form of physical symptoms and signs. They aren't yours, and they release as soon as you become aware of why they're showing up and whose they are. And now that you've connected intuitively with your dad and started advocating for him, you've set up a highway of connection with him to speak on his behalf.

But you still don't trust it.

And when the nurse wonders why his temperature is up and why he is a little groggier than he's been, you'll keep quiet. You won't say what your intuition is guiding you to say: He has a urinary tract infection.

You'll instead doubt yourself and think, "who am I to say this to her? I'm just a grieving family member. How would I explain it anyway? Besides, it's probably not that. I'm just thinking that because my bladder feels weird today."

Just over a day later, as he slips backwards on the consciousness scale, they will finally diagnose your dad's urinary tract infection and start him on the right antibiotics. Stunned, you'll kick yourself and think, "I should've said something. I knew, and I didn't say a word." Your elusive symptoms disappearing as soon as his diagnosis is made.

You had believed your intuition wasn't useful in intensive care. But you were 100% wrong. You're gaining confidence now.

Dad will then start to improve and they'll decide—too quickly—to discharge him from intensive care and send him to the neurology ward.

When he arrives, you know something is wrong. Mom suspects it, too. He's chronically drowsy and sleeping. His new ward nurse is dismissive: "Oh, that's completely normal. He's just recovering."

Connecting intuitively with your dad, you know in an instant that his brain is suffering—that he's in trouble—but the ward doctor dismisses your concerns. She tries to placate you, telling you to go home: "He's fine! Come back tomorrow. He just needs rest,"

Right in that moment, you realize you need to take a stand.

You need to trust your intuition. Not only when it suits you, but always.

You explain to your exhausted, worried mom that she needs to be on board with what you do next since she's the next of kin. She agrees after a little hesitation. She's very concerned, but she doesn't want to make an unnecessary fuss. Dad's failing condition soon convinces her, however, and she's prepared to stand her ground with you.

You stay quietly by your dad's bed after visiting hours end. The staff don't notice you're still there, waiting for the ward doctor to leave. When she's gone, you ring the bell for the nurse. "Page the on-call doctor," you instruct him. "Something's wrong with my dad. He needs another scan." The nurse blinks. Confused, he does what you ask.

The on-call doctor must attend when called. With a new set of eyes on your dad and his medical file and with you advocating for him, they finally call his surgeon who books another scan of his head. Sure enough, he is in the early stages of a serious stroke—a consequence of having had a hemorrhage around his brainstem. No one had noticed the signs. Untreated, this stroke would either kill him or leave him in a permanent vegetative state within hours.

This time you held firm in your belief in your intuitive guidance and took a stand for your dad in response to it.

YOUR INTUITION IS SPOT ON

They immediately transfer him to another hospital where specialized neurovascular surgeons can operate on the blood vessels of his brain and stop the stroke.

A couple of days later, it happens again.

This time you'll be ready, and your mom will stand by your side and agree without hesitation. With your encouragement, she will be the one who courageously speaks up and insists on another scan.

And the doctors will listen this time.

Sure enough, they'll need to operate on his brain a fourth time to stop another severe stroke they hadn't seen coming. The operation will be successful.

Intuition will save your dad's life. Again.

Each of these events will boost your confidence in your intuition and allow you to trust it more and more. Through the trauma, you'll learn just how valuable crystal-clear intuition is in an acute health setting.

You will learn to trust your intuition 100%

...no matter whether you're in a medical intuition session with a client or in intensive care, surrounded by skeptical health professionals.

You'll no longer care if your intuition goes against the grain with doctors, nurses, or other health practitioners. You'll trust it and be willing to take a stand for it.

All this time, you had been believing that intuitive guidance was great for minor questions or problems like why your knee pain has flared up, why you have a headache, or whether you should go on that retreat.

You thought intuition wasn't what mattered when it came to the crunch in hospital. That logic, statistics and reason were all that mattered in an emergency. That's what you were taught at university, after all.

But you couldn't have been more wrong.

Just think of how much more effective our medical teams would be if they were trained to use their intuition this way, combined with their logic and reason. How many more lives could be saved? What if they viewed their patients as whole beings, with a soul and a body, and could see and understand that our choices, fears, and beliefs are inextricably linked to illness or injury appearing in the physical body?

The health system as we know it would completely change; doctors trusting their nudges with the courage to speak up and act quickly and nurses feeling supported when they share their intuitive knowing about their patients.

And patients, as the central focus of their care team, being treated and respected as whole beings.

My dear, all of this will stem from this time of deep soul-searching and intuitive exploration after your dad's fall from the scooter.

It will be what gives you the confidence to create your ground-breaking Medical Intuition Practitioner Training course. You'll teach people how to use their intuitive eye professionally like you do to see inside their clients and identify the root causes and deeper meanings of their health and life issues so they can guide them to heal from within.

This can be taught. you are the one to teach it.

You are the embodiment of science merged with spirituality. Your first-hand experience on both sides of the hospital setting combined with your complete newfound trust in your intuition will set you up to create a world-changing course that doesn't downplay medical intuition to something only good for party tricks or looking up spiritual meanings on a chart. Instead, it will honor the role of intuition as vital to the care of the client in any setting, and understand its scope of practice so as to keep the client in safe hands.

You are ready to give it all up as you sit in that waiting room. To give up everything you hold dear. To give up your business and your belief in medical intuition. All of it. To just walk away and never look back.

But what happens in the weeks that follow only serves to strengthen your resolve that the health system needs to change and fortifies your belief and trust in medical intuition.

You step forward from this point in your life to create a wave of change that will sweep across the globe.

So this moment that feels as though it has knocked the wind out of you will be your making in so many ways.

Your beloved dad will spend a long time in hospital rehabilitation, but will come out the other side of it walking, against all his doctors' and physiotherapists' predictions. He will still crack dad jokes and offer sage advice, like he used to. He will be altered, but he will still be Dad. You will have the gift of more precious time with him.

Thanks to you trusting your intuition.

You've got this. You are deeply supported. Feel into the energy that surrounds you and draw strength from it. I am holding you as you journey through this dark night of your soul to discover the true unlimited potential of your intuition.

Love, Emma. xx

ABOUT THE AUTHOR

Emma Turton is a leading international medical intuitive and founder and director of Medical Intuition School. A rare combination of health-science nerd and intuitive bad-ass, she sinks her teeth into the place medicine and metaphysics meet. Emma uses her powerful intuitive eye to see inside people and guides them to heal from within, using medical intuition as a compass for life and health.

A two-time international #1 bestselling author and award-winning university lecturer with 20+ years of clinical experience as a physiotherapist and nutrition coach, Emma teaches a world-class IICT Approved Medical Intuition Practitioner Training course set to change the global paradigm for health and spirituality.

Connect with Emma here:

> *Website: www.medicalintuitionschool.com and www.emmaturton.com.au*
> *Facebook: www.facebook.com/emmaturtonhealth*

CHAPTER 6

FIONA STEVENSON & SHELLI BALTMAN

ear younger selves,

You don't know each other yet but you will meet in 2012 and recognize that you are destined to work together. While on maternity leave (coincidentally, at the same time!), you will co-found an innovation agency, which will become one of the fastest-growing agencies in North America. And then, six years later, during a pandemic, you will found a second company—built around your shared passion for energizing people—which you will create while pivoting your first business, home-schooling your children, and dealing with some of the biggest personal and professional challenges you have ever faced, all while spending 16 months in lockdown at home, with virtually no in-person contact with anyone outside your immediate family.

We're sure it all sounds a bit surreal. (It does to us too!)

But all of this will be possible because of your virtually boundless energy. You don't know it yet, but one day you'll realize that energy has been the driving force behind every success in your life.

So, what we want you to know more than anything else is this: energy is the key to everything!

Energy is the physical, emotional and mental fuel you have to do the things you want or need to do—and it matters, both in life and in work, because it is the key to creativity, problem solving, and influence, and the foundation of strong relationships. When you're in an energized state, you're more generous and fun, you have more ideas and solutions, and you make better decisions.

And decisions matter.

In the end, your lives are just a reflection of the decisions you make. And if that's true, don't you want to make the best decisions possible? That's why, more than anything else, you need to focus on growing and cultivating energy, wherever and whenever you can.

But where to start?

Get attuned to your energy: find out what makes you glow

If we could suggest one core principle, it would be to work out which things give you energy early—start now!—and learn to follow those signals. If you find an activity, a job, or anything at all that brings you energy, you're more likely to devote time to it, practice it, and eventually become great at it! Achieving your dreams happens when you put in the hard work—trust us on that one—and that hard work can take a lot of energy.

When you see someone pursuing their true purpose, you'll almost be able to feel the energy that comes from them. They glow!

At times, you will get sidetracked by the expectations set for you by society. You won't always invest sufficient time and focus on the things you love to do because they may not seem practical. As humans, we're often taught to work hard, to study hard and to get a good job so that we can buy a nice house, a nice car and nice things. But you will learn that the happiness that comes from material possessions is fleeting.

So, don't let shiny objects sidetrack you along the way!

True happiness is going to come from filling your lives with the experiences that bring you energy. From creating a life where you get to do things every single day that bring you joy. From finding your glow.

Use energy to find your passion and purpose

Some people are lucky and discover what their passion and purpose is early in life. And, if they're even luckier, they might also have the talent, privilege and perseverance to succeed in that chosen field.

But what about the rest of us?

You're going to hear many people tell you that you're supposed to find, and then follow, your passion—which makes it sound like your passion is a fully formed thing you can hunt around for and recognize instantly. But that isn't always how it happens! Sometimes finding your passion takes time. Sometimes it's more about working out what brings you energy and then going through a long, winding process of learning, experience, encouragement, mentorship and growth that slowly but surely evolves into a passion—or passions!—over a long, long time (sometimes years!)

The key to finding your passion is tasting different experiences. Try everything once! Spend time traveling, meeting different people, trying different activities and—this bit is important—making mistakes. Invest in experimenting, so that when you get to the other side of your next great adventure, you can work out what draws you back, and keeps your interest, and starts to show you the embers that could one day be your glow.

Ask yourself this: what would you do if you had to do it for free, with nobody watching and with no recognition?

Now, that doesn't mean that we're suggesting simply turning your favourite hobby into your work. Sometimes a hobby is just fun, and that's OK!

But spend time experimenting, and then using those experiments to spot your energy signals—when you're enjoying yourself so much that the rest of the world disappears, when you want to learn every single thing about something, or when you just absolutely have to try that thing again. When you feel the first glimmers of that glow.

Finding your true purpose starts with that spark, that glimmer of interest! And then, with time and exposure, learning and support, mentorship and experience, that spark can one day grow into a purpose.

Energy: Your superpower

There was a time in our lives when we didn't understand the value of energy. Maybe that's right where you are now!

One day, your university classmates will recognize energy as your special characteristic in a yearbook feature. When this happens, it will make you feel you somehow aren't enough—because you won't yet recognize its value.

If that hasn't happened to you yet, then do one thing for us: don't let it make you feel that way!

Because energy will become your superpower!

No matter what you're pursuing in life, energy will get you further. It will be a multiplier of your performance and your persuasiveness. Over the years, your energy will help you to punch above your weight and to achieve more than your skills and circumstances alone were ever supposed to allow. And, eventually, when people tell you they love your energy or that you make them feel energized—you will take it as the highest compliment.

Energy drives your belief in your abilities and the belief that others have in you. It fuels your optimism and helps you to fill in the gaps in your capabilities with moments of brilliance. It is that indefinable 'X-Factor' that grabs hold of opportunities and that gets you over the finish line.

Lightning bolts vs. sponges: the lightning always wins

Here's a secret. There are really only two types of people: lightning bolts and sponges. Those who give energy to the people around them and those who drain it.

We recommend you spend your life trying to surround yourself with lightning bolts. Lightning bolts are interested, engaged and are great at finding the fun in almost any situation. These people are magnetic—they draw everyone else towards them, and magic happens because of it.

Sponges tend to make everything about themselves. They constantly complain, tend to talk about others behind their backs and like to tell you all the reasons 'why not.' If you can, please avoid them!

You might not know it yet, but you are lightning bolts. Don't let anyone tell you otherwise.

But you have to bring that lightning to the surface:

Be kind.

Be curious.

Find the positive.

Choose gratitude.

And, most importantly, stop complaining and start finding solutions.

The value of amnesia: learn and let go

Holding on to negative experiences will drain a lot of your energy in your younger years. You will hold on to a piece of criticism, a mistake, or negative feedback for days (sometimes longer), and ignore all the other amazing things you are and that you have accomplished. Maybe you're still doing that now.

If so, please stop that!

Instead, embrace the value of amnesia. Now, we're not suggesting that you gloss over or ignore the negative experiences that life throws at you, because there's often a lot to learn from mistakes and failures. Instead, learn to live by the mantra, learn and let go.

When something negative happens, remind yourself that it has happened *for* you rather than *to* you. Take some time—24 hours max!—to reflect on it, feel and process your emotions around it, and to truly learn the lesson so that you don't repeat the mistake.

And then? Move on and start to think about what you will do next.

Living with abundance

Throughout your life, it will be difficult not to compare yourselves to others. In the future, people spend a lot of time watching each other's 'human highlight reels' on something called social media. This will make you feel envious, at times, and create a sense of scarcity, of lacking something, even if you don't know exactly what.

You will learn that cultivating a feeling of abundance—of focusing on and being hugely grateful for the things that you have—is a very powerful source of positive energy. When you focus on the things that you don't have, you're less likely to be generous and to attract good things into your and others' lives.

So, try making gratitude a daily practice. It will help you create that feeling of abundance. Look for opportunities to give to others and be creative about it (it doesn't have to cost you anything!). You can give smiles, support, expertise, or attention. Whatever you choose, focusing on giving to others is an incredible way to recognize the abundance in your own life.

What about work, though? By now, you're probably worried about how you're going to pay the bills. After all, it can be tough to feel abundance when you can't afford to pay the rent.

Energy as the tipping point: landing your first (and second, and third…) job

Don't get discouraged as you begin your job hunt and realize that you don't meet all (or perhaps any) of the qualifications for the job of your dreams, or don't have a secret backdoor way in. You will never be fully qualified for any job you apply to when you're just starting out. What will set you apart from other candidates will be your persistence, energy and enthusiasm.

This persistence comes into play long before landing that coveted job interview, as you'll need to cast the net far and wide, and then remain strong in the face of multiple rejections or—worse—the void of silence, when the vast majority of your applications seemingly fall into the abyss.

But when you land that coveted job interview, view it as the golden ticket that it is and approach it with the same drive to win it that (spoiler alert) Tom Brady did his 10th Superbowl. That's where your energy can be your secret weapon.

A good employer will recognize that a particular degree or job experience is usually a nice to have vs. a need to have, and enthusiasm, ambition and persistence are greater predictors of success. Because of that, energy is often a secret tipping point—one that can make up for a lack of experience, or help you outshine another candidate who might have credentials, but doesn't have your spark!

When you become an employer yourself, you will approach talent acquisition in the same way. You will feel so passionately about energy that it will become one of your company's core values—and your #1 hiring criterion.

So when you're going for your first job interviews, don't forget to bring your energy with you!

Energy and resourcefulness: the keys to success at work

When you ultimately land those early jobs, you will struggle with self-doubt. You might even feel woefully unprepared to do the job you've won —this is when you'll get your first taste of imposter syndrome.

Here's where your energy will be the difference maker again! Because you can harness it and your resourcefulness to take responsibility for closing the gaps in your knowledge and experience. This will be made easy by something magical called the Internet that will allow you to YouTube, Google or LinkedIn Learn (we promise these are all actually verbs!) your way to decoding acronyms, demystifying technology, and mastering the fundamentals of almost any subject or industry. While you can't claim to be an expert until you've hit your '10,000 hours' of practice, you can build the foundation necessary to grow your confidence and accelerate your learning.

And this will teach you that you never need to have all the answers— just the energy to go find them in the people or places they exist!

Avoiding the ultimate energy drain: inauthenticity

When you start your career, you're going to kick things off with a 'work self', which you'll consider separate and distinct from your 'real self.' Your motivation for doing this will be a combination of people-pleasing tendencies, a fear of failure, and a desire for some separation between your personal and professional lives.

And, understandably, there are parts of yourself that you will feel uncomfortable revealing to others at work. Work can be challenging, confusing and even intimidating, especially when you're just starting out. But holding back what makes you human and vulnerable every day to be seen as competent will drain your energy—a lot! After all, you will spend a third of your life at work—which is a long time to pretend to be someone you're not.

Trying to look a certain way—to fit a mold or to appear to 'have it all together'—takes a ton of energy, thereby preventing you from doing your best, most creative work, and negatively impacting your overall wellbeing. And this will become even more detrimental when you become leaders of others at work. You will learn that you need to role model authenticity and humanity to allow other people to do the same, and if you don't, it will be incredibly difficult for your organization to perform at its best.

So:

Speak up.

Take risks.

Be authentic.

Lead with humility.

Genuinely connect with others.

Showing up this way at work takes commitment, intention, and courage. But the cost of not doing so (on you, your team and your organization) is far bigger than the cost of doing it—especially when it comes to protecting your most precious resource: your energy.

Radiating positivity: how to build lifelong relationships at work

"I've learned that people will forget what you said, people will forget what you did, but people will never forget how you made them feel." - Maya Angelou

This powerful quotation is particularly true in the workplace. Ultimately, businesses and organizations are just a collection of people, and the details of the work itself—although they will be responsible for many sleepless nights at the time!—are later forgotten. But later in life, as you look back at the thousands of people you've worked with over your career, you will remember how each one made you feel.

On the positive side, you will have bosses who will motivate you to be your best self and fiercely advocate on your behalf, 'work BFFs' who will get you through torturous moments of insecurity but also just make work exponentially more fun, and leaders who will inspire you with their authentic and inclusive approach to leadership.

Equally, you will work with and work for toxic people—ones who will make you feel small or who will lose your trust because of the way they treat you or others.

So, commit to bringing positive energy to every single interaction in the workplace, every single day. And, in doing so, you will build a legacy that will follow you through the rest of your life.

The greatest test of your energy: entrepreneurship!

And then one day, you will make the bold leap to entrepreneurship. Walking away from the security of a salaried job at an established company, and into a realm where the chance of failure is higher than that of success will force you to draw from the lessons you've learned about energy up to this point. Building something out of literally nothing will expose you to a new kind of vulnerability. You will have to relentlessly persevere through all the adversity that comes with starting out, using every setback as an opportunity to learn, grow and propel your business forward.

You'll need infinite optimism and the highest levels of physical and mental energy to push through the challenges of business ownership and keep forging ahead, day in and (often very long) day out—sometimes against seemingly impossible odds. But, perhaps most important will be the energy you will need to put into your business idea—in order to turn it into something big and amazing—and this will be determined by your passion. Your passionate energy is what will unleash your creativity and brilliance, push you to go the extra mile, and fuel your every success. Ultimately, it's that passionate energy—not the products or services you're selling—that will attract investors, customers, and the most talented employees to you and your business, and turn them into lifelong champions.

There is a lot to look forward to in the future that awaits you! But don't rush to get there. Savour every beautiful moment along the way, even the hardships—the bumps and bruises will shape you, build your resilience, and make every success that much sweeter. Looking back, we wouldn't change a thing.

Love, Shelli and Fiona

ABOUT THE AUTHORS

Shelli Baltman and Fiona Stevenson share a passion for helping others to maximize their creativity and potential and become their best selves at work and in life.

In 2015, they founded a boutique agency, The Idea Suite, with a mission to unlock the creative potential of people and businesses through innovation. **The Idea Suite** has been recognized in the *Adweek* 100: Fastest Growing Agencies list, the *Report on Business* Canada's Top Growing Businesses list, and the *Canadian Business* Startup list.

After years of energizing cross-functional teams and stakeholders at some of the world's largest companies to deliver multi-million dollar products, brands and services, Fiona and Shelli founded **Energy for Growth** in 2021 to share their proven energy-building tools and techniques with leaders who want to unleash the potential of their teams and themselves.

Shelli started her career as a management consultant with Mercer Management Consulting in Toronto and then joined McKinsey & Co. in London, UK after completing her MBA at INSEAD in Fontainebleau, France. She joined ?What If! Innovation in 2002, where she built their Customer Experience Innovation practice and worked as Managing Director. Shelli is devoted to her family, loves spending time outdoors, and is also a passionate downhill skier.

Fiona spent more than a decade in brand management at Procter & Gamble in Toronto and Geneva, Switzerland, and in 2017 was recognized in the P&G Alumni Network's inaugural global '40 under 40' list. In 2020, she was selected as a delegate for the Governor General's Canadian Leadership Conference. A bestselling author, Fiona's hobbies include writing, improvisational theatre, travel, and being active with her husband and two children.

Connect with Shelli and Fiona at:

> **Website:** *www.energyforgrowth.com and www.theideasuite.com*
> **Email:** *shelli@energyforgrowth.com and fiona@energyforgrowth.com*
> **LinkedIn:** *www.linkedin.com/in/shelli-baltman and www.linkedin.com/in/fiona-stevenson*

CHAPTER 7

JACKIE WOODSIDE

ear younger self,

Hey there...

Happy to connect, and, oh my, there's so much to say to help you in your coming years!

I hope you're not looking for this to be some kind of handholding, coddle-you-to-the-breast, it's-all-going-to-be-ok missive because that's just not my style. Not only is it not my style, but I'm not sure it would help you get on in life. And that is what you want, after all, is it not? That's pretty much what we all want, just to get on in life—to find our way.

I can appreciate that, and after all these years, I could say it's what I've done, more or less. I've found my way. I suppose that will not make any big headlines: *Jackie Woodside: She Found Her Way.*

Anyway, I digress.

I've always said I'm more of an ass-kicker than a hand-holder, but still, I hope you find some solace, support, and direction in what I'm about to say. I will not sugar-coat this because, well, life doesn't sugar-coat itself. It just comes at you, full throttle, headlights blaring, like a semi-truck barreling down on the wrong side of the road, coming straight at you. You either learn to adjust and react, or you get barreled over along the way.

There you are, wide-eyed and hopeful while simultaneously uncertain and afraid. You're hoping to find ways to avoid the pitfalls in life, but the truth is there is no avoiding them. Life can be filled with landmines waiting to blow you up or see what you are made of. Yeah, I know, that's harsh, but the faster you realize that it's true, the better off you will be.

At the same time, and here's where things get really dicey, the landmines aren't outside of you. The problems you will face are not outside of you. The problem is you.

Hard pill to swallow, isn't it? You probably won't believe me. Younger people never do. Hell, most older people never really learn this one either.

There aren't really any "problems" in life; there are just circumstances to be dealt with. It's how you label and define them that makes the difference.

Losing your job isn't the problem; your fear of being destitute is the problem.

Your spouse walking out on you isn't the problem; your codependent need for that relationship and your fear of being alone are the problem.

Running out of money isn't the problem; not having faith that you will always have your needs met is the problem.

You see? Life is simply made up of circumstances, some of which you create and some just show up on your doorstep. Either way—circumstances just the same.

Don't get caught up with the immature notion that just thinking good thoughts will make your life go precisely where you want it to go. Sure, it helps. It's better than self-flagellation and despair. But all the good thoughts in the world won't stop cancer from coming or your child from experiencing mental health challenges, or your parents from getting dementia. Sometimes Life. Just. Happens.

While there are no easy fixes that guarantee a life of ease and endless satisfaction, there are a few things that helped me go from batshit crazy to the life I now profoundly enjoy. If you're still reading, and maybe a little curious, read on...

Since I already said that you are the problem, let me go a little deeper. There's one tenet I live by every day, all the time, and it is this:

Don't believe everything you think.

It's a fundamental truth that has the potential to change your life forever.

Don't believe everything you think because "what you think" is not the Truth. It's just what you think. Your thoughts are not anyone else's thoughts. Hell, they're probably not even yours! They are simply patterns of neurons firing. You behave like your thoughts are FACTS, and from those "facts," you determine the meaning, and from that meaning, you decide how to act, what to choose. And from those decisions, you get the quality of your life.

Hold on, Captain Wonderful. What You Think Is Not The Truth!

When I was 27 and my partner of five years walked out on me without as much as a day's notice, I thought for sure I would never be happy or love again. I thought my life was over. I thought, "Why does this always happen to me? I'll never find lasting love." I am eternally grateful that I didn't believe that thought for long because now I've been with my spouse for 21 years, and I am blessed to be the most happily married couple I know!

When I was 44, I thought I couldn't afford to buy my family cottage from my cousin when he told me he would put it on the market. Luckily, I pushed past that limiting thought and we have enjoyed 13 years of summers living there, and the property is now paid in full.

Be careful not to believe everything you think.

Mistaking thoughts and beliefs for facts causes more stress and suffering than any other facet of life. Do yourself a favor and get really skilled at distinguishing thoughts from opinions from facts.

This leads to the corollary of this point:

The stories you tell yourself become the life you lead.

How I wish I would have known this truth when I was younger. The stories you tell yourself about life, love, yourself, and the world become the experiences you create and the life you lead. There's no getting around it—you will always only do what is within your realm of belief.

Telling myself that life is filled with landmines isn't the truth. It's a story I've made up based on my interpretation of the circumstances I have experienced. That story used to disempower me, and I felt like and acted like the victim of life. Once I realized that it's all made up, I switched my relationship to that "story" and used it to empower me. Yeah, life can be challenging. That's not news to anyone, and God knows I have nothing to complain about. I'm a white, educated, middle-class woman who enjoys the perks and benefits of having money, health care, a happy marriage, and a stable income.

Once I realized that the story I tell myself creates the life I lead, I used the landmine story to empower and inspire me. It made me appreciate the easier times and face the hard times with a resilience that I had not previously known.

At the same time, it is crucial to give all of your feelings room to live in your heart. When you allow yourself to observe what arises in the contours of your soul with honesty and courage, perhaps the separation and division within our entire world will subside.

When you don't make room for all of your emotions to dwell within your soul, the world itself becomes a less hospitable place. Does that mean you can never indulge the angry, sad, hostile, blaming emotions that arise? No, far from it. You can bear and share as many difficult emotions as any human being, but do not let them dominate or take root in your soul. Observe them, feel them, and let them pass through, as effortless as clouds passing in the sky.

Allowing my emotions to be present, to feel them but not identify with them, led me to this beautiful and profound realization: Life isn't happening "to me." It is happening *for* me.

I remember feeling frightened and alone after reinventing my career for the third time and having absolutely no idea how to make a living as a speaker, teacher, and trainer. Hell, I wasn't even sure what I wanted it to look like. Did I want to be a keynote speaker in front of hundreds of people or a spiritual teacher leading workshops and retreats, or did I want to be a corporate trainer, bringing my teachings to the workplace? I was sitting in my uncle's farmhouse living room at Christmas time in 2011, not knowing how to make a living, not feeling the success I knew in my previous career and scared to death that I would fail at my new endeavor. Then all at once, it came to me—this was happening *for me*. I answered the call of my heart. I listened to the passion within, and every single event prior, and every event coming forth. All of it is happening FOR me, for my growth, for my greater good. Not only for MY greater good, but life is happening FOR GOOD.

That was a shift in consciousness, and as my consciousness changed, so did my narrative, and then my circumstances followed suit. I started holding empowerment seminars, got my first publishing contract, and was hired as a professional development speaker and trainer. Life happens for good. (Yes, even when it doesn't look like it).

Everything transformed when I changed the story I was telling myself. Watch what you say. Watch how you interpret your life events. Notice when what you are saying is your perception or a belief, not a fact.

This too shall pass...

You will have painful times, and you'll definitely feel as if you can't go on. Here is what you need to know and remind yourself every day: this too shall pass. Burn that statement into your heart and mind and let it soothe you when things are challenging, and humble you when life lifts you up.

When I went through one of my most painful breakups after graduate school, I carried a note in my pocket—a simple piece of crumpled paper, and on it was written this simple epitaph: *this too shall pass*. You can't control every thought and emotion that emerges as you stumble upon the landmines of life, so learn to make friends with them. They are what make you human. Learn to observe your inner world rather than be ruled by it.

The ocean of human suffering will always be here; whether you suffer from loss or grief from lost love, or anxiety for an uncertain future, or addiction to help you deal with the pain, it doesn't matter. Be less concerned with the circumstances of your pain, sorrow, or joy, and get very interested in *who you are* concerning those circumstances and in life itself. Through it all, be comforted and humbled by this one simple yet profound truth: *This. Too. Shall. Pass.*

Let your passion be your strength.

You will find more solace in your calling than you can imagine. The pains of life melt away when you're engaged with doing what you love, and more so being who you came here to be. Here's the thing you need to know: Hard work is overrated, but passion is not.

When what you do is who you are, you never have to work a day in your life. Remember that. Reread it. Imbue it into the very fiber of your being. Never let your calling become a burden, or you will be burdened most of your waking hours of life.

Your calling is a *sacred self-expression*, so bring your whole self to it. The last thing you want to do is simply "make a living." No, that simply won't do. You are here to design your life—each incredible, painful, and precious moment.

Let your calling propel you through your days and illuminate endless possibilities when you realize the infinite potential in each moment. When you work, let there be a spring in your step and a lightness in your heart. Use your work to lead you to the definitive knowing that life is endlessly magnificent, and that you contribute to the long line of human experience.

Yes, the same can be said of your relationships, and your family and how you spend your time. But your calling and your work are yours alone. Let it emerge from you like a *soulprint* into the ethers of time. Let your passion live *you*, and your work express the very depths of who you really are. In all you do, live your truth.

When you live this way, the outcome is that you will succeed. Not because you possess any particular skill or talent, but because when you live your passion, you are bringing forth the vibration that you were born to create and express into this world. Which leads to the last simple truth I want you to carry with you in life...

You will always have what you need, but you will have to go after what you want.

Don't allow yourself to be lulled into the illusion that you will someday "be discovered." Instead, spend your life discovering all the ways you get to express yourself during your brief stay on earth. Allow yourself to become much simpler, relax a bit more, and for God's sake, find some patience for the things that matter.

The solution to going after what you want is straightforward but not always easy: go into your inner chamber, listen, plan, and then act. Don't overthink what you must do. Use your intuition to guide you and your heart as your compass. You can't think your way toward the fulfillment of passion because passion isn't an intellectual game. Living your passion requires something different altogether. You have to be willing to go where other people won't, to live on the edge, to honor and trust your inner voice, and to honor your simple slice of eternity.

Place high demands on yourself and then go out and fulfill them. Don't wait to be motivated to act. Don't think you need to have the courage first. Courage comes from doing what scares you. Just get on with it. Inspiration and motivation are highly overrated. You can be filled with uncertainty and fear and still act, anyway. That is what passion does for you.

And while you will be vastly driven to achieve, please, please remember that sometimes all you need to do is "be" and live out the passion in your heart that makes you alive. Passion leads to fulfillment and true happiness. That, and a bit of peace, kindness, and a lot of love, will make your life profoundly complete.

Remember the hot summer day sitting in a large, stuffy conference room in New York City, being called out by a determined and powerful seminar leader. He spoke boldly in front of over 200 other participants and told you that, "you simply have to decide who you are going to be and how you want to show up in life." I was simultaneously chagrined and inspired. He then recited these profound words by George Bernard Shaw that molded and changed my life since that very day.

"This is the true joy in life, the being used for a purpose recognized by yourself as a mighty one, the being a force of nature, instead of a feverish, selfish little clod of ailments and grievances complaining that the world will not devote itself to making you happy. I am of the opinion that my life belongs to the whole community, and as long as I live, it is my privilege to do for it whatever I can. I want to be thoroughly used up when I die, for the harder I work, the more I live. I rejoice in life for its own sake. Life is no brief candle to me. It is a sort of splendid torch, which I've got held up for the moment, and I want to make it burn as brightly as possible before handing it on to future generations."
- George Bernard Shaw

Your strength lies in your ability to look life in the face, with all the landmines that lie ahead, and with cold determination and passion, say, "Bring it on! I've got what it takes."

Be great. Be strong. Go light your world.
Jackie Woodside

ABOUT THE AUTHOR

Jackie Woodside is a bestselling author, TEDx speaker, expert guest on television and radio, Life Design coach and trainer. She is the founder of the Curriculum for Conscious Living and the Conscious Living Summit, and trains coaches around the world to deliver this life changing work. Jackie is a certified professional coach and licensed psychotherapist with 30 years' experience in both fields.

She has authored three best-selling books and 25 training curriculums: *Calming the Chaos: A Soulful Guide to Managing Your Energy Rather than Your Time, Time for a Change: Essential Skills for Managing the Inevitable, Money Vibe: Your Financial Freedom Formula Whether You Have Money or Not.*

Inc. Magazine selected "Calming the Chaos" as one of their top ten motivational books.

Jackie offers professional development training, keynote speeches, and retreats around the country.

You can connect with her at:

> *Website: www.JackieWoodside.com*
> *Facebook: www.facebook.com/JackieWoodsideSpeaker and www.facebook.com/groups/VibeTribers*
> *LinkedIn: www.LinkedIn.com/in/JackieWoodside*
> *Twitter: www.twitter.com/jackiewoodside*
> *Instagram: www.instagram.com/jackiewoodsidespeaker*

CHAPTER 8

MARISA MURRAY

ear younger self,

I can hardly express the excitement I feel for you as I watch you throw your academic cap up in the air to celebrate your graduation from high school.

You look so happy and confident about taking on the world.

You can't know this yet, but after the class parties, and a day or two to recover, your 18-year-old self is going to start thinking about what it really means to venture out on your own. The excitement you feel right now will mellow and expose your fears.

You don't know the challenges you are about to face or how lonely and confused you will feel as you try to make so many important decisions.

But through the magic of writing, I get to come visit you.

I'm coming to take you for a nice long walk along the path that follows the lake shore—the one you've walked a thousand times. I'm going to bring you a message-in-a-bottle. A message from me to you, from 30 years in the future.

I've spent a lot of time thinking about this and I've distilled everything I want you to know into six principles. The most important lessons that I have learned; to guide you on your way; so that you don't need to learn them the hard way, like I did.

Shall we start our walk together? Let's begin with principle number one.

Principle #1: Never have *enough* of learning

After finishing engineering school, I was fortunate enough to have several job offers. Most of my friends were scheduled to begin their careers within a month of graduation, but something didn't feel right to me about accepting this smoothly paved path. Don't get me wrong, I craved the security of the paycheck, but the offers were contingent on me starting right away, so I declined them. Instead, I travelled to Italy, to study Italian and the Renaissance, and then I met up with a friend of mine to travel across Western and Eastern Europe and into Russia.

One afternoon, I called home from Prague and my parents began urging me to return. It had been months: "Haven't you had enough?" they asked. That seemed like the most peculiar question to me: "How could I ever have enough of learning so much?" Not only had I not had enough, I would never have enough of learning.

When I returned home, people teased me about whether I had 'found myself', and asked: "Are you finally ready to join us in the real world?" What struck me, when I looked around, was how lost they seemed. Many were already bored in their jobs, not learning much of anything, but they were staying, none the less. My self-education that year clarified that my life would never be boring because I was going to be focused on learning.

There will be opportunities that come to you that feel safe and maybe even smart, but this principle will guide you to choose experiences that support your growth. It will help you avoid getting distracted by perks or comfort because if you focus on your growth, you will end up having both. I'm warning you, though, when you will need to make a choice, you will be distracted. You will not know what to do, so I want you to have no doubt. The first principle is to never have enough of learning. When you are at a crossroads, ask yourself: "What will help me grow?" Always choose to learn; it is your key to evolving.

Principle # 2: *Tickle* your curiosity

About a decade later, thanks to principle number 1, I had built quite a life for myself. I had an impressive career, a husband, a home, and kids. In fact, for several years, I thought I had it all, but somehow, I started to hate it all. I couldn't quite believe that everything I had worked so hard for wasn't as satisfying as I hoped it would be.

One Saturday morning, my youngest son came to me and said: "Mommy, come tickle me!" and I felt drained and burned out by his request. I thought: "What is happening here?"

Despite career advancement to leadership positions that provided me with financial stability and a beautiful life, I had started to hate my job. I tried to keep this dissatisfaction from spilling over into my personal life, but it wasn't working. My inner-voice was screaming "make a change," but my rational mind kept drowning it out. What about the mortgages, the amazing lifestyle, and the freedom my family was enjoying? Then my heart began to whisper: "you must change what isn't working or it will ruin everything else."

I didn't know what to do, so I decided I needed to *tickle* my curiosity.

I quit my job, without a plan, to tickle my potential, tickle what excited me and tickle my way to a new path.

I found the way to launching my own business and embarking on a new career that I love. It took work to re-build the professional and economic aspect of my "all" but I never had a single regret.

You might find that you will need to recreate your all, more than once. You may worry that the cost of rebuilding is too great or too risky. You will hear overwhelming consensus from those around you, telling you not to do it. Principle number two will remind you to pay attention to those whispers, to tickle your curiosity and trust that you will find your way.

Principle #3: Be the *steward* of your thoughts

At a holiday party, a little over a year after starting my business, I ran into a few of my former colleagues. One of them asked: "How is your new business going?" I said: "Great, actually, I have clients I love working with and I'm learning a ton..." I barely finished my sentence when I was peppered with questions: "What kinds of clients?" "Surely you can't be making any decent money serving them?" "You must miss the challenges of a real job." "Don't you think you should look for something else?" I froze, stunned by the looks on their faces, full of skepticism, disapproval, and determination to prove me wrong. Wrong about what? I don't know! I could tell that they were not happy for me. In fact, it almost seemed like they saw me as a threat.

After the verbal firing squad, I whispered to my husband: "Do you mind if we go home? I'm tired."

On the drive, my eldest son asked: "What was their problem with you mom? Why were they mad at you?" I didn't know what to say. I wasn't in a good place; my brain was already attacking me. Repeating their words, hearing their doubts and triggering feelings of embarrassment, shame and rejection. I couldn't respond to him; my brain was spinning.

The next morning, I felt a hangover from the negativity. My brain was not bouncing back, so I knew I needed to take my brain-matter into my own hands. To do that, I needed to become the *steward* of my thoughts.

I learned the importance of being my mind's *steward*. Being the steward means to be responsible for, to govern, to take care of and even to protect someone or something. In this context, it means protecting my mind from unhelpful thoughts and other people's opinions that can knock me off track.

I took up meditation and wrote my own affirmations. I began to discern between helpful and unhelpful thoughts, and I trained my brain to release negative thoughts and adopt empowering ones. I want you to learn to be a steward of your thoughts. Take the time to teach your mind how to think. When facing negativity or the judgements of others, be the steward, protect your mind, free it from self-doubt. Your brain is a powerful tool, but it is your responsibility to keep it on track, focused on creating your future.

Principle #4: It's called a *body of work* for a reason

After publishing my first book, my business began to take off. I was being invited to do more keynote speaking and getting more visibility. My family began to notice my self-inflicted stress and said: "Slow down." They were right about my stress, but I didn't want to rest.

I loved the impact that I was having on my clients. I wanted more, not less, but I had to admit that being out there, expressing my views in such a public way, was exhausting me. I realized that there was something deeply vulnerable about constantly pushing myself outside of my comfort zone as I brought my ideas into the world.

I started going to my local yoga studio to catch a class as often as I could. One morning, the instructor mentioned an information session for yoga teacher training, and on a whim, I decided to show up. When I arrived, I felt a sense of warmth in the studio. It was not from the heating; it was in the energy of the people. As I listened to the past students' stories about the benefits they experienced by deepening their yoga practice, I wanted in.

Over the year-long program, I studied anatomy, postures, and breathing. People thought I had lost my mind: "Don't you have better things to do? Is business so bad that you need to become a yoga instructor?" I hadn't lost my mind, but I was rediscovering my body.

I learned to breathe through my stress, regain my flexibility, and enjoy more freedom of movement. My body and my brain began to attune to each other, and this fortified me. I was no longer living only from the neck up. I was tapping into my body's stability, agility and strength in the real world. I felt more courageous in my self-expression because I was grounded in my body.

You are very smart, so it will be easy for you to live in your head. Your intellect is an amazing gift, but it is called a body of work for a reason. You need to bring your body to the table. Yoga practice is not the only way for you to stay integrated. Find the physical activities that you enjoy, ones that make your body come alive. Remember to be proud of your body, celebrate it and nurture it. There are two halves to your whole, and you will be bolder and braver when you leverage both.

Principle #5: *Toast* to *symbiotic* relationships

Four years into my business, I was in full swing. I was working with more senior leaders. I was winning larger and more challenging mandates, and my clients were raving about the positive impact I was making. I felt so grateful and wanted to give back, so I made a sizeable donation to a charity that was raising money to train women entrepreneurs in the developing world. I also signed up as their lead sponsor for their annual fundraising event. The investment was a stretch for me and it made me nervous, but I wanted to do it, anyway.

I bought tickets for more than a dozen of my clients. People that worked with me in my first year of business. I was thrilled to be with them that evening because I was so grateful for their faith in me right from the very start.

Surrounded by this amazing group of people, I caught a glimpse of one of the board members from the charity: a prominent lawyer and a bit of an icon in the city. She caught my glance and joined our circle saying: "Nice to see you, I was just looking for you to thank you for your dona-tion." I smiled, and she continued: "Seems like you have built a wonderful business, and I read your book, it's amazing, what's next for you Marisa?" I said: "Well I'm not sure, but I've always kind of wanted to do a TED talk." She immediately raised her glass and said: "Well, let's all toast to that."

About a year later, out of the blue, I received an email from her intro-ducing me to the curator of a local TEDx event looking for speakers. I applied and was unbelievably excited when I secured a spot. The TEDx experience was incredible. The highlight of the event was seeing my husband and sons beaming with pride. When I stepped on the stage, I saw the rows and rows of my clients and friends there to support me. I felt the power of all the symbiotic relationships that had brought me to this moment.

I want you to be aware of this power. Opportunities open up when you are taking action and they show up even more quickly when you are making a difference for others. Be as generous as you can. Share your knowledge, your resources, your network, your compassion, and your positive energy. Toast to your future with people that inspire you and get ready to welcome all the symbiotic helpers that come into your life.

Principle # 6: Make *time* for the tulips

Much to my delight, my business continued to scale, and I was now being asked to do more than executive coaching and workshops. I was hired to design leadership development curriculum for the entire enterprise. The work was so engaging, although admittedly a little intense, especially as the launch date approached. I was heads down, running seven days a week for at least a month when one evening, my husband suggested we take a walk together. As we strolled along the public garden and turned the corner, I was shocked at what I saw—I gasped!

The tulip garden was a field of half dead leaves. With my hand over my heart, I said: "I missed the tulip bloom!"

Tulips are my favorite flowers. I adore them and every year for a few short weeks, this garden is filled with them. I'm always taken aback by their beauty, their variety, and the colors. But this year I had gotten so busy, I forgot to take a moment just a few steps from my home, to take them in.

This may seem a little dramatic to you, but missing the tulips threw off my year. The joy, the energy, the renewal that these spring flowers bring. It impacted the way I experienced my summer, fall, and winter that year.

Most people wouldn't make a big deal about this. They justify missing tulips for years in a row. These same people later bemoan that life is short. They couldn't be more wrong. What I want you to know is that life is deliciously long. It is the most beautiful long journey, when you are present to every moment and deeply aware of every season. You have to make the time to take in the tulips.

This sixth and final principle is critical. As your life gets busy, there is a risk that you sleep-walk through it. So many people do. They feel pressured to move fast and get stuck running in a loop. They fall asleep and the beauty passes them by. Some of that beauty will never repeat itself like a baby's first steps, a violin recital or a grandmother's last smile. That is why you must stay present to life.

Don't stray too far from life's nurturing source energy. If you distance yourself too much, a part of you will darken inside. Detaching from life will make you lose track of your essence: your passion, your purpose, your joy. Over the past 30 years, I have learned that nature is my greatest teacher. She shows us exactly how to embrace every moment of life powerfully and joyfully.

If you get stuck in your inner world, and it starts to feel dark, remember that it is breathtakingly beautiful and bright outside. Appreciate life's forces. Let them energize, animate, inspire, and guide you. It doesn't take long to take them in. Make the time to experience this incredible, wise and inspiring partner. Attune to the seasons, be present to every experience life brings. Say "Yes" to life and make time for the tulips.

It's hard to believe but we've reached the end of our walk together! I have to leave you now. I'm so happy I got this chance to visit.

I've shared a lot, probably too much to take in. You might still feel a little worried or uncertain. Don't be. I promise that if you keep these six principles in mind and let them guide you, your life will be everything it is meant to be:

A powerful and joyful experience.

I wish you well as you embark on your adventures. Remember to develop your gifts; meet fascinating people; celebrate and synergize with life. Keep this message-in-a-bottle close to you, so that your life will be everything that you want it to be.

Love,
Marisa

ABOUT THE AUTHOR

Marisa Murray, CEO and Founder of Leaderley International, provides executive coaching and leadership development programs for organizations including Accenture, Bristol-Myers Squibb, Molson-Miller-Coors, Pratt & Whitney and McGill University. She is the author of two Amazon bestselling books on Leadership: *Work Smart* and *Iterate!*

Following Marisa's TEDx talk, Madhavi Mantha (Partner at Deloitte Consulting) said: "She is an incredible executive coach and speaker because she combines her personal experience as a former partner at Accenture with her experience working intimately with top leaders. Marisa's tools are insightful, relevant and practical. You want her working with your team, because she gets results."

Connect with Marisa at:

> *Website: www.leaderley.com*
> *Facebook: www.facebook.com/murray.marisa and*
> *www.facebook.com/LeaderleyInternational*
> *LinkedIn: www.linkedin.com/in/murraymarisa*
> *Twitter: www.twitter.com/murraymarisa*
> *Instagram: www.instagram.com/murray_marisa*
> *YouTube: www.youtube.com/channel/UCs5KKVtKm-*
> *teRsbjJ16keWA*

CHAPTER 9

MATTHEW THRUSH

ear younger self,

Control your mind, control your future.

If you pursue one thing in life, make it the pursuit of mindfulness and knowledge. *For out of the abundance of the heart the mouth speaks.*[1] You will have many inputs coming your way, trying to persuade you into their agenda, plan, and thought process.

Resist all of them when they do not align with your calling. People always have an opinion regardless of their motives—but it rarely serves your best interest. Even good intentions lead to hardship if you're not careful and diligent with testing everything that comes your way.

You only have one life, make it count by removing the unknowns, confusion, obstacles, and poor paths. As your older version, I've lived these experiences already so you don't have to. I will save you years of stress, anxiety, pain, regret, fear, and longing through these few pages.

If you listen to my counsel, you will live an abundant life in every aspect: influence, impact, love, relationship, friendship, wealth, and purpose. Fail to abide by these simple truths and principles and you may find yourself taking a less-than-direct path to your destiny, and a much longer journey than you need to.

Let's save you the time and burden and do it the easy way. I've broken the top lessons learned over the years into pillars for success to act as your guide post and course correction to make your quest easy to navigate. Each pillar will serve you in a specific area of your life to accomplish everything you set out to do.

Let's begin.

Trust God

You will achieve nothing without God's support, provision, blessing, favor, and protection over your life. You will be tempted to go astray countless times in your life, but every time you've returned to your faith and placed your complete trust in God, He's never let you down.

You will prosper in everything your hand touches and take dominion over every area your feet tread.[2] This means that God will multiply your endeavors for His glory so that you will be a blessing to others.

God loves to bless His children. Give your life to God as soon as you can and never stray from His side. Devour His word, think on it constantly, and speak it. Don't rely on your own wisdom, especially your emotions, doubts, or feelings—they will ruin you every time.

Don't believe your experiences as the truth over what God says because you cannot see the full picture; God can, and He knows what's best for you and where your path leads. Listen to and do what God says in His word—period—even if it sounds counterintuitive or you haven't seen it work for someone else. Never question it, just obey and take action. You will succeed where others continuously fail.

It will ALWAYS work out for your good even if in the moment it appears you're failing, hurting, or going backward. Don't waiver. For God said His word will not return to Him void (it will always accomplish what He sent it to do).

What appears to take years, decades, or no results at all at the time is God's divine timing, and you'll be glad you waited. Surround yourself with God-believing people who pursue truth, believe what God says, and live it out. If God said you can do it, you can. He gives you access to the invisible realm where everything is possible for those who believe.

Mindfulness

Your soul (mind, will, emotions) is the gateway to everything. You will live or die with what goes on in your mind. Guard it above all else and refuse to let the enemy get a foothold.

Block negative influences as they will damage your resolve, curse your spirit, and pollute your mission—this includes toxic people, small-minded friends or family, gossiping neighbors or coworkers, and above all, stay away from the news media and social media! Question everything by seeking truth. Even God says to test His word for yourself to prove Him faithful, and to test everything in life to protect yourself.

The best way to increase your mindfulness is to study the most successful people, model what they do in their lives, study God's word and implement it into your life every day, and read.

God said His people are destroyed for lack of knowledge.[3] But if you do not have that knowledge, how will you know when your thoughts don't align with your goals and higher calling?

If you commit your life to consuming as much knowledge and truth as you can, you will succeed where most will fail or give up. Life is not easy, but it can be simple. It all begins in your mind. If you believe it, and you can see it in your mind (deep within you), you will achieve it.

Some will call this *the law of attraction* or *speaking destiny into your life*. There is truth to this, but the reality is that this comes from God. He is the one who told us we must take every thought captive and hold it against His word to gauge its worth, validity, and power.

If you guard your mind and control your thoughts to the right ones that serve you and others, your mouth will speak that into existence, and your subconscious mind will handle the rest as it directs you through rotary motions every day on autopilot.[4]

Habits

The things you do every day will dictate your future. These serve as your milestones to calculate how well you're doing in a certain area.

Not as strong or fit as you'd like to be? Maybe check the food you're eating, the places you're living, how well or how much you're sleeping, who you're hanging out with, listening to, watching, and whether you're engaging in rigorous exercise on a weekly and daily basis to hit your goals.

Habits extend well beyond diet and sports. You'll be trained and conditioned to hyper focus your energy and goals on being strong to attract hot chicks and dominate in sports, but the better goal is to increase your reason for being fit and the best at sports for a higher calling.

Once you get married, have kids, and achieve your goals in sports, what will there be left to motivate you with the same vigor? You'll easily fall into a rut and this will suck the life out of your body, mind, and spirit.

To guard against this, develop daily habits and never quit. Start off every morning with drinking cold water to activate your body's nervous system and hydration. Then, immediately make your bed as though your life depended on it. Make sure the corners are tight, and the top flat with no wrinkles.

Set small goals like this every day that are easy to achieve within a few seconds or minutes, and do them without question. These small wins will trigger your mind with an overflowing abundance of confidence that will enable you to crush any obstacle during the day.

Use these small habits to develop the necessary ones to achieve any goal in your life by working backward. If you want to become a billionaire, find out what it takes to achieve it, then do those action items every day until you hit your goal. This works for every area of your life.

Health

There will come a time in your life when you will not be the alpha like you are. Your body will be weak and sick. You'll lose radical weight in a short period and look like a skeleton. Doctors won't know what's going on and won't be able to help you.

Your life, friendships, and marriage will suffer because of it, but you don't have to go down his path at all. Do not neglect the things you once did when you were younger and in sports. Continue to work out, eat food that energizes you (get rid of the sour candy or reduce it), and take supplements that boost your immune system.

The best thing you can start taking and never stop is acemannan. It'll supercharge your immune system and eradicate disease from your body. If you're proactive with this, you will not get sick. Plus, when you look good, you feel good. And that confidence and agility wills serve you in business.

Mentors

If you want to shortcut and bypass all the mistakes, obstacles, and time to achieve your goals faster, find mentors immediately. The sooner you surround yourself with coaches and people who can help you get to your goals faster, the sooner you'll achieve them and with a lot less stress and burden.

Use mentors for your sports, your marriage, your finances, and your business. Mentors, coaches, and counselors are gold mines for you and exude dominance and strength. But only partner with those who have the same beliefs as you, think as you do, and are where you want to be.

If they aren't, do not align yourself with them. They will teach you things that will only hinder your growth and keep you trapped in the mediocre life that most people live, and never realize there's something else for them.

Find mentors in books, courses, workshops, masterminds, and events. You'll find them easily when you start looking. And start when you're a teenager as you can become a millionaire and influencer before you ever graduate high school and college.

Books, Growth, & Power

You'll develop a love for books at a young age, and will find mentors who will come alongside you to develop your skill with writing. Lean into their teaching and spend more time with them. Write every day as it'll lead to a prosperous life and equip you for the mission of helping thousands share their stories in books.

Always carry a book with you wherever you go. Not only will it level up your mind, but it'll give you something to do for all of the long waits. You'll redeem your time this way.

Books will act as your gateway to knowledge and the tools to accomplish everything you set out to do. You'll be enticed to read mostly fiction, but I encourage you to consume as much nonfiction as you can about relationships, marketing, investing, life insurance, wealth, taxes, influence, and leadership. You'll thank me later—just trust me.

Examine the wealthy. All of them are prolific readers, but they don't just read, they consume things that build their minds. Be selective with what you read and don't read what others do for mere entertainment. Everything you do has a purpose and leads to your goals or away from them.

Pay To Go Faster

This is one of the most important truths you must master and engrain into your mind before you ever graduate high school.

If you develop this habit and mindset, you will dominate. Don't waste time trying to learn everything to do it yourself, pay someone who's already a master and expert to do it for you. You still will continue to develop your knowledge and skillset, but pay people to get you to your goals sooner while you learn. Plus, you can learn from them the right things instead of testing or trial and error.

You don't need to be the best or the expert at everything to influence people, make a ton of money, or live an abundant life. You just need to surround yourself with the best team of people who can get you there and serve people at the highest level. Be the best at serving and empowering people and you will rule the world and bless millions in the process.

Choose a Mission You Cannot Achieve Alone

The way you will determine whether an idea is yours or God's is by whether you can do it alone. If you can do it by yourself, it's a shallow dream and you should throw it out as fast as possible, or multiply it by ten. If you cannot do it on your own and it impacts others (not just make you a lot of money), that's a God calling.

We're meant to do life together and in community. One of the titans of your day, Tony Robbins, will say, "If you want to be wealthy, serve people better than anyone else."

A passion you'll develop is helping people eradicate poverty mindsets and beliefs, debt, increase cash flow, and build generational wealth. The way you do this is by finding mentors to level you up, help you on your mission, and bring others with you.

Generosity Above All

The more you give in life, the more God will provide you with to keep giving. You never know when your kind gestures, acts, and speech will leave a lasting impact on someone's life, or serve your higher calling in the future.

We're all interconnected, and you always reap what you sow.[5] Make sure you're sowing life, abundance, perseverance, hope, kindness, and friendship into others.

A common thread you'll discover is that the most successful people around you (not just financially) are also the most generous people you'll ever meet. They give more than their money, but also sacrifice their time, talents, skills to lift people up, remove burdens, and teach people to prosper.

Training your mind and your habits around generosity will enrich your life beyond anything you can imagine. Don't take my word for it and find out for yourself. Live a life of generous giving and watch how the windows of heaven open up for you to change people's lives.

This doesn't mean everything will always go perfectly, but even in the storms, you'll walk with a smile, an air of confidence, and will continue to ruction in the habit of generosity despite your circumstances and experiences.

Never Settle & Resist The Herd

When you know what you want in life, pursue it with complete vigor and focus. You'll see many people who aren't living life at the fullest. They've given up on their dreams, and they live for the weekends. Do not be a weekend warrior, but live life with excitement and longing for the next day.

Every day is a gift. Don't waste it. A life of mediocrity is stagnant and actually means you're dying. Most people will pursue comfort over growth because it's easier, but it's also destroying them. The better reward is to never quit, always pursue more, and use it to give back.

This means you'll be tempted by the masses to do things like they do. They'll offer unsolicited advice on how to make money even though they're broke, or marital advice even though they've had five divorces, or how to raise kids even though they don't have any or their kids never talk to them.

Do not listen to people who aren't where you want to be. They're poison to your soul and purpose. They may mean well, but it's toxic and it'll imprison you like it has them. This leads to my final two points.

Say, "No" Frequently

It may seem harsh to tell people no, including yourself, but you must if you want to reach your destination with the least amount of roadblocks, heartaches, and meaning.

You'll be taught that you should become a people pleaser, but this is the last thing you want to be. It'll only suck the life out of you and leave you empty in the end. The better option is to focus on things, habits, people, and opportunities that move the needle for your goals faster, and with integrity.

The sooner you restrict external inputs, others agendas, and give your time one hundred percent to your mission, the sooner you'll wipe out needless burdens, obstacles, pitfalls, negative people, toxic relationships, and rocket to your goals.

Have a friendship that's one-sided? Drop it. In an intimate relationship that's going nowhere and leaves you drained, get rid of it. In a job that's not moving you forward as a person or you're surrounded by leeches, quit.

It won't always be easy to do these things, but it'll save your life —literally.

And lastly...

Create Leverage With Money To Build An Empire

Time is on your side in building wealth and never having to worry about money again. You'll be tempted to spend everything you earn, like 99% of the population, but don't follow the crowd.

Invest early and watch your money soar. If you invest just $10 a day when you're twenty years old (you'll spend more than this anyway) at 7% average return, you'll amass more than $1,198,019 by the time you retire at sixty-five years old.

If you start at thirty years old, that number will drop to only $581,582. That's a $616,437 difference you'll miss out on. Just think, if you increased it to $20 per day, that'll net you more than $2,396,038. You will have double your money by leveraging money you would have spent anyway, but you placed it into an investment vehicle that was unaffected by the volatile market's ups and downs, it grew tax free, and you can access it anytime (even before you retire), tax free.

But here's the secret...

This is only one tool you'll be able to leverage to create a lasting impact and wealth. Don't spend to consume, but spend to build. Learn what the wealthy do and follow their example. They aren't using 401(k)s, IRAs, mutual funds, and working as a W2 employee their whole lives.

They run businesses, and they store, protect, and build wealth in other vehicles like life insurance, trust deeds, real estate, mobile homes, storage units, and tax strategy, to name a few.

This is what you'll pursue in your journey. If you follow these principles and advice, you'll not only be a multi-millionaire in your early twenties, but you'll live a vibrant life, and will influence millions.

The choice is yours. If you follow the same path I took, you'll accomplish massive goals, but if you use these shortcuts, you'll bypass the nightmares and get there faster, and surpass me while you're still young to use that youthful energy and limitless belief to change the world on a grander scale.

Make the right choice. Learn from me, "be fruitful and multiply, and fill the earth and subdue it; and have dominion over the fish of the sea and over the birds of the air and over every living thing that moves upon the earth."[6]

---

1. Luke 6:45
2. Joshua 1:3 & Deuteronomy 11:24
3. Hosea 4:6
4. Philippians 4:6-7
5. Galatians 6
6. Genesis 1:26–28

ABOUT THE AUTHOR

Matthew Thrush is a magician in writing books that sell and change lives. He's written over 200+ bestselling books to date for his top-tier clients and has left a mark on the world with the massive impact those books are generating. He and his partners have helped launch over 1,000 authors and books to the Amazon, Wall Street Journal, USA Today, or New York Times best-seller lists, and he's on a mission to help over one million people share their knowledge, expertise, thought leadership, or stories in a book to impact one billion lives.

His work has been awarded Editor's *Pick of the Week*, been published in multiple online magazines and blogs, literary journals, and even used to promote Blockbuster movies. His one story has grossed over 1,000,000+ reads and used by Hollywood producers and directors to promote Season 8 of *The Walking Dead*, *Pride & Prejudice: Zombies*, and *The Boy*.

However, Matthew gauges his success by how well his clients' books perform. He's fortunate to have worked with many of the best minds, talents, professionals, and world changers. One of his clients' *based on true events* Science Fiction Thriller was adapted into a graphic novel with artwork by Marvel, DC, and Image designers, and is in talks for adaptation to the big screen and/or a video game.

Matthew wants to help you, too. Schedule your *FREE 15-MINUTE BESTSELLER BRAINSTORM CALL* and be ready to have your mind blown!

www.calendly.com/matthewthrush/bestseller-brainstorm-call

CHAPTER 10

MELISA KEENAN

ear younger self,

Covered in silty dirt from head to toe; arms crusted over with blood; in the back of a pickup truck going 70 miles per hour along the highway in the Nevada Desert, staring at the vast sky. You are hitch-hiking at 12 years old. Somehow, you know that the three large Paiute women in the truck will bring you to safety. The stern lectures they gave you about the dangers of walking alone on the desert highway came as welcome reassurance. For now, you are safe, being held by the universe. You were only recently orphaned following the death of your beloved Daddy battling cancer, and just prior to his death, your mother lost custody of you, leaving you in the care of relatives. However, on this fateful day, you were visiting her for the summer on a court appointed trial period when things took an unexpected, violent turn where your life, and more importantly, your heart was at stake. Today, for the first time, I will put a tangible and clear picture on the vague message of peace that miraculously settled into your bones in the bed of a pickup truck full of angels.

Picture This

You feel so alone right now, my Melisa. But you would not believe the life you have created at 33 years old. You are going to find love with a fiercely devoted husband, willing to slay his own dragons to be by your side, be surrounded by joy with four carefree children who think you are their superhero and best friend, and have a business where you help people daily because of all you have been through! Above all, you will cherish your life, because you know who you are: a radiant feminine woman, a visionary spiritual healer, and a powerhouse force for good, and you walk side-by-side with Jesus Christ daily. Can you see it, Melisa? I am convinced that part of the peace you felt in the back of that pickup truck was my voice transcending time and space. In fact, maybe it was this very chapter reaching back to you some 21 years earlier to let you know that your life is full and that I need you to stick around to live it.

Shattering Generational Chains

When the car window glass shattered all over you in the backseat from the rock your mother had just thrown, you believed your life was in danger at the hands of your own mother and fled. The rock grazed past your hip and cracked the car door plastic. Any hope of living with her again completely dissolved. Despite the chaos, there is nothing more familiar than the bosom of your own mother. And even at 33 years old, I still shed tears writing these words because it is sad. The next six years of zero contact were so sad, too. Your great big heart always sees with eyes of compassion, and paradoxically, Melisa, my love, you were set free in the sadness. Let me tell you what else shattered in that moment: the pain and dysfunction that had been passed down from parent to child throughout generations were obliterated because of you! Generations of sexual abuse, incest, molestation, addiction, dependency, the nose-to-the-grind-stone work-until-it-kills-you mentality, and the need to repeat unhealthy patterns were no more. Also, the generational beliefs that life is a drudgery, or that a woman must compete with or fear men shattered right there for you and for the entire feminine lineage. The women before and after you call you blessed. When everything shattered, you were set free.

Shadow Gifts

The most haunting part of this experience came when you looked over your shoulder to see your mother, now far in the distance with her head in her hands, sobbing and shaking. Hearing her shrill screams, demanding of the world at the top of her lungs; "What is wrong with me?!" That horrifying instant when your mother let you come face to face with the darkest part of her shadow. The scariest part was not her rage but the depth of her inability to see who she really was; her greatest weakness being fully exposed, her shadow permeating the entire desert valley with her screams. The answer to her question seemed to come to YOU, as if *you* asked the question. Your darkest shadow met hers, and the answer was, "Melisa, what is wrong with you is that you are not enough. Never forget this," leaving you with that voice in the back of your mind and a fire to your feet to prove yourself worthy in each new encounter you experienced. This voice came with you when you went on to start a new life with your guardians. Later in life, as you found an eternal companion, the voice bound itself right into the marriage. That voice, there again, at the birth of your first, second, third, and fourth child. "Don't forget!" It was a constant companion as you stepped into your business to help women in their femininity and intimacy, and shadowed over your courageous decision to charge your first client $997 for a program you were not even sure would be helpful to her. It stuck around as you saved marriages and helped women liberate themselves from their cages and lies... and then years later, as you created a high-level opportunity and charged $10,000 for your first time. "Just remember, Melisa: no matter how much you do and accomplish, you're still not enough."

Your mother believes that the best things she gave you were normalcy, family life, trips to the lake and Disneyland, love, and warm, healthy meals in the first few years of your life. Those things mattered tremendously, of course. However, years later, in your twenties, you had a vision that taught you a part of her divine mission and role in your life. Part of that mission was to show up with her full shadow as your mother, Melisa. So that, from such a young age, you knew what it felt like as a human being and a woman -- to face our deepest, darkest fears and insecurities. It is because she showed you her shadow, and by default, showed you yours so clearly, you can now help women create massive transformation in their lives. For it is by consciously going into our shadow and bravely facing all aspects of it, that we create space for the flow of intimacy, abundance, and goodness we are all born for. Without the depth of the darkness, we will never know the fullness and richness of the light. As we allow it to carve out our inner vessel, it floods us with light that spills onto everybody we encounter.

Divinity Within

At this stage, your experience shifted away from your mother. She had lost track of you and you entered your unique refiner's fire. After running a couple hundred feet away from the road and all the horrors there, you halted at a barbed wire fence where you began shoving the flesh of your wrists against the barbs. You wanted to escape the pain inside by any means possible. This was not the first time you wanted to flee this life, but it was the first time you acted on it. How many times you had asked God to let you trade places with your daddy, telling yourself it was because of how much you loved him, when really, it was because you were carrying pain that was ripping your soul apart—literally tearing at the marriage of your spirit to your body. Self-inflicted pain can be like that. Maybe we think we would not have to experience the internal pain if we create external pain. Perhaps we do it to punish ourselves for the suffering of others. Perhaps we are just seeking a strange sort of solace where we can find peace, or somehow find ourselves again. Maybe just maybe, there is a part inside of you that knew that you were not made for this. You are made from the stuff of gods, and your experiences were not reflective of your divinity. That part wants to go to a higher place where it resonates again, while your human body and mortality beg you to stay, to merge, to feel it all, and to make it work. Paradoxically, they are both wise —your body and spirit, your flesh and divinity. Maybe we are meant to realize we are heaven on earth, amid all of life's experiences, which is exactly what you woke up to next.

Miracle of the Heart

You left the barbs behind, and after running about the length of a football field deeper into the desert, you dropped to your knees behind a hill and instinctually began begging for a miracle; a relief from the pain on the inside. The moment you finished your prayer, you fell unconscious on the desert floor. Miracles of the heart seemed somewhat easy to come by, but physical miracles filled you with curiosity and confusion. Your holy-roller, faith-filled ancestors included you in many-a-prayer-circle, pleading for tangible miracles. But God seemed choosey with these kinds of miracles. After all, he did not save Daddy from cancer. It turns out, Melisa, a miracle of the heart is the most potent kind, and this day, you experienced both. You awoke to wounds that God himself dried up. The physical cuts were not as deep as they were before. But more than that, you realized you had been granted another chance at life, and suddenly your life clearly had meaning since God preserved it. It felt as though you had just remembered your crown. And so, a fire that burned bright with purpose was planted in your heart. It was not your time to leave this earth. And you arose, embodying purpose and sovereignty.

Sovereignty

There is nothing like the dry blazing heat of the Nevada sun in the middle of summer, with only sagebrush and mountains visible on every turn to make someone feel they are alone on the planet. But even there, with grit and war paint for survival, you learned that you could surrender, soften, and arise as the feminine queen. It was as if God the Mother and God the Father, the mountains, sagebrush, and the dirt beneath your feet whispered with each step, "I've got you. You know who you are. You are cherished and carried." This knowledge penetrated so deeply that when your marriage was dangling from a thread later in life, during a six-month separation, with three little children all in diapers, it was like you were back in that desert. This time, exhausted with an infant on your hip and two trusting toddlers, their eyes begging to know why we were in the middle of the desert, and where Dad was. You had asked him to move out, believing again that you were all alone. Then, the sagebrush, mountains, and God all called to you again and said, "I've got you, Melisa. Remember." You were then guided even deeper to your truth. This time, to the deepest intimacy of your life, recognizing your husband, even in his perfectly imperfect humanity, as the perfect king to rule alongside you as the queen in your equally perfectly imperfect humanity. You were often perceived by others as a heretic -- and with a burning passion inside of you – you decided to do something big to help women. People would often scratch their heads and say, "What? I don't even understand what you are doing." You felt so alone and yet you forged your business' path with this whisper still in your heart, straightening your crown and persevering. When your circumstances around you try to convince you that you are alone and must therefore only be harsh, fierce, and ferocious, remember that if you will sink into your feminine for just a moment, you can hear the elements all around you reminding you of who you are and how precious you are.

Warrior Goddess

With nothing but a crude prayer and a sovereign faith, something in the inner-most parts of yourself, a knowing voice, told you to return to the highway. Your sacred and stumbling prayer—like a mantra—on repeat was, "Lord, please no assholes." It was your Captain Marvel moment, walking across the vast Nevada desert wearing bright blue. You came back to life and back into the sight of the highway, fearless and determined. You knew you needed to get back to the highway and back to safety. It seemed impossible, but you began walking, taking one step at a time. Your blood ran cold as you watched your mother's blue Blazer zoom past, miraculously leaving you unnoticed. You were unstoppable, impenetrable, and invisible. Like Captain Marvel with what felt like a million darts, bullets, and arrows rushing your way, with your shield of fierce belief in the impossible, a queen's shield, you made it safely to the highway. Your life, my Melisa, though once fraught with pain, it is now full of lasting and enduring joy, and from the beginning it has been full of magic and miracles. Because this is what little girls, and women, are truly made of.

Inner Knowing

Your inner knowing manifested everything you needed. You walked on the highway for just five minutes before your angels made a quick U-turn to pick you up; prayers answered. The inner knowing came to walk to the highway, you acted, and quickly the results of your trust in that voice came to fruition. Remember? It was that same intuition channel that came to you a year earlier. While the rest of the family in the living room shouted, prayed, and cried around 11-year-old you and Daddy, laying on his hospice bed, God spoke to you and told you when your daddy would take his last breath. You shared his last breath with him when no one else knew. Melisa, ten years later that inner knowing spoke loudly through body and soul that you were supposed to marry this man... and then came to you just five years after that, when you asked him to move out because your marriage could not continue with where it had started. And again, it spoke through your soul and told you it was time to invite him back in, even though you did not have everything figured out. And look at your marriage now! It was your inner knowing that pulled at you to start a business—to go help women with their marriages and their identity. That same intuition, your feminine intuition or inner knowing has served you all this time. It is your constant. Listen.

Honor Your Lineage

The three large Native women were never identified. Amid a tiny reservation, they were not to be found. The only logical conclusion was not logical at all. My great Aunt Betty, a spiritual matriarch of our family in her own right, declared that they must have been angels. Melisa, they were women who came to carry you and take care of you when it did not feel safe. Despite your mother's instability, women still felt safer than men. Who else was there with you that day, carrying you, tending to your wounds and mending your broken heart in the back of the pickup truck? Your grandmother who died after enduring a horrible affair, breast cancer, a mastectomy, and Parkinson—both of your great grandmothers from either side who died young of heart attacks when their daughters were only twenty years old. Your great grandmother Saphronia, whose husband left with nine children and two of his cousins to raise when he ran off with another woman. The spirits of your unborn children and grandchildren, helping carry you along. The spirits of your living ances-tors, even your mother's, always connected to you even when their human form was not in alignment with their truth. And lest you think your lineage cares about your survival only, think again. Repeatedly, you receive the knowing that they are present and want to see you thrive with joy and success in your marriage and business. Money was never a part of your ancestors' story and neither were solid relationships. So, every chain you break and finish line you cross, you will sense them cheering you on and helping you. You are liberating the entire lineage. You are the result and answer to the desperate prayer they said for themselves and their posterity. The veil seems to become increasingly thinner, even though sometimes you forget to pay attention to the support all around you. Your feminine lineage is full of women who are orchestrating a life for your greatest and highest good. As you remember who you are, you liberate women everywhere to remember who they are too. Honoring your lineage blesses all feminine lineages throughout time.

Today, a family car full of six drives along, gleefully singing family road trip songs. We pull over onto a dusty dirt road unfamiliar to all but me. We go beyond the barbed wire fence, and I kneel and tell my children and husband that this land is sacred. Something holy that transformed the way I see life happened here. The tears fall, anointing the sand with the gifts I embody now because of this place and my mother; permission to claim joy, divinity, sovereignty, intimacy and femininity, no matter the circumstances. My kids clamor around me, using their sticky fingers to wipe the tears of gratitude from my cheeks as my husband's solid gaze meets mine. Thank you, my Melisa. My heart is full and I am whole.

Love,
Me

ABOUT THE AUTHOR

Melisa Keenan is an international feminine intimacy coach, visionary, and Keynote speaker. She is the trailblazer of a movement of women who pursue the fullest experience of life by embodying intimacy and leading with their feminine in both business and marriage. While only three short years ago she was a stay-at-home-mother of four without a penny to spare, the exponential growth and success of her business make her an inspiration to heart-centered entrepreneurs everywhere. Melisa's power lies in her ability to heal and claim joy for herself and others, through the tremendous life experience she has overcome. She enjoys dancing, singing, working, and praying at her hobby-ranch in Northern Nevada where she lives with her husband, CJ, and their four children Elisagrace, Christopher, Daily Abundance, and Evelyn-Joy.

Website: www.melisakeenan.com
Email: support@melisakeenan.com
Facebook: www.facebook.com/groups/2239709656292481

CHAPTER 11

RON MALHOTRA

 ear younger self,

At this stage, it may not be easy to conceive that your difficult childhood experiences have been preparing you for something special.

I know you want to achieve a lot and I do not want to end up living an average life. I feel that somewhere deep down, you also want to do something meaningful because you wish to be a people's champion even though sometimes you feel you cannot trust people.

I want you to know that the journey ahead will bring many challenges significantly different to the ones you have faced in the past.

The new challenges will shape your destiny if you make a sincere effort to learn from them.

Not only will the new challenges bring many revelations about yourself, they will also come with lessons that will enable you to guide others. I know you see your future version as someone commercially and financially astute, but there is an element of your future that you do not see yet.

That element is the impact you will have on others. There is a reason you have never felt inspired by athletes and entertainers as much as you're inspired by people who stand for something bigger than personal achievement.

You will achieve, but your achievements will not satisfy you because you will crave something much deeper. Your thirst for meaning and purpose will not diminish; it will only get stronger as you accomplish your financial goals, and throughout your career. It's likely hard for you to imagine, but a spiritual quest is not out of the question for you. You have always been curious, and that curiosity will serve you well.

It is important for you to understand that the experiences you consider undesirable and unpleasant are essential for the development of character that you are going to need to enable you to raise others.

Your struggles in jobs and your need for variety will create chaos and havoc in your life, but...only for the short term. You will see how your curiosity and your unwillingness to settle will turn into a blessing later in your life.

I know you won't have a problem having faith in yourself and your abilities, but don't forget to keep the faith in something much greater than you. Where possible, remember to observe the play of divine intervention in your life. The more you acknowledge it, the more frequently it will become in your life. Don't forget to occasionally take the time to be grateful for all that you have, whilst you so vehemently strive for everything you desire.

Your prosperity will come from combining production with integrity —production, not labor. Labor is all about what you put in, but production is all about what outcomes you produce. Keep asking yourself, "How can I add value to others in a way that uses my passion and skills?" and prosperity will come to you in abundance.

Since you have an interest in finance, learn everything that you can about money; not only how money is made, but also how it is multiplied. This is an area that most people have not mastered. Carefully observe and analyze habits, behavioral patterns, attitudes, and the skill-set of people who are financially successful. Use your gift of sifting through complex information to extract simple yet powerful insights that will change people's paradigms around money.

Get your money right, but don't stop there. Share what worked for you and enable others to do the same. That is what will separate you from others who have created inter-generational wealth, but don't necessarily want to share their financial wisdom.

Find mentors who have the results you want and learn from them with humility and openness. There is a lot you have to learn, and remember to not let feelings of insecurity impede your learning. By remaining curious and humble, you will remain in a state of continuous learning. This is important and will cause a deep understanding of principles that govern life. It is also the only way to wisdom. You must never stop seeking.

Here are the three factors that result in holistic success and deep fulfilment. The magic happens when you develop yourself in all three areas. It's the integration of these three factors, which is key.

Number one: An understanding and mastery of self. This includes being clear on your life's purpose, your passion, your unique strengths, your vision, your mission, and your goals. It also includes understanding your emotions and mindset and their connection to one's results.

Number two: An understanding and mastery of spiritual laws. This includes an understanding of energy, frequency, and vibration. It also includes the desire to understand and acknowledge what goes beyond the physical—mainly the metaphysical and paranormal. It also involves understanding that we are more than matter. Our connection to the world is important, and when we don't understand this, we may become clever, but wisdom may elude us.

Number three: An understanding and mastery of business and financial fundamentals. Since we live in an economic world where having sufficient money allows more choices and options, it is important to master the language of money and business. The lack of money can be a source of stress. Develop high income skills, but keep in mind that the skill of making money differs from the skills of keeping and multiplying money. The most important thing about mastering money is that it allows you to contribute to causes and people you care about.

Whilst success may mean different things to different people, there are some key contributors of success which are universal and apply to everyone, including you. The key contributors to success universally start with identifying your life's purpose and dedicating yourself to living it by aligning your occupational or career choice to your purpose.

The second one is to continue to strive to maximize your potential. This will require you to be mentally tough—persistent in your goals—and to remain agile so you can bounce back after challenges and adversity. Adversity strikes everyone, but not everyone responds to adversity the same way. When adversity strikes, you will either break or break records. If you maintain perspective and don't lose sight of your goals, you are more likely to do the latter.

Finally, make a difference in the world by solving a problem you deeply care about. These three factors are common amongst successful people with a high level of fulfilment in their lives.

It is best to treat success as a stopover, not as your final destination. Why? Because success by itself doesn't bring joy. If you want to experience real joy, not only fulfillment, then aim for significance. When you reach significance, you feel real joy in giving, because you have taken care of your psychological, physiological, emotional, social, and financial needs first. This allows you to strive for something far greater. Something that goes beyond your needs. Something that will bring you unparalleled joy. Whatever you do, don't bypass personal success. Many people do precisely that: they pour into others' cups without first filling their own. This is delusional and not wise if you wish to leave a positive footprint that makes a great impact on others.

Work on your communication skills continually. Identify the nuances in your thoughts and words. The more nuanced you become in your communication, the more people will notice, and that will add to your influence. Many people wrongfully assume that building influence is driven by vanity. What many do not realize is that influence is a great enabler of impact.

Influence is simply how many people know you, know about you, trust you, or respect you. The more influence you have, the better your chances to make an impact. You can influence people, policies, beliefs and even the strategic direction of groups, teams, and organizations. Great leaders always have influence and influence gives you an opportunity to lead positive change. Think big and set your sight on vision of such magnitude that you have no choice but to grow into the person you need to become in order to achieve that grand vision.

Make time for the important things. The five pillars of life are non-negotiable. They must be prioritized and everything else should be treated as secondary or delegated.

The five pillars to always prioritize are your mental well-being, your health and nutrition, your relationships, your career, and your finances. If any of these pillars are unstable or neglected for too long, your life will feel and become unstable. Occasionally, you may drop the ball on these pillars. However, as long as you pick up each pillar every 30 days, you will be fine. Everyone drops the ball and there in no point in beating yourself up over it. The principle fact to remember here is that as long as you don't neglect any of the key areas in the long term, your quality of life will be better than most.

Life is brief and short. How short?

Well, the average person will live less than 80 years or 4,000 weeks if they are lucky. That is all the time we get—maybe a little more or a little less. Keeping this fact in mind will create a sense of urgency for you to fulfill your dreams. Whilst many people claim that they have ambition, the true test of ambition is revealed in the level of the sense of urgency one demonstrates in going after their dreams. Make no mistake, not all action is equal. There is action...and then there is 'immediate' and 'massive' action. The first one creates momentum, but the second one brings big outcomes.

Since time makes up life and time is finite, life is therefore finite. So, treat your time with respect. Only exchange your time for activities that bring you growth, inspiration, or joy. You can either waste your time, spend your time or you can invest your time.

Most things you do will be a waste of your time. We must standardize daily activities into a routine as much as possible, so they take the least amount of our mental energy or time. Decide what activities will bring you growth, inspiration, or joy, and start planning and designing your life in such a way that you mostly exchange your valuable time for the highest value activities.

Never be casual about time, as time squandered will never return.

Learn to maintain an optimistic disposition about your future as much as possible, but do not let it distort your current sense of reality. The ability to remain highly optimistic about your future, whilst at the same time remaining brutally honest about your current situation is a superpower worth developing. It will allow you to keep your head in the clouds and have a bold vision for your life, whilst having your feet firmly planted on the ground and remaining realistic.

Determine your primary value because you will always be naturally motivated, disciplined, and organized when you are engaged in activities and tasks that align with your values. Many people will tell you to work on your weaknesses, but it is futile for you to work on traits and tasks for which you lack a natural gravitational pull, or at least some form of interest or intellectual curiosity.

The principles discussed are simple to understand, but they are not easy to remember, and certainly not easy to apply. Therefore, it's best to take these seriously, reflect on them regularly and apply them consistently so they become a part of your habitual nature and personality.

When that happens, you will be ready to conquer the world, because you conquered yourself.

Your older friend,
Ron Malhotra

ABOUT THE AUTHOR

Ron Malhotra enables ambitious professionals, visionary entrepreneurs, and business owners to magnify their influence, wealth and profits, so they can achieve a reliable plan to secure their financial future.

He is an award-winning wealth expert, managing director of Maple Tree Wealth Management and Black Footed Business Advisors and an author of several bestselling books.

Ron was voted as one of the Top 50 most influential men on LinkedIn in 2019, 2020 and Top 50 most globally admired Indians in 2018 by Passion Vista.

He has been featured in many mainstream media, including Entrepreneur, Forbes, Money Magazine, Personal Investor and more.

Website: www.ronmalhotra.com
Email: info@ronmalhotra.com
Linkedin: www.au.linkedin.com/in/ronmalhotra
Youtube: www.youtube.com/ronmalhotra
Twitter: www.twitter.com/ron_malhotra
Instagram: www.instagram.com/theronmalhotra
Facebook: www.facebook.com/ronmalhotrainternationa

CHAPTER 12

ROSIE CHEHADE

This is a call for the pioneers, for the innovators, for the ones who are audacious enough to be in the fire and stand for something they can't even make sense of. Dedicated to those of you who want to break the chains that are keeping you small, so you can truly rise to your next level.

ear younger self,

Here you are! You've dreamed of walking the Camino de Santiago for a whole decade and now you're about to board the plane and press start on the next chapter of your life.

This moment is everything. You intuitively know that you're at a turning point, and you're equally petrified and excited because you don't know what life is about to bring you.

You know this journey is going to shift everything—your business, your marriage, and your comfortable, secure life. And while you know this needs to happen, I know how uncomfortable and scary it feels.

Although the timing of your journey makes absolutely no sense, trust me when I say that your Camino experience couldn't have come at a better time (who would have thought when you booked your ticket all those months ago that this would be exactly what your soul would need —how's that for Divine intervention?).

Despite deeply knowing that you're on purpose in your work, and having tried everything to take it to the next level, your business has still hit a plateau.

You're experiencing your slowest months ever, and there's a not-so-comfortable imbalance between the money coming in, and the money going out.

You feel lost in how to get to where you want to be, and how you can tap into the wealth you desire.

I want you to know that although you feel you're at your all-time low and are struggling to see a way forward through the fog, this journey is going to shift *everything* for you.

You will know what it feels like to have the financial freedom you crave BUT you will never know what that feels like if you first don't allow yourself to come into the truth of who you really are.

THE INNER JOURNEY LEADS TO OUTER SUCCESS

Your focus needs to lie *within*, my love.

Not outside of yourself. Not in the strategy and 'doing.'

But within, because all the answers you seek are within you.

Trust me when I say that this journey—this physical *and* inward journey—will all be worth it.

It's time to reconcile and revolutionise all the parts of yourself that *still* hold you small and safe.

As soon as you do this, you'll redesign your business, revolutionise your relationship with money, and hit six figures and beyond, not long after.

But you won't get to where you want to be on your journey with wealth by having all your ducks lined up in a neat little row on the outside.

All the work that needs to be done is on the *inside*. In your heart.

Your heart needs you to listen to her. To nurture her. To love her. To go deeper on your journey with her as you explore your identity and expression as a woman.

This is the choice you now face and need to make for us. For our future.

DEEPLY TRUST YOUR INNER KNOWING. THIS IS YOUR COMPASS

It's a weird feeling isn't it—being equally called to do something and frightened by it, at the same time? Feeling as though the safe option would be to stay put and push through in your current reality *and* having a deep, intuitive, and nonsensical knowing that doing so would only push you further away from your truth; open to what may come *and* desperate for an immediate concrete resolution simultaneously.

I see you and I honour you ...

When societal conditioning would have you believe that sticking it out, ticking the boxes, and continuing to take action is what you need to do to get the clarity you want for your life, you're trusting your inner knowing and getting on that damn plane.

And that's scary as hell.

Do you know how many people turn around and retreat into predictability?

Do you know how many people choose fear over trust?

Do you know how many people choose pushing and 'doing', over pressing pause and allowing their inner wisdom to drop in?

Many people, my love. MANY.

But you've chosen to do things differently and, my god, I'm cheering you on.

I know it's hard not to think about everything that's weighing on your mind, but I want you to try your best to be here now. This moment is *all that matters*. Trust that this trip—this pressing pause on your daily life as you know it—will illuminate your next right steps forward.

I want you to remember that whatever unfolds because of your journey is exactly what is meant for you.

Yes, it may mean that things in your marriage, business, lifestyle (all the things!) get a shake up, but I want you to trust that you've got this.

Whatever life dishes out to you, you can handle.

Know that investing time and energy into doing this for yourself will reward your life tenfold … hundredfold!

I know your journey hasn't been easy, nor have the years/money/energy/blood/sweat/tears you've invested left you with the abundance you desire, but I want to give you a spoiler alert. What you will come to know wholeheartedly off the back of this journey is this:

A thriving business doesn't just require proven business strategies to support it to succeed; it needs the leader at its helm to have done deep inner healing and transformational work.

Not something you'd typically be told, right?

(Double spoiler alert, sweet one—you're going to understand and embody these teachings so fully, that they'll one day form the basis of what you teach and how you serve in this world!)

CHOOSE YOUR HEART OVER YOUR HEAD, EVERY TIME

So often in life we make decisions from our rational minds, based on evidence that we can see and experience (it's a human thing!)

But you're beginning to understand that the next evolution of your Self needs you go beyond this. It needs you to consider the idea that the possibilities for your life, wealth, and abundance are greater than you've ever allowed yourself to imagine and feel.

You've listened to your heart your entire life, and it has never led you astray.

Listen to her now, trust her, and allow all the external noise to drop away. As you board your flight, leave all rationality and logic at the gate.

Remove your armour, remove your labels of Coach, Teacher, Speaker, Wife, Sister, Daughter, and let your heart shush your mind.

In your heart is where the magic happens.

Your life needs you to go within, not look outside of yourself for external guidance and validation.

I know you want to retreat to what you know, because you feel safe in the familiar, but do NOT doubt the shit out of yourself.

You're being stretched and expanded and it's normal to be feeling uncomfortable.

Your energy and vibration are going through a mammoth growth spurt now because your heart is playing with the idea of up levelling your life in a way you never thought possible for yourself before.

Trust the discomfort. Go inwards.

Everything you have been through does not have the final say in your financial success, future reality, and what you create from here.

Your next chapter begins right now.

EVERYTHING UNFOLDS EXACTLY AS IT SHOULD

None of what you're going through right now means that you've fucked something up, or that you're failing. None of this means that you are bad or an imposter. None of this means that it's all falling apart. None of this means that it is all downhill from here.

Everything is unfolding exactly as it should, even though I know it feels really shitty and scary in the eye of the storm.

Whenever you take an action that doesn't serve your highest purpose, stray from your authenticity and integrity, or make a decision that isn't attuned to a vibration of your complete and utter worth and Queendom, you'll come up against roadblocks like these that will feel like failures.

But they're simply messages and signposts for you to check in with yourself, reconnect with your true self, and then take your next step from this place of knowing and alignment.

Ask any person you admire if they've experienced hurdles in their life and they'll respond with a deep and resounding YES!

All the greats—Richard Branson, Elizabeth Gilbert, Oprah—have had to overcome many feats to get to where they are today. Rejection, self-doubt, epic pivots, financial stress, relationship breakdowns, identity crises—you name it, they've experienced it.

What most will tell you in hindsight though, is that their journeys have unfolded in an almost Divine way (even if they felt anything but Divine at the time!)

As Steve Jobs once said, "You can't connect the dots looking forward; you can only connect them looking backwards. So you have to trust that the dots will somehow connect in your future. You have to trust in something — your gut, destiny, life, karma, whatever. This approach has never let me down, and it has made all the difference in my life."

THE KEY TO YOUR FINANCIAL LIBERATION

This next phase of your journey will completely transform you, how you serve, and the way you run your business, and you must be willing to let go of everything you thought you had to do to be successful, and birth your unique way forward.

The things you're clinging to are giving you the illusion of safety, and instead of expanding you and supporting you to be the woman you want to be, they're keeping you anchored in the small. They're keeping you stuck.

Honey, the reason you haven't yet reached financial liberation, is because YOU'RE NOT BEING YOUR TRUE SELF.

I know you've been taught that it's not safe to be your true self—to openly express your emotions, set huge goals that most people can't even fathom, take up s-p-a-c-e, and share vulnerably and intimately—but these things will be crucial to your success going forward.

You've never felt safe to be who you truly are, so you've spent years pretending to be someone you thought you needed to be to make money, find love, or be happy.

It's why your business has plateaued.

It's why you're in a marriage that isn't lighting you up.

It's why you feel stuck, lost, and hopeless about your future...

...because the actions you've taken and the people you've called in haven't been attracted by the *you* that exists as the highest expression of yourself.

You've been attracting experiences and people to the person you pretend to be, not the woman you are at your core.

As much as your rational human mind is telling you to stay put and try harder, it's your time to be bold, and rise to the occasion by trying something new.

As Albert Einstein said, "The definition of insanity is doing the same thing over and over again, but expecting different results."

This is not a time to wish things away, to hide or retreat to that constant set point of safety.

It's your time to arrive at the altar of your life, and rise gracefully to the occasion that's presenting itself.

When you do this, the success you desire will find its way to you.

LET YOUR TRUE SELF SHINE

You've been having the wrong conversation with yourself. One that says, "when money comes in, I'll feel safe to be my true self."

But the truth is the exact opposite: when you feel safe to express your true self, the money will come in.

Your only commitment to make from this day forward is to remain true to your authentic self. That's it. From there, the financial liberation (everything!) you seek will find you.

Right now, you're living your worst-case scenario—your business has flat lined, you have no money coming in, you're pretending to be someone you're not, and you're making yourself small when your inner Queen is screaming to be unleashed.

But guess what, my love …

You're still standing!

YOU ARE A POWERFUL GODDAMN GODDESS!

Don't you ever forget that!

The Camino will leave a trail of evidence that will prove to you that you can do anything you set your mind to. That you can rise from the ashes and be reborn. That you have what it takes to be the woman you deeply want to be. That you can build the wealth you desire.

You are creating your legacy RIGHT NOW.

As Elizabeth Gilbert said, "If you are brave enough to leave behind everything familiar and comforting and set out on a truth-seeking journey, and if you are truly willing to regard everything that happens to you on that journey as a clue, and if you accept everyone you meet along the way as a teacher, and if you are prepared – most of all – to face (and forgive) some very difficult realities about yourself... then truth will not be withheld from you."

That's what's in store for you. Stay open and receptive.

It's not meant to be comfortable or predictable. It's expansive for a reason—your future self needs you to be stretched in these ways so she can be revealed.

You will go into emotional spaces you're not used to and delve into realms of your being you haven't looked at. And when this happens, I want you to shut down your eyes, take a big breath and trust that on the other side of this tidal wave of discomfort is a deeper connection with your most authentic self, and that is where your wealth lies.

I remember reading once that people will have to move two mountains in a single lifetime and that these feats will forever set the trajectory of their lives.

You already climbed your first, when your major health crisis showed up, and derailed your life.

Your second mountain is here now, calling you to arrive in your fullness. For you to climb this mountain, parts of you, and your life as you know it, are going to have to die.

I want you to embrace this journey and hold your highest vision for yourself in your mind's eye and heart.

As you'll come to experience, the woman you're about to grow into flies courageously towards her highest vision of herself, with her arms wide spread, her commitment relentless, and a full embodiment of who she truly is.

This has been where my heart and journey have taken me, in my identity as a woman, as a leader, and as a human being, undoubtedly committed to serving humanity.

FEELING YOUR DREAM LIFE MAKES IT YOUR REALITY

My love, I want you to shut down your eyes and go within right now.

How would it *feel* to live life as your most true and unadulterated self?

How would it *feel* to do business your way, not how other people tell you it has to be done (that, let's be honest, feels crappy)?

How would it *feel* to have a beautifully full bank account that supports you to be of service, look after your loved ones and live a luxurious life?

And, my love, how would it *feel* to be financially independent and have complete autonomy over your finances so you never again feel trapped or forced into a corner?

FEEL INTO ALL OF THIS JUICINESS!

Don't question how. Don't let your monkey mind pipe in with its barriers and hurdles.

Simply imagine that all these things already exist and *feel* it in your body. *Soak. It. Up.*

Your poor nervous system is shot, and your mind is exhausted from constantly fearing and worrying. Instead of focussing on what's going wrong, it's time for you to focus on what you want to call in, so you can get into a state of receptivity.

This practice is how you do it.

Nothing in your business, your relationships, and within you will ever be the same again. And this is a beautiful thing.

Lean in. Embrace it all. Especially the bits that hurt, because they need your love.

Everything that has happened and is about to happen is for your highest good. It's all in your favour. It's all adding up for you.

Trust yourself. Trust the process. And believe.

You've got this. I love you. I am so happy you are reading this.

It's time to board and start your next chapter, beautiful.

Buen Camino!

ABOUT THE AUTHOR

Rosie Chehade is an international bestselling author and leading transformational success + master coach, speaker, and mentor in the coaching and consciousness industry.

She has empowered hundreds of leaders + soulpreneurs globally to grow their impact-driven business and quantum leap into their next-level success + wealth. She is internationally renowned for leading the best women's spiritual retreats and transformational group intensives in the world and is a spiritual advisor and business coach for some of the highest level CEOs and conscious entrepreneurs, authors, and multiple six-to-seven figure businesses.

Her powerful work is the first of its kind combining conscious and sub-conscious reprogramming with step-by-step strategies. She takes a D E E P holistic approach to biz by blending the mental, emotional, financial, and spiritual worlds.

Her principal focus in life is to support people in awakening to their wholeness and lead more open, happy, and fulfilling lives.

Website: *www.happinesslifestyle.com.au*
Facebook: *www.facebook.com/HappinessLifestylewithRosie*
Instagram: *www.instagram.com/rosiechehade_coach*
Email: *rosie@happinesslifestyle.com.au*

CHAPTER 13

SUE DONNELLAN
THE GIFT OF BEING UNAFFECTED

ear younger self,

You are magnificent! You have marvelous health and the vitality of youth. You are brimming with the innocence of naïve confidence. At this point in your young life, you maintain a carefree, idealistic existence.

You are both fearless and cavalier; and will soar through life in the certain knowledge that when you leap, the net will appear. This will be key to your entrepreneurial spirit and to your success in both business and life.

You'll enjoy a life lived unaffected by the criticism of others, by your own self-doubt, and by what society tries to dictate. None of those inputs will ever compare to the inner compass that illuminates your way.

Beware, though, your youthful self-assurance may be just an illusion that needs to be tested before it can become real. These tests will be disguised as challenges that arise from missed opportunities, pre-judgments, and selfish behavior. Adversity will dare you to take a stand, determine what you believe, and decide whether to sell out when tempted by the easy chance to do so.

The Opinions from Others

Freshly armed with your bachelor's degree in advertising, you promptly land a dream job in advertising sales for a trade magazine. Bursting with anticipation, it's finally your turn to experience a busy travel schedule, lunches out with colleagues, and important client meetings. How thrilling to finally be in charge of your own budget, filling in your new leather planner with work events, and reading *Advertising Age* on the commuter train from CT to NYC. It all feels so grown up.

Your joy lives up to the post-college dreams you had while slogging through school. You're sitting on cloud nine as you enjoy life exactly as imagined, with all the fun and money you ever thought you'd have access to at your age.

Soon, though, and with unexpected urgency, the day comes when you begin to feel disillusioned and restless. As you survey your tiny cubicle, you'll ask yourself the inevitable questions:

"Is this tiny cube going to be my home-away-from-home for the next thirty-five years?"

"Will there always be a minimum of six people within earshot, ever-ready to critique my foul-mouthed conversations with friends?"

"Will I constantly be judged by the eavesdroppers over my ability to make the sale when I slam the phone down from a rejection?"

As your youthful dreams begin to tarnish, you'll chafe at the constraints of a work life that has become a grind and wonder how to remove yourself from what has taken on somewhat of an intolerable situation.

Gut instincts that have been present, but not yet fully heeded, start to express themselves. Flashes of thought emerge telling you there has to be another way. Should you stay in this job and submit yourself to a lifetime of this work environment? As you cautiously share your private thoughts with others, testing the waters by saying out loud that you're unhappy, you are met with swift dismissal from your peers.

This is your first significant test. Will you recoil into the daily job grind or shut out the voices of your co-workers, friends, and family who insist that you've hit the jackpot with your dream job? Even while it sounds as though they are trying to convince themselves.

While on that fateful business trip to New Hampshire, you go for that run. Jogging in the White Mountains, you decide to stop listening to everyone else and instead take that leap of faith. You breathe in the fresh mountain air, with your mind numb from the meditative effect of exercise, and the first of many messages from your inner wisdom burst through. In that pivotal instant, the idea to start your own business crystalizes. No amount of money will ever repress your freedom and happiness again.

You excitedly share the news with your inner circle and encounter every conceivable unsolicited opinion about your decision:

"Why would you leave a great-paying job?"

"Don't you know that over 50% of new businesses fail?"

"Who risks their entire savings on such a gamble?"

Instead of feeling minimized, you embark confidently on your new investment in yourself. You pass this test, never letting others define or restrict you. Just as you've shrugged off the doubt from those you trust most; you encounter the next level of naysayers. The tradespeople who you'll depend on for new information to get your business off the ground —bankers, vendors and marketers. There will always be those who say:

"It's not done that way."

"Your idea won't work."

"No, it can't be done."

Those sentiments are merely other people's oppositions and fears. Don't make them yours. Resistance often arises when someone lacks the creativity to find alternate ways of solving problems. The joy stealers will not triumph. As you surround yourself with an advisory board of the people who support you, you learn how to fortify your resolve to do what inspires you. Let that voice inside your mind drown out the ones trying to assail your psyche. When living life by your own rules, you are unaffected by the pessimism of those who only espouse failure.

While carving multiple new paths to create something from nothing, you'll come to fully embrace the knowledge that every rule is only conceived by another person, just like you. Rules can be changed, broken, and even ignored. When you live confidently in your ability to be unaffected by others, you take risks, blast through barriers and create opportunity for yourself and others. That's when you'll know you are living fully in your power.

The Opinions from Our Self-Doubt

Just as you revel in the newfound independence of running your own business, your college romance will become more serious. Your future partner has chosen a career in the military; undoubtedly one of the most restrictive, least independent careers. While you've taken steps toward the freedom of entrepreneurship, you will now find yourself faced with the difficult decision of whether to pursue a deeper relationship with the love of your life or choose to build your business.

The old phrase, "If the military wanted you to have a spouse, they would have issued you one" will ring in your ears. You're told by trusted mentors, "There's no way you can combine an entrepreneurial lifestyle with the stringency of military life." Military spouses don't work; instead, they raise families and support their military member—forever relegated to dependent status. Moving every two years, as well as supporting a man who chooses to pursue a combat-focused specialty and who will deploy to combat five times, is not synonymous with being able to successfully run your own business.

You'll begin to doubt if you can commit to the military lifestyle, even second-guess yourself as to whether he is the right person for you after all. How will you choose between your newly formed business and the love of your life?

Remember that you've waited your whole life, until this point, to find this type of unconditional, true love. Relive the instant connection you experienced that moment in college when you first glanced his way and recognized your soulmate from across the room, even though he was still just a stranger.

Ignore the noise of the detractors who will maintain that you cannot have the best of both worlds. Making decisions based on what others think and do has never defined you. You are blessed to be deeply intuitive, and this has served you well throughout your life. Your internal knowing is something you come to realize everyone has, but not everyone can accept or understand. Know that when you are in sync with yourself, your relationships with others will deepen. By consulting with your inner knowing, you'll make your final decision after being led to ask yourself this simple, yet profound question:

"How does life feel without him?"

The clarity is immediate! You marry him and all else falls into place.

The Opinions from Society

So far, you've enjoyed total control of your life; you've been firmly in charge. You've figured out how to be unaffected by the opinions of others and how to ignore your own self-doubt.

On a routine pregnancy visit to your doctor's office, you'll experience your most life-defining moment when your doctor shares the shocking news:

"You're having triplets."

Your second pregnancy delivers babies two, three and four to your family along with your 2 ½ year old. The triplets are in addition to your full-time business and your deploying husband. The unaffectedness you've achieved by not listening to cynics or giving in to your self-doubt will be challenged by yet another demand on your hard-won freedoms. You'll get no less than hundreds of well-meaning inputs on the expectations of a mother of four:

"You'll never have time to shower."

"Make sure you socialize them because triplets can be socially awkward."

"You won't be able to run your business *and* be a mom to four kids, three at the same time, that'll be impossible!"

By digging even deeper, you'll find the ways and means to remain unaffected by what society says your life needs to look like. Continuing to follow your inner knowing, you'll make the right decisions for you, redefining how motherhood, entrepreneurialism and being a supportive spouse can and do co-exist beautifully. No one else can provide the answers that build your successful life. They can only come from you.

The opinions of society are meaningless. They suggest you need to give up your business, or that you can't handle a husband in the military while also being an entrepreneur—that you can't have it all. Be unaffected by society's rules and re-write the book for women in the 21st century. You are beginning to figure out that there is no cookbook recipe to follow. You gave up looking for leadership from anyone else when you realized it doesn't exist.

Leadership - Your Most Valued Asset

Finally, apply these lessons on how to live an unaffected life by incorporating them into the role you take on for others. This requires that you embrace the unique value others offer through their own experiences, just as you pull from your own.

We are all interwoven, yet individually autonomous. Some people in our lives will stay for a lifetime, some will be more fleeting. But they will, in their own way, all add value and meaning to your journey as we will to theirs. Sometimes you'll take on the role of teacher in another person's story, and sometimes the roles change as you find yourself learning from those you taught. Sometimes the journeys will overlap or run side by side, but ultimately, our journey remains our own.

Only by staying authentic to your distinct, unaffected voice, will you be given the courage to reject the buzz of irrelevant judgements, preconceived stereotypes and intolerance from the crowd. Out of that position of strength, your specific value and leadership will freely emerge.

Nurturing the gift of true love, being open to it and inviting it into your heart will be the most significant event in your life. From that foundation, you will be able to meet the challenges before you.

Becoming a mom, and a mom of four over-night, will catapult you into learning many of the most illuminating truths in your life. It will pave the way to become the leader and role model you are meant to be, even taking it to the next level. Motherhood and the uncertainty of entrepreneurialism will also exponentially increase your ability to understand a variety of thought processes and perceptions, while developing your empathy beyond measure.

Children, especially your own, will relentlessly shine a mirror on you that will force you to question what you say, do and feel, and in the end will be the greatest reward for committing to a life unaffected by noise.

When you no longer care about what others think about you, you take back the power you've given them over you. By not being consumed or distracted by the chatter of others, you will become immune to it. This immunity to other people's judgments will enable you to assume control of your own life, decisions, and happiness. Learn to harness this power early, and you will start to soar. When you are unaffected by someone offending you or disagreeing with you, you have ultimate control over yourself.

You will discover with time that the lessons you learned from living your unaffected life, building a successful business, raising kids and having a fulfilling, happy marriage will empower you to come firmly into your own fearlessness. You will share that courage with others through your leadership.

During moments of adversity, always strive to retain ownership over yourself. No amount of investment in others, no matter how much you love them, will take the place of the investment you make in yourself.

This letter has been written to you from the wisdom that comes from time and perspective. If the tremendous value of trusting yourself and being unaffected by all external influences could be put into a little gift box, then this letter would be in that box. Treasure this; it holds the secrets to your happy, successful and fulfilled life.

ABOUT THE AUTHOR

Sue Donnellan is the mom behind *Ask Mom Parenting* and the author of the International #1 bestselling book, *Secrets to Parenting Without Giving a F^ck*. She is a mom to four children (including triplets), founder of 3 businesses, and wife of a career military officer.

Sue knows how it feels to parent while submerged in stress, how to overcome and how to get the job done with humor and wisdom. If she can emerge triumphant, so can you, and she'll show you how.

Her Ask Mom Parenting platform has become sought after for its personal parenting classes in the form of mentoring. Sue's results-based, no-nonsense program helps parents who are drowning, just like she was.

She teaches the transformative parenting mindset that helps end tantrums, eliminate back-talk, neutralize sibling fights and build lasting relationships of lifelong trust and respect with your kids.

FUN FACTS: In her free time, she's also a mom to two dogs. She's discovered a cure for hiccups and created a family recipe for sleep dust. She appreciates great comedy and is passionate about living healthy.

FREE 20-minute Mentoring Consultation:
   www.calendly.com/suedonnellan/consultation
Take the Parenting Survey: www.AskMomBook.com
Website: www.AskMomParenting.com
Get the book: www.amazon.com/Secrets-Parenting-Without-
   Giving-Non-Conformist/dp/0578843838
LinkedIn: www.linkedin.com/in/suedonnellan
Facebook: www.facebook.com/AskMomParenting
Instagram: www.instagram.com/askmomparenting

CHAPTER 14

TAMALA RIDGE

ear younger self,

Hey, Girl, I see you over there, dancing high up in the air on that huge speaker in the corner of the nightclub, letting your hair down, embracing your inner rebel—totally absorbed in the lack of pain you feel in this moment, and I celebrate that feeling with you.

I want you to know that it's so ok to seek that space; the space between your thoughts, your pain, your suffering, your victimhood... It's a great thing to seek.

I am in awe of your commitment to finding those spaces. You are the Happy High Seeking Queen.

All this playing, experimenting, and eventual addiction will be your learning ground. It will be the space where you get down and dirty in order to rise again. You will become a supreme spiritual athlete and this training is the platform from which you will jump; the edge from which you will fly, and the fire from which you will emerge.

I am here to tell you that you are going to make it. Just as the Phoenix rises from the ashes, so too will you, my love. You will never stop chasing that illustrious HIGH. What you are doing now is discovering every single avenue that will eventually bring you to your knees. It will all take you to a place of absolute surrender and it is all a necessary part of your initiation into the higher realms.

You will eventually discover many natural highs that will take you to places way beyond where you are now. But you will need to dive through the dark to discover the light. This is your doorway—your rite of passage —and you WILL MAKE IT THROUGH.

You will eventually learn to dance without a concoction of drugs and alcohol to find that 'zone'– that portal of freedom, bliss, and a tribal knowing that the movement is actually a powerful way to move anger, grief, sadness, and fear out of your body. You will also use it with intention in ritual, celebration, and sacred devotion, COMPLETELY SOBER AND HIGH ON LIFE!

"Sober dancing! wtf?" I hear you say.

Lol! Yes, babe, sober dancing will become your thing!

You will discover oxytocin—the love drug, the hormone that will become the basis of your medicine, the opposite of cortisol and adrenaline. You will ultimately uncover the pathway to turn your addiction to pain, suffering, stress, and self-doubt into an addiction to love, celebration, and joy, and then eventually share this with the world.

You will become a pioneer in the world of addiction, inviting others to consider an alternative story than the one that has been told so far – that we are more addicted to the come-down than we are to the high.

I see you now on your 30th birthday, dancing on top of that speaker, doing your best to distract yourself from the grief of losing your beloved Papa Bear only five days ago. I want you to hear that your medicine has now been activated. EVERYTHING you do from this day forward will be a process to add more and more powerful ingredients to your potion. You will no longer be drawing from and depleting it. You have activated the centrifuge, the process of spinning off the dross; the old beliefs, patterns, and traumas, to re-align with the purity of who you truly are. Separating yourself from your ego.

You have begun the process of alchemising your pain, removing the dross from the precious metal, in order for your medicine to become the GOLD.

The grief you are experiencing now amidst the thick veil of intoxication will be the catalyst that shifts your spiritual seeking to a new level. It will begin the removal of the veil and an ascension into the magical, sacred, and devotional, mind-altering practices that don't involve a comedown.

FINALLY, you will begin to seek those happy highs that come from within and you will become a devoted *#spiritjunkie, #detoxjunkie #mindfulnessmaven* and *#loveaddict.* You will dive deeply into yoga, chanting, mindfulness, dancing, meditation, circles, bodywork, massage, counselling—all sorts of physical, emotional, mental, and spiritual healing modalities, and they will become your new addiction.

You will learn that every human is hard-wired to become addicted to things, and this will be your greatest discovery—how to get addicted to the things that bring you closer to Heaven, love, and God.

You will come through this as an absolute warrior, a teacher, a leader, a change-maker, and an activist. The medicine you will eventually offer the world will become so refined that it will no longer seem to be of you, but of God, flowing through you. You will become committed to purifying your physical vessel for this to happen and you will support others to do the same.

As you lie there on your father's bed after leaving the nightclub, the room still spinning, sinking deeply into the moment your father left you—a devastating time-collapsing, heartbreaking, earth-shattering moment—I have my arms tightly wrapped around you. I know this feeling well—when the veils between the worlds are so very thin and all you want to do is die. You desperately want to join him in his freedom, peace, and ascension.

No one else in the world gets you. No one has ever understood you. No one has ever related to you like your dad did. The conversations that you had were out of this world—expansive, philosophical, and deeply spiritual. You were able to explore together, seek the truth, and dance around the edges of this reality.

Who the fuck was ever going to replace that?

I feel you slipping away; your desire to follow him is so unbelievably strong. You feel as though there is no purpose to your life without him.

Even though your dad was far from perfect—sometimes violent, aggressive, emotionally absent, and unavailable—the one thing you could do with him was to be yourself, and he really got you and you got him.

There is unbearable loneliness in your stomach even amongst family and friends. It is more than loneliness, it's terror—a deep empty void of nothingness that is utterly terrifying.

You are afraid.

Grief-stricken.

Frozen.

Nothing makes sense anymore. You are questioning life and you feel as if you might go insane.

You are trying to connect with him and there is nothing but a vast, fearful, excruciating emptiness.

I feel you. No one can comfort you, even though many have tried and offered. But nothing will take away your pain and yearning to leave this world.

And you know what? No one will replace him. But you will absorb him; take his soul deep into yours as you become one with him.

Please know that this pain will slowly lessen. The grief will become not so all-encompassing. Yet, for as long as you stay a believer in this 3D reality, it will never truly leave you.

This is not your time, because welcoming death as an escape from the pain of life is not the answer, my love. When your time does come, you will be in a space to leave this world because you have embraced ALL of life and you are not afraid of death. You will welcome it as a celebration of your experiences and a welcoming of the transmutation of this 3D reality. A welcoming of the eternal infinite consciousness that is true and blissful peace. You will not be running from Hell; you will be running towards love.

You will soon discover that Heaven and Hell are not places that you go to when you die. Everything is in the eternal moment. Heaven and Hell are right here, right now and my precious self, you are in Hell now.

And as daunting as this seems and perhaps it may even fuel your desire to leave this realm even more, I want you to know that you will eventually discover this profound truth and it will become the message you share to the world, supporting others to discover Heaven here and now. You will become a true believer and champion for Heaven on Earth.

This pain will become your greatest gift, your greatest opportunity for awakening, the ingredient that will set you free and your medicine on fire.

The severity of the pain is necessary to make you question the pain itself. It will push you up against your edge of sanity and is a necessary doorway that will support you to entirely shift your perception of the meaning of life and death. The pain will trigger a switch in you that will activate you to think, feel, and act differently from here on in.

The edge of pain will lead you to discover that pain and Hell are ultimately a choice and it is not the truth. As *A Course in Miracles* states, "Nothing real can be threatened, nothing unreal exists." You will discover that loss is not real, only a perceptual concept born from the belief that we are just a 3D body.

Oh, and by the way, that book has been sitting on your bookshelf for ten years now and you will pick it up many times before you choose to commit to its teachings. It will become one of your greatest spiritual teachings.

The question is...do you really want to come back and do this all over again?

This is your opportunity to discover the truth of who and what you are—answers I cannot reveal to you now; they are up to you to discover on your own.

So, I will ask you some questions instead:

WHO OR WHAT ARE YOU?

You are more magnificent than you can possibly imagine right now and when you learn to heal your broken relationship with God, you will have the answer to this question. I invite you to ask yourself this question upon waking every single morning: "Who am I?"

WHAT ARE THE THINGS YOU ARE REALLY GOOD AT?

Keep doing them with fervour and enthusiasm. You were always the life of the party, the one who gathered the tribe and created the momentum for people to follow. You were always the last one standing at the end of the night, making sure everyone was ok, and gathering the remaining few to join you on the next adventure. You had stamina, enthusiasm, and a lust for that elusive HIGH.

You will create programs, trainings, and workshops—in your 40s—that will feel like a party. Everyone who attends gets to feel HIGH, because you will support healers, coaches, and practitioners to heal from their self-sabotaging addictive behaviours and patterns. You will support others to increase the potency of their medicine. You will become a divinely sought-after coach's coach.

HOW CAN YOU BEGIN TO NOTICE AND RELEASE GUILT, SHAME, AND UNWORTHINESS?

These are the elements that will slow you down and create the most suffering in your life. They are the ingredients that will dilute your medicine for many years, so remember that whether or not you hold onto these feelings and limiting beliefs is your choice." (ie. having or experiencing them is not a choice, but how you respond to and process them is the choice)

When you begin to dismantle and separate yourself from these distractions of the ego, you will step into the role of spiritual mentor, leading the way for other medicine women to follow. It will ultimately become about supporting other leaders and coaches to release their deep beliefs that they are unworthy of heaven.

HOW CAN YOU HARNESS YOUR FREE WILL?

Free-will is your one and only God-given power. It is your ability to choose love over fear at any point in time and space. But first, you must discern the difference between love and fear.

You will spend many years grappling with this distinction, and when you get clear on it—BOOM, sista! It will be the most commonly asked question by your students and you will support them to discover the answer for themselves with crystal-clear clarity.

When you realise you have the God-given free-will power to create your own reality, you will begin to manifest HEAVEN on Earth and support others to do the same

WHAT DOES YOUR INNER VOICE TELL YOU?

What kind of thoughts are you having? Are you your own best friend or your worst enemy? When you take charge of this, EVERYTHING will change. You will become a mindfulness teacher and you will often be quoted as saying, "Mindfulness is the medicine for everything!"

And finally, WHAT IS YOUR RELATIONSHIP TO GOD?

You will spend many years rejecting God, which is ultimately a rejection of yourself. Have you thought about redefining your idea of God? What are the characteristics of a divine, sovereign being that you could rely on, trust in, and fall in love with? You get to choose, you have the power, and you already have all of the answers. It's time to let go of the way religion, family, friends, and anyone else defines God and dive deep into your own intuitive knowing. This is where you will find Him/Her and believe me, you will fall in love again.

So, I am holding you whilst you lay on the bed, just days after your father passed over. I've got you; you can do this. You are braver than you think, stronger than you can ever imagine and more powerful than you can dream of.

This is not your time to die, to follow your father. This is simply the beginning, a giant leap in your spiritual development and one of the greatest and most profound experiences of your life.

And deep down, you know this to be true. As you looked deeply into your father's eyes as he took his final breath, you felt it—I know you did. That moment when time stood still, reality as you knew it melted away and you connected deeply with his and your immortality.

You saw and felt universal, infinite consciousness that has no beginning or end.

As you experienced this new revelation, this new deeper understanding of the meaning of life, you now have a clearer goal post. Your direction has pivoted and you will now do everything in your power to stay focused, guided, and clear on your direction—straight to Heaven, baby, and you don't need to die to find it.

Your father left early so he could be with you, protect you, guide you and comfort you in a more profound way. He will be a lot easier to access now that he has moved to the ethereal realm. You will have him on-call, 24/7.

He will speak to you and through you; he will have the opportunity to live vicariously through you as you continue to work on and heal aspects of your father wound with him. You will also do this in preparation for your children to come—yes, they are coming.

This is the crucial moment in your life where you transmute:

- From wild, crazy, irresponsible party girl to devoted and reverent space holder
- From spiritual seeker to spiritual mentor and leader
- From depression and anxiety to excitement and celebration
- From victim to empowered leader

GET UP, GIRL!

For many years from this point, you will paint your dad—our dad—as a monster. You will focus on his wrong-doings, his violence, his anger, his egotism, and his abandonment of you, your sister, and your mother. The reason you will spend so many years focusing on his faults and betrayals is because you were so fucking ANGRY that he left you.

After years of him leaving the family home; multiple times, you had finally formed a functional and loving relationship with him in your 20s; where you felt safe that he wasn't going to abandon you again—and then he goes and bloody dies! He was only 56, and yet he used to say, "I'll outlive you all!"

If you focused on his earlier abuse, neglect and violence then you might be able to cope with the fact that he is no longer here.

But truth be told, you always saw through that. You always saw his seeking soul, the wounded child within him, the gift that he gave to you. You always saw him as your hero—a clever, strong, and intelligent man.

This is the gift that will carry you through life. It's the gift that will fuel an incredible career as a drug and alcohol counsellor because it's part of your medicine to see the good in all, no matter how destructive the crime; to see the wounded child, the pain, neglect, and trauma from people's pasts. You will have great compassion and people will feel safe with you.

It had to be this way. He came to play this role for your learning and discovery of how to heal from abandonment so that you could support others to do the same.

You will stand proudly at his funeral in a week's time and announce to the crowd of hundreds that you will see your father again, that you will smell him, touch him and be with him. As strange as this may seem to those listening, I want you to know that this is true.

I see our dad every single day, I smell him, I speak with him, I hear him, and I laugh with him. When you learn to let go of the importance of the physical and embrace the energetic, you will end your suffering.

You will begin to embrace your black sheep-ness, your secret love of shaking others up, going against the grain, pushing the limit on society's expectations and norms. You will spend many years reclaiming your sovereignty and freedom when the world's egoic systems try to take it from you.

When you embrace the fact that you see the world through a different lens to most people, you will stop feeling so alone at night—separate— and like you don't belong here. I know you feel as though you are looking through the eyes of God and that there is no one else out there. This is far from insanity, my dear self; this is closer to the truth than you could possibly imagine.

The one thing that makes you feel so different is what, in truth, makes you so connected.

All of these poignant moments, tragedies, epiphanies, separations, and connections are building an incredible alchemy, an elixir of the soul, your divine medicine. Soon enough, you will offer this medicine to the world. You will support others to connect with, own, and deliver *their* unique medicine with utmost spiritual integrity.

Every event is significant and as much as things feel painful right now, just know everything is happening for a reason; a shake-up, a healing, a nudge closer to your awakening. Yes, yes, it really will happen!

I've got you, girl.

I am celebrating you.

I honour you.

And...

I love you.

See you on the dance floor... *Let's do this!*

ABOUT THE AUTHOR

Tamala Ridge is the founder and director of the Institute for Spiritual Companioning. She is an international best-selling author, addictions specialist and spiritual mentor.

Tamala is the a highly sought-after coach's coach, providing training for leaders and practitioners who desire an up levelling in their space holding skills. Those who work with her quickly stand out as experts in their field by becoming qualified as Spiritual Companioning Practitioners.

Her mission is to inspire others to experience Heaven on earth through the sacred art of her physical, mental, and emotional cleansing programs. After her own battle with addiction, she has become a self-confessed #detoxjunkie and #spaceholdingmentor who now gets high on the sobriety of her untainted soul.

Website: www.tamalaridge.com
Email: tamala@tamalaridge.com
Facebook: www.facebook.com/tamalaridge1

CHAPTER 15

TARSH ASHWIN

'The wound is the place where the light enters you.'
~ Rumi

ear younger self,

If I were to look back on one of the most profound turning points in your life, I'd find you floating in the bathtub on a wintery night in 2018. You have two bottles of red wine marinating in your system. Your ex-partner and toddler are asleep in the house and you are the closest you've ever been to ending your life.

The addictiveness of depression surprises you. The feeling that you could (un)happily stay in this state of numbness for a very long time. This space of ultimate presence where there is nothing but you and your misery. You had spent your evening sitting on the balcony, under the full moon, smoking cigarette after cigarette and drinking glass after glass until you'd concluded that enough was enough.

You wanted out.

You had described the feeling as one of 'cosmic homesickness' and you fantasised about the freedom that might come from being free of your body. This place didn't feel like home anymore and you would sit, under the moon, and wonder where exactly that home that you craved was.

And so, as you float in the bath, you make the drunken decision to die.

It's at that moment something curious happens. The timeline of consequences of that decision flash in your mind's eye—your toddler finding his mother floating dead in a bath of red water and the impact that your decision would have on his life. The bone aching agony of your ex, with whom you still share great love. You begin to realise that this isn't a timeline you want to subject the people you love the most to, yet the density of this experience feels unbearable.

As I peer back through the layers of time to this pivotal moment, I see a woman in the grips of Post Natal Depression. A woman who has never experienced such devastating lows before and who is floored by the experience. A woman whose transition into motherhood has rocked her to her core.

In your proverbial 'bathroom floor' moment, I see you perceiving the veil between worlds starting to thin. You suddenly experience an overwhelming knowing that you are not alone. That your unseen support team has chosen this time to make their presence known. You imagine that it's your recently passed grandmother reaching out from the other side. You can almost hear her speaking softly in your ear.

You wonder if it's the booze. You hope that it's not. But I bet that in a million years, you'd never consider that the presence you feel might be me, your future self.

They say we have to hit rock bottom before we find the courage to climb back up. I'd love to share with you some things you have no way of knowing right now, but you'll come to deeply understand as you lie in that bath at the biggest crossroads of your life.

If you cast your mind back to that night in your late teens, in your favourite nightclub. You're lining up for the bathroom and the woman in front of you turns, locks eyes, and whispers in your ear, 'I believe that at every point in our lives we are exactly where we're meant to be.' She winks at you, spins on her heel, and enters the cubicle.

Her 17 words changed the next 10 years of your life.

Those words percolated in your mind and acted as a catalyst for you, encouraging you to take actions that you'd been otherwise afraid to take —traveling the world with nothing but your backpack and living intuitively, based on what felt *right* in the moment. Those words helped you to understand the intricately connected nature of life and helped you embody the knowing that life is not made up of random coincidences, but intricately connected synchronicities designed to elicit key life lessons.

Soul lessons, if you will.

But I see you've forgotten this knowing. I suppose it's fine to believe these things when life is easy; it's when life gets hard that these insights tend to go out the window.

Let me gently remind you. At *every point*, you are exactly where you're meant to be. Even now.

Charlie's birth, as traumatic as it was for you, had to happen as it did. It set in motion a cascade of events that converged right here, right now. You see, you've spent your life existing in the space of neutrality. Your 'happy-go-lucky' demeanour has meant that you've found it difficult to process any emotions other than positive ones. You've become a master at pushing your traumatic experiences, and the consequential pain, to the depths of your subconscious, shoving it away from prying eyes.

As you lie in that bathtub, your heart is cracking wide open and it's more painful and beautiful than anything you've ever experienced before.

Beautiful, you say? *How can this be beautiful?*

Because this moment is teaching you how to *feel* again and it's in your capacity to *feel* that your power resides.

So stop avoiding it. Feel it all. Even the shame. Let's go there together...

The shame you felt after your babe finally made his dramatic entry into the world and you didn't experience the overwhelming love and adoration that everyone said you were supposed to feel.

The shame you felt when your bank account dropped to double digits and it was rent day and the bills were stacking up and you couldn't for the life of you ask your parents for the money because you'd portrayed this act that everything was fine and you were doing well, thank you very much.

The shame you felt that your relationship was in tatters and your toddler saw you throwing a glass at his dad which spilt red wine all over the wall like blood. The final straw.

The shame you felt when you had lost yourself in motherhood and daydreamed of buying a one-way ticket to the other side of the world and reclaiming the freedom you felt all those years ago.

These are the darkest days of your life but you will come to greatly appreciate them.

Because of these days, you will find the courage to seek support and undergo a profound journey to reclaim your power, piece by piece. This reclamation will skyrocket you into a place that, right now, you could never even dream is possible.

There will come a time when you realise that being separated from your ex is causing you both more grief than happiness and you will reunite, stronger than before. He will become the rock that supports you as your second boy is birthed in your living room in the most empowering and ecstatic experience of your life. Once again, you'll be floored by the overwhelming intensity of motherhood and birth. But this time, the healing that will take place in those moments as you work to bring your baby earthside will be so deep that you'll find you can't articulate it. The raw, primal, power will cascade through your body and wake up every ounce of self-determination you possess. You will feel like a superwoman in the months following this experience; as if you can do absolutely anything you put your mind to.

(Because you can.)

With hindsight, you'll understand that the two (totally different) birth experiences of your babies will act as powerful initiations. Right now, as you're in the throes of the first initiation. It feels like you're dying because, in many ways, you are. This is the death of the maiden as she transitions into a mother. Right now, the responsibility of mothering another soul lays heavily upon you because it doesn't come as easily as you had believed it would and you so desperately don't want to fuck it up. Let me tell you, you *must* release the shame and guilt that has kept you frozen in fear. Then, and only then, the resistance you feel will melt away as you truly surrender to this powerful role of Mother.

Indeed, over time you will come to see your role to be the greatest path you could walk.

One day, in conversation with a friend who laments the necessity of putting her child in care five days a week so she can return to work, you stumble upon a life-changing realisation. You realise you don't want to return to work. You don't want to put your child in care just so you can enter the rat race again. Whilst you've always had a side business, it has come secondary to your job which provided financial security. But why did it have to be that way? What would it take to create a business that supports you financially *and* provides a way for you to keep your babies at home while they're young?

These questions spark a tenacity within you unlike anything you've ever known before. You will dive headfirst into re-birthing your business and come to find it on par with motherhood in how challenging yet satisfying it is. Through building your business, you'll learn the simple art of *asking for what you want*. Claiming your desires with the tenacity and courage that is backed by powerful self-belief. Hear me, the woman that your current moment is forging believes in her ability to create magic. You will come to know inherently that *you* are the source of your success, be it in motherhood, relationships, or business, and you will stop looking outside of yourself for that approval.

Life will seem to come full circle when you decide to open up a publishing company. Memories will resurface of when you were a girl, locking yourself away in your room with the latest Harry Potter book, resurfacing 12 hours later once you'd devoured it. Memories of filling piles upon piles of journals with your stories and innocent musings on life.

Ashwin Publishing will be born; your third baby of sorts.

This is why you will come to believe so powerfully in what you do: the world that you are currently living in, and the world that I live in three years later has changed dramatically. Censorship is rampant in today's day and as a woman who has always been a fierce stand for disrupting the status quo, your publishing company will give a platform to the conscious entrepreneurs who are actively standing for an essential paradigm shift. The leaders who dare to say the things that people are thinking, but no one is saying. The changemakers who deliver the powerful healing that the world needs to shift course from fear into love.

Those will be your people whose words and transmissions you publish. You must not let their voices be silenced.

Indeed, there is a global battle currently taking place between love and fear. It is subtle, masterful, and highly divisive, and you will come to feel as if everything you've been working toward has prepared you for it. There will be times when you feel as if you're going crazy. Times where you wish you didn't truly see the truth of what was happening. But these times will further concrete your belief in the work you do and the voices your company helps amplify.

What I want you to know, as you lie in your bath, is that you have a purpose that is far bigger than your current pain. It is essential that you learn how to connect to your purpose here and your motivation. This will act as the anchor that tethers you when the craziness of the world becomes too much. Hold on to the vision you have for the more beautiful world you believe is possible because this is the world your children will be inheriting. When your confidence dips, ask yourself: do I want my children to grow up in a world that is full of love or a world that is full of fear?

You have no way of knowing right now, but there is so much ahead of you. Developing the ability to *trust* that everything will work out is essential. Trust that the universe is always responding to you and is listening to the signals you're giving it. Your intuitive knowing is the most powerful GPS tool you have. Listen to it, trust it and always act on it, even when people around you think you're crazy. When you can learn to stay in this space of deep trust, life becomes a dance between listening and responding.

At the end of the day, I'll leave you with the best advice I can offer you. Life is a game so stop taking it so seriously. Find the courage to embody your raw authenticity and have fun with the precious time you have here. Strive toward work/life balance and recognise that you have workaholic tendencies. Your children will grow up so quickly and they are the true legacy you will leave. You don't want to get to the end of your life and wish you had spent more time being fully present with them.

It's time to gather your courage because you're on the precipice of great expansion. Like the phoenix who is reborn from its ashes, you will rise and fall, again and again. But each time you rise, you will get stronger. Each time your self-belief will harden a little more and each time you will move one step closer to creating the life you deeply desire.

Remember, there will be times when you're standing on the edge, about to leap into the unknown. I'll be there to give you the loving push you need to take the action that scares you the most, but that you know you need to take.

You can thank me when we finally cross the threshold between life and death. But now, my love, is most certainly not that time.

ABOUT THE AUTHOR

Tarsh is an international bestselling author, business strategist, and the CEO and founder of Ashwin Publishing. She provides a platform for conscious leaders and entrepreneurs to share their message with the world, elevate their authority and effect global change.

She specialises in guiding soulful women in business to grow their impact-driven business and step into empowered leadership. Her work is a bespoke fusion of inner mindset work, energetic transformation, and outer strategy implementation that paves the way to purposeful profit. She believes in the incredible power of publishing to grow heart-centred businesses that are committed to effecting transformational global change.

Tarsh lives in Newcastle, Australia, with her partner and two young boys.

Website: www.tarshashwin.com
Facebook: www.facebook.com/tarshashwin and
www.facebook.com/groups/businessalchemycollective
Instagram: www.instagram.com/tarshashwin
Email: tarsh@tarshashwin.com

CHAPTER 16

VIRGINIA SADA YORK

A JOURNEY OF TRANSFORMATION

"Life can only be understood backwards; but it must be lived forwards."
- Soren Kierkegaard, Danish philosopher

ear younger self,

It is very poignant writing back to you, age 35, in your shattered life. Love is broken and work is fragile. Love, work, health—these are the foundations. Yours are shaky.

Though it's a terrible time right now for you, know there is destiny unfolding right now for you. Writing to you takes me back to re-experiencing the pain of waves of upheaval in that time—the passing of your beloved grandmother who anchored you so, your vibrant marriage ending so sadly, and now you are poised to leave your demanding corporate role plus moving house too—all within 18 months. So much change. I promise you, it will make sense backwards, you will see the purpose for your learning. You just need to keep living forwards right now, in this dark storm, where you are feeling quite lost.

I know you are reeling—losing the sense of who you are or how to manage each day, somehow having to perform in the fast slipstream of demanding life up a skyscraper. This age of 35 marks a new era for you, a deepening and widening that plants the seeds of the magnificent oak tree your life will become. It brings up everything in you to investigate, to reform, and rework into the beautiful sculpture your life will later become. But it's painful right now.

Your marriage of 15 years has shattered spectacularly and sadly in the 18 months before this, and daily grief and upset are tearing at your insides. His new partner was unbearably cruel to you, writing without prompts to your work email and calling your work mobile with insults and taunts, so there was double upset and trauma to deal with. Many sleepless nights. Such sadness at what was lost with your former husband. Pain is high.

You have so much to learn at 35. How to be alone for the first time in your adult life; how to set up a business, for the first time in your life; how to find a new social world; how to practice new skills like meditation; how to live alone in a big house when he moves out.

This time of rebuilding your life will bring you to your knees frequently. Now is when you will dig deep to find ways to calm your mind using new skills of meditation. Some resting of the busy mind is helpful. You will learn meditation soon, which brings some peace. You will learn how to dance to release your grief and rise again into a new era of your life.

Life is a training process.

Life is its own training process and this difficulty and turmoil will build compassion, empathy and understanding of the challenges of life. This becomes a great asset for your future. But at the moment, managing each day is hard. You just work harder to lose yourself and numb your pain.

I see your sensitivity right now will make you a more talented therapist in the years ahead. So it's all messy right now, but you will learn so much!

How to be alone, but not lonely;

How to balance your life with work and home life;

How to trust your intuition; and

How to flourish, celebrate, and use more of the creative person you are.

Be authentically you.

You will never be a hard-headed business person—hell no! Your intuitive, creative, bohemian, free-spirited, right-brain self will lead you to dance a unique path in your life and work. Your creativity develops insight that will access transformative processes for your future clients.

Your deep conversational skills (a sweet reframe from being a talkative child and later adult!) mean you can find the story and material for working within any person and unravel deep learning for all types of people.

And because you will go on to rigorously study in many modalities, you will offer a potent container for learning and change and many of your clients will work with you for years. You will play a part in their journeys. Remind them of the unseen layers of existence. The heart of vulnerability. I tell you all this because in many ways you are just setting out on your journey, changing and investigating, drawing out the gold of learning from your own life.

Transform your first career.

You took the safe road and majored at university in education and literature at university, then you landed a great role in book publishing as a young junior editor. Later, you trained in PR and advertising and video production, and soon you are flourishing in a busy career in PR, then advertising and corporate communication. Now, age 35, life has expanded you. You take on more responsibility, enjoying seeing your capability grow. Then bang—life delivers the next level of challenge, in business and personal life.

I want to focus on a pivotal moment in your life—one that wakes you and surprises you on the path of change. Can you recall this one?

...you heard the booming yet invisible voice, right?

"You are going to be a dance therapist in the corporate world."

Well that was weird! A shock! This is a defining moment in your life, and it will take many years to make sense. I see you looking up from the free-form ecstatic dance meditation you are doing for the first time in a crowded room, during a six-month-long personal development course you are doing in the raw months after your 15-year marriage ends. You are close to a decision to leave your demanding corporate job to set up your own company. You are bravely diving into personal exploration as you reel about such a major change time in your life.

I see you in my mind's eye—hair disheveled, panting at the end of an intense dynamic moving meditation, looking up into the ceiling in the crowded room of sweaty bodies, trying to understand where that almost-audible mysterious voice came from. The sky? Your head? Another dimension?

"What?" I hear you saying inside. "Where did that voice come from? What does that even mean? What on earth is 'dance therapy'? I know both words—dance and therapy—but how does that combination of words and even sentence make any sense?", you ponder. Well, honey, yes, it did all come true. Many years later, yes. But that day was the start of a huge next chapter for you. Here you begin the alchemy journey, learning to let new ideas and material bubble in your life, activating rich learning experiences.

My greatest pride in you is seeing how you become a queen of bravely enduring and courageously sustaining yourself, navigating to a new life. I want to send you some ideas and guiding wisdom to help you along the way to your future.

Know that you will be sent wise beings—high-calibre teachers who inspire and teach you. Ken McLean, your Aikido sensei in Sydney, will come into your life soon when he agrees to come each Monday morning to your fledgling company, to begin each week with an Aikido session for all staff. This will be the beginning of a new body language, such as learning to centre and blend, looking for harmony through conflict and interaction, and to radiate energy and follow the line of Ki, a teaching stream you will be in throughout your life.

Another is Dr Marcia Leventhal, famed US dance movement therapy pioneer and PhD clinical psychologist, who opens you to the Quantum world through dance movement training. You studied classical and modern ballet for years but now you train long and deep to the top advanced clinical level in dance movement therapy, and this will sustain you and become pivotal in your work ahead.

Alchemy, or transformation, becomes the theme of your next business in your 40s—assisting others in a truly transformative way. First, you will have to experience being transformed yourself, from married to single to partnered to married again. From training as a teacher, to a career in publishing and communication, into a master leadership development coach. And become a qualified and experienced dance movement therapist as well! Then finding your voice in your poetry and your dance. You even uniquely blend dance and movement practice and principles into your special style of leadership coaching in the corporate world.

Right now you are only 35, and it is still a couple of years before you will meet a dance therapist for the very first time. You are intrigued to explore some sessions in dance therapy for yourself and eventually become drawn into the study of it to become a practitioner yourself. In your first session, despite years of dance training, you cling to the walls of the art deco hall in Melbourne, scared to be so fully visible, so free to express, with another person fully gazing at you. It is powerful and terrifying, this dance therapy thing, but magically draws you in.

The reconstruction of a new life, single for the first time as an adult after 18 years in a couple, will prove an extensive process, hard and disorientating. Your work life continues frantically as national head of a busy corporate communication team in a skyscraper of a global professional services firm. Married when you started; not when you left 3.5 years later!

Horror hours, horror demands, 90 hour weeks often, occasionally down to 60 hours. You get by with the great team you assemble, enduring the assault of deadline after deadline. Late nights and sleeping on the floor for 10-minute grabs at 4 am—you call it doing a "Winston Churchill." He had a way with naps, apparently. Shove on more lipstick, drink black coffee, and press on.

You will soon resign from this oppressive corporate role and after a terrifyingly quiet start, successfully set up your own company, We're With You. Once again, you will quickly be in a volcano of work and deadlines, with seven staff and a $1.5 million annual income. Days of momentum will be filled with output and stress, with major corporate banks, utilities, and insurance companies as demanding and focused clients for seven years. Now, the forging of the core of your own leadership framework and philosophy begins in a practical way.

Your work/life balance will be tested. Again and again. You know the world of fast deadlines, but now the company is yours and there is no one else there to share the burden or stress. The aloneness, no partner or business partner, gives you compassion later on for the sense of isolation a CEO can experience.

You will go through many more challenging times in the next two decades, including a serious head-on car crash, loss of pivotal business accounts in a fiasco of internal politics, finding yourself after several great loves learning to settle in a new marriage, belonging to disparate social tribes, and riding the waves of cashflow worries in a small business. Yes, it is a journey full of highs and lows. You learn your depths, your weaknesses, and that your potential is high and vibrant!

Career Number Two appears.

Towards the end of your big corporate job, you watch a top-notch presentation company lead a multi-million dollar tender rehearsal, badly, and realize, "I can do that! And better!" And here is birthed the decision, from frustration, to start your own method of presentation work, morphing that deep encounter work into a leadership development experience, and this lands you in a few years pioneering your way experimentally from presentation training into leadership coaching.

A wise teacher said to you, "Just because you can do something, you don't have to keep doing that." There is a pivotal moment coming for you around age 42 when you realize: yes, stop. Just Stop. Focus. Centre on your deep spirit. What gives you the most joy and flow?

So you will stop production work, offload staff, choose the intimate relational work of coaching and people development that is building naturally for you. You will choose the less adrenal work, opening up space in your life. This is a brilliant decision. And a total transformation of how you spend your days.

Your coaching business has thrived for over 20 years now, grown by word of mouth, with long-term clients around the world leaning into your expertise in the journey of leadership.

It is a next stage you can't even imagine at age 35. And there is more coming!

Celebrate this magnificent journey.

Here is another pivotal moment I want to share with you in this letter, younger Virginia.

This "aha" has just happened this week, in this very reflective process of deciding to write this letter to you.

Driving down the Clyde Mountain from Braidwood just outside Canberra, as I have so many times over the past 24 years, arcing into the curves and sway of her beauty, I realized that I first came to this mountain with my first husband in the late 1980s! After our marriage ended, I bought rural forest land on the far south coast and so began the regular drives down and up the Clyde—in pea-soup fogs and mists, in tumultuous thunderstorms, on beautiful balmy summer nights, in high winds and pouring rain alone at midnight. I learned to love the mountain drive, with its precious spotty gum forest and burrawang cycad undergrowth and sea glimpses.

Last year the forest was burnt badly all down the mountain, but the resilient bush is regenerating. The cycle of life goes on, from ash and cinder to new growth and rebirth. There was devastation but now there is renewing. I want you to see the metaphor. Just as periods in your life will bring immense heat and challenge, you will keep regenerating. The trees lining the pilgrimage trail down the Clyde are a reminder of the sacred journey of transformation.

You and I have been curving down the bends of the sacred mountain for a long time now, and it has been magnificent. It awakened your love of nature. Every drive amongst such lovely forest has been a spiritual journey of renewal. And now you live somewhere just like that –rejuvenating, lush, calm, nurturing.

You understand transformation.

You will deepen along the way, learning to relax into the unknown.

Though fires of transformation will be fierce in your life, you will find gold!

Though you are a born teacher, your clients will also teach you. As your people development consultancy business, Your World Within, grows over 20 years, you will become an expert in perceiving themes and creating material to help business and private clients navigate change. You will work with what you know: communication practices, energy and time balancing, mistrust and poor culture, overload and exhaustion, overwhelm and anxiety, resistance to change. You will become strong and clear yet tender in your teaching style, to penetrate like a sword to help wake people up to what they want to see, learn, transform.

We are our own worst enemies, you will teach.
Learning to become our own best friends, you will add.

I struggled with this for so long. Why the lack of confidence? Systemic sexism? Being raised to doubt myself? Inner voices of fear? Self-limitation is insidious. Cultural. Ancestral.

I have learnt that hesitating to believe in yourself is the biggest hurdle to overcome. So back yourself, be your greatest love and cheerleader.

From suffering comes wisdom.

From experience comes insight. Finding your authentic path will take courage and getting out of your way. That is how it is for each of us. Get out of your head. Let life reveal itself to your spirit and heart. Let knowledge and experience combine into wisdom.

I have always been a spiritual person and have found the corporate world full of spiritual people on their journey. I have learnt that my capacity to talk about the visible and invisible dimensions of life, to stay with human vulnerability, and to share others' journeys must come from the heart, the authentic and courageous self. When people feel my authenticity, it inspires them to trust their authentic self.

Follow your unique path.

Know that you will have an unusual path, my dear. Don't hold back your creative spirit. You have a natural intelligent talent. Trust that you are enough. Many times you will question what other folk would even consider success to be. Loving your work in the world? Being passionate about learning (for you and your clients)? Persisting through many challenges? Believing in yourself is the longest test and the deepest gold you will find. There is a third career cooking in a crucible right now. It blends everything into another path you will travel -with eyes wide open, blending your past into a new future.

Do you remember stumbling over these words in your first job in publishing, working on a reprint of E.J. Banfield's book, Confessions of a Beachcomber, quoting Henry David Thoreau (a favourite of yours and Banfield's!):

> *"If a man does not keep pace with his companions, perhaps it is because he hears a different drummer. Let him step to the music which he hears."*
> *- EJ Banfield, Confessions of a Beachcomber*

What great advice! I promise you'll have lived this by the time you get to my age.

Would you ever have thought that you, a somatically trained, body-oriented dance-therapy-informed coach, would work fully online in the corporate world with global clients?

Trust you are a powerful change-agent because you are different.

Your empathy, your sensitive observing eye, and rapport arise from your colourful life experience. Your power with words, naming and making meaning for others on their learning journey will grow. Your willingness for intimacy and connection means people will trust you as they pour their lives out for reflection in sessions. These are not SOFT people skills! They are hard skills—the true heart of what makes for rich living, for humanly talented leaders, who risk vulnerability.

Embodiment is your gift—using attunement and presence, meditation and centering, breath and impulse, movement and flow. You will integrate this skilfully from dance movement therapy, mindfulness practices, and other modalities of training, making a unique teaching style that integrates emotional, spiritual, and social intelligence. Your difference will become vital to leaders you coach and train.

You will spend years learning how to manage energy and time in the fast flow and stress of deadlines and long hours. You will remind yourself and your clients to return to the centre, to tend the body, to calm the busy mind, to integrate the heart, mind, feelings, and to live well in the body to create a healthy flow in life and career.

Your creativity is your power.

You use words with artistry and potency. You dance with verve. You have a poetic style, an eye for beauty. Express it fully! Family, friends, and clients will see this. Clients will quote back to you YOUR quotes that touch them. There will be discussions with coachees based on your spoken and written words and ideas. Keep being inventive and outspoken.

"Leadership is simultaneously an art, a philosophy, a practice, and a learning experience."

- Virginia Sada York

When you're 36 and in the United States, you will buy a copy of the famous Letters to a Young Poet, by Rainer Maria Rilke, and it will inspire you to back your own creative way in the years ahead. This exquisite poet still takes my breath away and inspires me as I write back to you, to give you glimpses of your learning ahead.

Here is the gold from the crucible of our life together, in every age younger Virginia:

As within, so without. Stay true to your uniqueness, your vitality, your passion. The poetry of your life will spring forth in your career. Learn to be your own best friend. Back yourself and your intense, passionate, creative, brilliant, sparkling, insightful way. It's your journey, all yours. There is more coming.

Rilke can end this letter now for us both. Please go out into the years ahead with this insight; trust in your inner knowing for your life. You will learn well, radiate and activate much in the world, in the days to come. It is going to be magnificent.

"You are looking outward and above all else, that you must not do now. Nobody can advise you and help you, no one. There is only one way: Go within. Search for the cause, find the impetus that bids you write ... Go within and scale the depths of your being from which your very life springs forth. ... It is always my wish that you might find enough patience within yourself to endure, and enough innocence to have faith... Believe me, life is right in all cases." - Rainer Maria Rilke, Letters to a Young Poet

ABOUT THE AUTHOR

Virginia Sada York is the CEO and founder of Your World Within. Her work catalyses CEOs, entrepreneurs, visionaries and business leaders to grow and flourish in the artistry of their leadership, radiating success on all levels.

In this vibrant global practice, Virginia is master teacher, executive coach, team development expert and therapist, working with large global corporations, start-ups, and individuals ready to transform their lives to flourish with skilful success and deeper harmony and flow.

Virginia is also CEO of Alchemy Publishing which activates transformation for conscious business by sharing stories from potent business leaders about their journeys.

Formerly a city-dweller, she lives in a tranquil rural valley, enjoying deep nature with her husband, two border collie pups, three horses, and a plethora of Australian wildlife.

Email: virginiasadayork@gmail.com
Website: www.virginiasadayork.com
LinkedIn: www.linkedin.com/in/virginia-york
Facebook: www.facebook.com/virginia.s.york

CHAPTER 17

ANGELA C. LALANDE

ear younger self,

You have had the heart of a champion since your very first breath.

A feeble three pound babe born two months early along with your twin sister. You fought for life early on, spending a month in the hospital as you gained strength to go home. Your parents did not even know you were there until your twin sister was born.

A surprise baby—a surprise to everyone but God. He knew you. He formed you in your mother's womb.

You knew what it was to persevere early on—to struggle through an obstacle. The word "through" shows you did not stop short but that you reached the end.

Remember, a champion is not merely a winner; a champion is someone who has been forged and formed through the fire and has not been overcome by the flames.

For with a champion, the flames only propel you. The flames may etch marks in you; but they are marks of beauty.

And courage grows from ashes.

I am going to share some things about you, some things you are going through now, and some things that you will experience in the future. The purpose of sharing is so you can be better prepared to weather some storms of life when they come and to know that though your journey may not be smooth, it has developed such character within you. They say with age comes wisdom. Sometimes it comes through experience.

You will experience ups and downs, will become nearly derailed from walking out your destiny on this earth, but you will rise above these moments and you will be a better person in the end. One who can more easily have compassion on people. One who can more easily take a step back from a situation to see the bigger picture. One who develops immense courage. One who will find her way back to God and will know the authority she carries as a citizen of Heaven.

Today you are 14 years old, saturating in your insecurities. You look down at your body and see only a gangly, rail-thin frame. You still have a touch of the lisp that you worked hours and hours as a child with a specialist to overcome. You don't feel you truly fit in or that you are really good at anything other than loving your family and the people around you. You are an athlete but you still feel awkward being you because you are trying to figure out who you are and what your purpose is.

You love to write. You love to read.

You love resting in the realm of the imagination.

Getting lost in a book and finding yourself in its pages.

Hidden away from a world that can be loving yet uninviting at times —whether or not it was intentional. In this realm, you feel you can be whoever you want to be.

In the realm of the imagination, you are accepted.

You are smart enough.

You are good looking enough.

You are confident.

You are brave.

You are resilient.

You are known.

Oh, darling, let me tell you right now that you *are* all of those things!

Here and now! You are *all* the things that you don't believe about yourself in this time.

Allow these truths to marinate in your soul. You will need them to overcome the lies of the Enemy when you are older.

This is a tough age—a time where there seems to be an uprising of voices who whisper over and over that you are not enough.

Many carry this skewed mindset into adulthood. You will. But a person with the heart of a champion never carries it too long.

In a few years, you will pick up the sport of javelin. In case you are wondering, it is the spear looking thing in track and field. Your very first meet will be one to remember. I wish I could tell you that you will win this one but you won't. In fact, after this meet, you will want to quit—and hide—but you won't. We both know Mom and Dad raised you better than that.

In that meet, you will be so nervous, as you look around to see a sea of eyes staring at you, expecting to see the spear fly. You will rear back for your first throw and the javelin will hit your back as you are following through, landing only feet from where you started.

It will be an embarrassing yet humbling time, and you will learn an invaluable lesson through that experience.

Don't let a failing moment keep you on the ground. Those moments are merely stepping stones to your success.

Dear child, we all have failing moments, but it's only failure if you don't get up. And the great thing about you is:

You get up.

You rise after a fall.

Heart of a champion.

In the javelin, you will become a champion. You will work hours and hours after church on Sundays with Dad and your sisters, perfecting the technique. Mastering the art. Your senior year in high school, you will win almost every track meet, set several meet records and win the state championship at Louisiana State University, holding the title of LHSAA (Louisiana High School Athletic Association) 2A State Javelin Champion.

Would you like to know something else about yourself? You're an attorney.

I know, I know. Try not to seem so shocked. I can already feel your gawking reaction. All of that reading and writing actually paid off!

As I sit here and write this letter to you, I am filled with such an array of emotion—because the journey to get to this point has not been easy. It has been an exceedingly difficult road.

But whose road isn't? As you get older, you will find that many of the people around you have felt pain as deeply as you have. Some more. People can tend to keep silent about it, but you are not alone in this. Keep your heart open when you want to seek isolation. There will come a day when you will be able to bring healing through the words that you speak. That is the power of testimony.

In law school, you will feel like a fish out of water most days. But it's okay—you finish!

At 28, you will find your way into a wilderness season and for a time you will feel completely lost.

Broken, cast away, flailing your arms aimlessly under the waters of failure, rejection and sadness, with the heaviness stemming from choices you made tormenting you. You will flail for a long time without the full resolve to go upwards, because somewhere in the back of your mind, you will believe you deserve to sink.

But since I am the author of this letter, you can tell that you did not sink to the bottom of the ocean, never to be seen from again. You indeed found your way back to the surface. An overcomer, a survivor, a champion.

The swim will make scars, some more hideous than others; some deeper than others, and it's okay. They will merely be reminders of where you had been, who you thought you were during your lost season and who you know you are now.

You will marry the love of your life at 32 and this time you will do things right.

This is when you will enter a season of birthing.

You will have three beautiful daughters and gain a stepdaughter.

You will miscarry a son.

Miscarriage—the word stings. It carries a weighty grief, a sound of heaviness as this word penetrates the ears and pricks the heart deep down, nuzzling itself into one's life experience.

It will nuzzle its way into yours and you will know what it feels like to be robbed of a perfect blessing of life.

You will throw yourself into work so quickly after the miscarriage in an attempt to not dwell on what just happened or make what happened even more personal. Remember, grief must be experienced. It is a part of loss. It is a part of healing. You must acknowledge the loss...acknowledge what happened...and please do not take so long to name your son.

Rhys Everett is his name and he lives in Heaven.

You will see him again.

What's so interesting about a season of birthing, whether it is with a career change or physical birthing, is that it is a time where things are developing and growing on the inside, a time where newness sits on the horizon and a sense of change will fill the atmosphere. If you are sensitive enough to the Spirit and to your surroundings, you will feel the shift.

One chapter in your book will begin to close. Another page will prepare to turn.

It is generally when we feel this way—no longer comfortable where we are—that a season is about to change.

So stay sensitive. Feel what is going on around you.

Sometimes the answers we seek are not given in words.

You will birth a business out of obedience. By saying yes to a God-dream that will be dropped into your spirit. Partnering with God in His grand scheme for your life.

That's right—it is a partnership. You cannot sit and merely wait for a blessing to come. You must take action on your part. That's what you will do by stepping into uncharted waters. Just like a sailboat seeking to cross a body of water—even if the wind comes to take the ship so it could move, if you don't put a sail up, the ship won't go anywhere. Remember this.

You will open a real estate closing company called Lalande Title and sign a two-year lease for office space without knowing if you can even pay the rent. You hope you can. You pray you can, but you do not have any real assurance in the natural that you will. It will be an arduous time, because you will be leaving a steady job with a steady paycheck, stepping out into the unknown with no guarantee of success.

Two weeks later, you will give birth to your second daughter, Ayla, 5 ½ weeks early. She will be in the NICU for a short time, as her lungs will be underdeveloped and she will need oxygen for the first several days of her life post-birth. The morning of her birth, all the beds at the hospital will be occupied so they will have to transport her by ambulance to another hospital across town. You will be separated, although you will see her through a live feed from the hospital.

You will be so scared—for her and your family's financial future.

You will lie in bed after giving birth, with a flood of thoughts coming to mind. One of those thoughts will be, "Can I *really* do this thing?" Lalande Title. You will be reminded how you were a "nobody" in the real estate closing world.

That will just be FEAR talking though. Something you will learn to take authority over.

Later that day, you will leave the hospital with the resolve to do. *This. Thing.* To be a courageous business owner. One who looks fear in the eye and tells it to bow!

You will go home and pretty much go straight to work. It will keep your mind off your little NICU baby—wondering how she is doing, picturing her in that incubator with all of those tubes, being warmed by a machine instead of your arms.

Eight days after Ayla is born, you will have your first closing. You will feel as if you don't know what you're doing. And you don't! But that's okay! You will learn along the way and it will be fine.

No one comes into a field a master. Remember, one must become a student of the art first—wise words your father will tell you when you first learn the art of javelin throwing.

Just like with the javelin, you will learn this trade.

You will form wonderful relationships with people in your community and all over the world.

You will love them, serve them well and you will help to give them the courage to dream big dreams and go after the things that appear to be out of reach. For your story will give them hope and allow them to see the truth:

That what lies within you also lies within them:

A heart of a champion.

Sincerely,
Angela C. Lalande

ABOUT THE AUTHOR

Angela C. Lalande is a real estate attorney and owner of Lalande Title, a real estate closing company offering home buyers, realtors, lenders and builders title insurance, escrow and closing services for residential and commercial properties. Her main mission is to provide excellent and engaging personable service in every closing and to make the closing process smooth for everyone involved in a real estate transaction.

You can connect with Angela at:

> *Website:* www.lalandetitle.com
> *Facebook:* www.facebook.com/AngelaCLalande and www.facebook.com/LalandeTitle
> *Instagram:* www.instagram.com/aclalande and www.instagram.com/lalandetitle

CHAPTER 18

ANN GOMEZ

ear younger self,

Headstrong.

That would be one word to describe you as you are right now. Before you debate it (because we both know how much you love to debate), may I remind you what you said to Dad when you were 18 years old? *'You can't tell me what to do. I'm an adult now.'*

As the older, wiser version of us, I smile—just like Dad smiled that day—thinking about how misguided it was to think I had life all figured out. Heck, I'm *still* figuring it out!

I know you like to figure things out for yourself. But I hope you'll make an exception to listen to me; your older, wiser self.

After all, I've learned some life lessons I wish I knew earlier. This letter is a gift from the future. A chance to help you make the most of this incredible life.

On that note, here are my top ten suggestions I'm choosing to send back in time.

1. Be selective

I used to jump on all the tempting opportunities vying for my attention. Write a book? *Yes!* Build a company on the side? *Yes!* Learn to speak Spanish? *Yes!* All at the same time. Plus, seventeen other projects.

You can imagine how this played out. I was overcommitted, spread thin and frustrated.

Focus is far more effective. The tighter you concentrate your effort, the better your results.

With priorities, less is more.

When you concentrate on a select few priorities (I recommend no more than three at any time), you make faster progress and you do them exceptionally well. You spend less time in catch-up, *"Where was I?"* mode. You have fewer frustrating, languishing piles. You eliminate all the tasks and meetings related to these extra projects, giving you time to breathe.

Thankfully, saying 'no' is easy in many situations. Join the tax committee? *No, thank you.* Edit the company bylaws? *That's not my strength.* Sing a solo at the holiday party? *Absolutely not!*

But saying 'no' is harder for all of those good opportunities and even harder for the *really* good opportunities. *'This could be fun.'* Or *'I could do such a good job!'* Or *'Everyone else is going.'*

Yet saying 'no' is essential. Just because something is a good opportunity doesn't mean it makes sense to do it now. If it's not a 'hell yes', say no. This may not be easy, but it is simple.

Once I finally figured this out for myself, I started training others to do the same. Every busy person who is overloaded and spread thin faces the same challenge—they are juggling too many projects at the same time.

When you're trying to make a big splash, say 'no, to the vast array of time-burning distractions.

Don't jump on every opportunity.

Be selective.

2. Be unreasonable

My former colleague was exuding excitement. He had reinvented his career in the golf industry. His reason? He loved golf. So, he made a career out of it. As I stood there listening to him, my jaw hanging open, I remember thinking, '*Wait, you can do that?*'

At the time, I had been stuck in a job for too long. A job I should have loved. A job I should have been grateful for. But the truth was, I didn't and I wasn't.

Should is a funny word, often masking regret and guilt. '*I should be happy living here. I should take this job. I should be grateful for this project.*'

You'll spend roughly 90,000 hours working throughout your life. It seems perfectly reasonable to do work you love. Don't settle for good enough. Don't accept a career best described as *meh*. Be open to a career swerve. As Michelle Obama says, "We can have many lives within a life."

Instead of doing what you *should* do, go after what you *want* to do. What you love to do. Your career should feel like a perfect fit.

But when it comes to goals, I encourage you to be *un*reasonable. Don't hold back. Don't play small. Don't underestimate yourself. If your goals don't scare you, at least a bit, they aren't big enough.

Ironically, I have more to learn from you on this topic. When we are young, we believe we can achieve anything. Ask any child and you'll hear dreams of being astronauts. Or Olympians. Or both.

But somewhere along the way, many people start to scale back. We start playing smaller. We tell ourselves it is impossible. We tell ourselves we don't have what it takes.

On the contrary, you are capable of doing anything you set your mind to doing. Ok, maybe you won't play in the NHL. But physical constraints aside, don't accept limits. You will only rise as high as you can picture in your mind.

Dream big. Be bold. Once you set your goals, double them. And then triple them.

Be unreasonable.

3. Don't be afraid to fail

'Failure is not an option.' That is the lie I used to tell myself early in my career when the word 'fail' sent shivers down my spine.

I couldn't have been more wrong. Failure absolutely IS an option. In fact, failure is an inevitable part of the journey. We stumble. We fall. We break. But then we rise. We recover. And we come back stronger.

Every success is built on the heels of setbacks and challenges. It's tempting to compare ourselves to others' highlight reels. But know they have had their share of setbacks, stumbles, mistakes and obstacles. Everyone experiences failure.

This doesn't mean we seek failure. It just means we find the lesson when we *do*—and we learn the most when we fail. Any one failure isn't your final step. Rather, it is a natural step—possibly even your most essential step.

If you're not failing regularly, you're playing too safe. If you want to live an incredible life, get comfortable with failure.

4. Be a lifter

When I advanced to pay at my preferred coffee shop, the friendly employee told me the car ahead of me treated me to a coffee. I'm smiling again as I recall this kind act.

You will be on the receiving end of good karma more times than you can count. But know this: lifting goes two ways. Do your part and find opportunities to help others. Connect them. Champion them. Roll up your sleeves and dig in. Not because you owe them a favour. Not because they can do you a favour. Help simply because you can—because you have gifts to share.

If you notice something you admire about someone else, tell them. If you can't find a trait you appreciate, dig deeper. When you seek out the best in others, they will show up better for you. Never miss a moment to share your appreciation. You never know how it will resonate with them.

In our interconnected world, collaboration is a multiplier. The most successful (and also happiest) people go out of their way to support, champion and empower others.

Life isn't a zero-sum game. You aren't depleting your resources when you help others. When you lift others, you both benefit.

Be a lifter.

5. Find your lifters

As a toddler, I would declare, *'No! I do it!'* while riding my new two-wheeler long before I was ready. I maintained this approach throughout school and into my first career. I thought success was tied to individual performance, and I was determined to prove myself.

Little did I know *who* we know is more important than *what* we know. Knowing how to play nice in the sandbox is a lifelong skill. Research confirms this—our success almost completely relies on our ability to work well with others. Shawn Achor, best-selling author of *Big Potential* says success is "not about survival of the fittest, it is survival of the best fit."

Life is not a solo game. Sadly, school and most workplaces emphasize individual performance, through grades, rankings and individual recognition.

On the contrary, your lifters motivate and challenge you to reach higher. They share your passions and celebrate shared wins with you. They offer diverse perspectives, unique expertise and valuable lessons. You don't need to know everything or do everything on your own.

Don't let intimidation, jealousy or a competitive spirit prevent you from surrounding yourself with outstanding people. Instead, be inspired. They are modeling what you are capable of doing.

Find your lifters and nurture these relationships. They are there in the wings, waiting for you to invite them onto your stage. In the game of life, these connections count more than any accomplishments or material possessions.

6. Find inspiration in flossing

One tooth. Once I committed to flossing just one tooth, I started flossing all of my teeth and I conquered a long-term battle with this ritual.

If you find yourself procrastinating (spoiler alert: you will, like every other human), you may be waiting for inspiration or an extra burst of energy. Instead, find small wins—the kind that are so small you can't fail. Small wins can give you the push you need to quickly break through. Small wins are the perfect complement to your bold goals.

Progress is a powerful, yet underestimated, source of motivation. Teresa Amabile and Steven Kramer, authors of *The Progress Principle* have found: "Of all the things that can boost emotions, motivation, and perceptions during a workday, the single most important is making progress in meaningful work."

Don't wait for motivation to start. Motivation, like willpower, is a fickle aide. Sometimes it shows up; other times it slacks off. Instead, get started and your inspiration will catch up.

Progress is the fuel for feel-good emotions. When you take tiny steps towards goals that are meaningful to you, you build momentum.

You don't have to have it all figured out to get started. Instead, focus on taking your next right step. And then another.

Ultimately, the secret to getting ahead is getting started.

Start today. Start now. Just start.

7. Pay yourself first

Savings before living expenses. You're off to a great start, which I'm grateful for, many years of compound interest later.

But there is another, even more important, formula I'd love to see you master much sooner than I did. Pay yourself first *with your time.*

I know your days are full right now, but the demands on your time are about to multiply, without any more supply of minutes. You'll soon realize there isn't enough time to do everything.

Hold on, because there is good news. You actually have an abundance of time, but only if you narrow your focus. After too many years of being overcommitted and chasing time, I started proactively blocking time.

I suggest you do the opposite of what most people do. *Stop* reinventing each day. *Stop* reacting.

Instead, create routines around what you value most. Assign your prime time to your top priorities.

Live your life by design, rather than by default. Create, versus react, to your day. Plan for, rather than hope for, an ideal day. Start your day with your hardest task, which is almost always associated with your most important work. If your goals were easy, everyone would tackle them.

You'll always have a list. Instead of trying to finish it all, prioritize what is on your list. Relegate lower value activities to non-prime time—or eliminate them all together.

Pay yourself first. This is a concept that makes the most of your money. And it works even better with your time.

8. Curate your stories

I was running late for an important meeting and was at risk of losing my window. My previous client showed up late, setting off this domino effect. Another car inched ahead of me in traffic, and I was infuriated! Sadly, this traffic irritant happened a lot, given how much time I spent in my car.

Then one day, a colleague shared a perspective that immediately shifted my mindset. *'What if the other driver was rushing to the hospital?'* Suddenly, this mild inconvenience no longer annoyed me.

We are natural storytellers. We tell stories to connect, to understand, to learn and to find meaning. But this doesn't mean we're always accurate storytellers.

We're fighting against a natural negativity bias, along with every other human on this planet. We notice negative events faster and more intensely than positive events. We also dwell on them and remember them for longer. This ingrained bias served our early ancestors by instantly alerting them to immediate threats. But in our lifetime, where life and death threats are less of an issue, our negativity bias can be misplaced.

Thankfully, we also have the ability to *choose* more empowering thoughts. For example, we can choose to see *opportunities* instead of problems.

Think this is merely semantics? I thought so when I was your age. But 'problems' tend to make us feel annoyed, inconvenienced and regretful. On the other hand, 'opportunities' make us feel excited, hopeful and creative. It's clear we prime ourselves for better outcomes when we reframe our thoughts.

When you plant your feet on the floor in the morning, choose to declare it will be a beautiful day. Replace "I can't" with "I can't yet." Replace "I'm nervous" with "I'm excited." Replace "impossible" with "challenging" and remind yourself you've done many hard tasks before.

For many years, I believed life generated our stories, but it's actually the other way around. Curate the stories you tell yourself. Your stories create your life.

9. Don't underestimate this sweet joy

Forty-five minutes. That's how long I rolled while playing craps. The buzz among my fellow gamblers was electric. In craps, the entire table tends to win or lose together. The dealers said they wouldn't see such dice-rolling good fortune again for a long time. A clear Vegas veteran asked, *'did I miss it?'* just as the table was breaking up.

There are some clear moments in life that take your breath away: the birth of a child, the excitement of a coveted job, the intrigue of exploring a new country. Or the tiny moments like the cherry blossom trees in the Spring, the first bite of a delicious meal or sharing a laugh with a friend.

There is another source of happiness we can easily tap into every day —the joy of easily finding what we need. No searching; no wondering; just pure and simple immediate gratification.

Yes, I'm talking about being organized. This might sound insignificant, but I assure you, it is powerful. After all, the goal is to *do* your best work—not waste time looking for it!

The more you have, the more you complicate life. As the heir of all your stuff, let me be clear: less is more.

So let go of those binders you'll never crack open again. Purge and digitize your files before they burst out of your drawers. Consider keeping only a selection of Grandma's thirty antique glass insulators.

Create discrete 'homes' for anything from project notes to gardening tools. Maintain one central to do list, your Master Action Plan, instead of miscellaneous notebooks (unless you like burying information). Clear your inbox—it is not your to do list. Establish an 'external brain' to digitally record key notes you swear you won't forget but inevitably will.

Above all, keep your systems simple so you can indulge in one of life's sweet joys—being able to quickly retrieve things when you need them.

Pure bliss.

10. Savour your burpees

"Ann, just try it!" my friend insisted in a can't-ignore way. I begrudgingly complied, even though I wasn't convinced it would make a difference. I didn't think my busy mind was suited. But I didn't realize meditation would be so life changing until I embraced the habit.

Sleep, exercise, gratitude, breaks, nutrition and a mindfulness practice. Our wellbeing is the foundation of all the above nine recommendations. Wellbeing unmistakably elevates our performance and our life.

At this stage in your life, you are committed to both running and restful sleeps. But spoiler alert, you will succumb to fair-weather wellbeing habits. Despite good intentions, you'll sometimes struggle to find the time and motivation.

The irony is if you don't have time for wellbeing, you definitely don't have time to be unwell. So, let's revert to tip #7. Pay yourself first. And don't forget tip #5. Find your lifters, from gratitude experts to workout buddies. They will help you find a way to savour your burpees.

I'm closing with what I argue to be my most important recommendation: prioritize your wellbeing. When you invest in yourself, every aspect of your life is enhanced.

As your future self, I am thanking you now.

I wish you a wonderful adventure and a life well lived.

Love, Me

PS: Don't put off that backpacking trip through Europe. Soon enough, you'll have those four incredible kids that will keep you semi house-bound for a few decades. Yes, four. Breathe. You've got this.

And one more tip: buy Bitcoin, plus stock in Apple, Amazon, Facebook and Google.

ABOUT THE AUTHOR

Ann Gomez is an engaging speaker and the founding president of Clear Concept Inc. She is passionate about empowering the world's busiest people to perform at their best. She is also the best-selling author of *The Email Warrior*, an active blogger and media spokesperson.

You can connect with Ann at:

> *Website: www.clearconceptinc.ca*
> *Facebook: www.facebook.com/clearconceptinc*
> *LinkedIn: www.linkedin.com/in/anngomez*
> *Twitter: www.twitter.com/clearconceptinc*
> *Instagram: www.instagram.com/clearconceptinc*

CHAPTER 19

BRIGID HOLDER

ear younger self,

The midnight train pulled out of your bedroom almost every night from ages seven to nine years old. Almost as if your body sensed that something was not quite right in your home.

Your Mum called it the midnight train because it was always close to midnight that you rose from your little girl bed and shuffled toward the bathroom even though you didn't need to use it.

Intuitively, you gave your Mother a welcome reprieve, a moment of peace as she left her discomfort and guided you back to your room.

On one particular night during a midnight departure, you discovered packed suitcases on the porch. The fear shocked you awake when you realised that the man you idolised, the man you built up to perfection in your mind, was leaving.

You asked him not to go, and as tears rolled down your cheeks, you begged him to stay. Even though you had no idea where he was going or for how long, somehow you just knew it was forever. As he looked at you, you could see the tears streaming down your mothers face, matching your own. Your mind wondered why he would want to leave you and your family or how you could live without him, but your voice didn't have the language to explain it.

Somehow you convinced him to stay. He said he would stay, only for you, and he promised to bring his bags back inside and unpack them.

It would have been much better if he left.

Later in life, you will twist yourself inside out with guilt about that night. About how you convinced him to stay. At how him unpacking those bags would mean many more years of your Mother suffering at his hands.

But know this my dear, you didn't know how cruel this man was and could be. You did not learn how he inflicted physical pain on your Mother. You were just a child in her pj's, roaming around an unsettled home in the middle of the night. It's not your fault, but you won't forgive yourself for a long, long time.

Two years later you were 11 years old. You had the coolest pushbike, it had handlebars with long tassels that blew in the wind. That bike gave you a taste of freedom and you loved riding around in your flare jeans and flowy tops. You had everything you needed though your family were not wealthy by any means. Some might even look down their noses and think 'poor' but you didn't feel it. After school you and your friends would ride and swim and explore. The world growing and expanding the way it does in your pre-teen years. Then the bubble burst.

One afternoon riding with a friend to her house, the two of you get into a squabble about some adolescent meaninglessness. In retaliation, she threw some town gossip in your face; that your Dad was having an affair. Your world shrunk again to consider your hero was a cheater and a liar.

Your friend started offering up details which made it all too real. She said it was your former babysitter, not much older than your eldest brother. And to make it worse, you adored and looked up to this lady.

Mortified, betrayed, angry, and scared you accused your friend of being the liar. How dare she spread rumours and talk about your Dad like this! You may not realise it by now, young one, but your intuition is strong, and you knew she was right. That was a lot of grown-up information to process as an 11-year-old. You didn't know what to believe or how to act, nor should you have. Do not blame yourself for any of your actions that would follow.

Riding furiously to your Mum's store, the stress and worry increased as you thought about what to do, how to tell her. You wondered what her reaction would be. Would she blame you? Did she already know? Is it even true?

No young girl deserves to be the messenger of news like this. No child should have to watch her Mother's eyes swell with tears. When you told her what happened, you could see through her body and witness her heart breaking. You could see it in her posture, in the energy surrounding both of you. The impact of those moments of that day would be your blueprint. A cycle you'd be doomed to repeat if you stayed unaware.

Watching your Mother crumble caused anger, hatred and rage to rise in your gut. You wanted so badly to protect her when you really needed protection yourself.

You hated your Father and in an attempt to spite him, you started acting out. Drinking and smoking because you knew it would make him angry. Dear girl, the only person you were hurting was yourself but I understand why you did it. You didn't have the support you needed, and hiding behind that numb veil allowed you some distance between you and the pain. And I'm so sorry that it would only get worse for you.

Until the cheating was out in the open, you had only heard your Father yell. Now the violence would ramp-up in front of your eyes. It had only been happening behind closed doors until that point. You would stand in their bedroom doorway begging him, this time, to stop. Stop hurting her.

"Fuck off," he told you over and over again. But you stood in that doorway for the next six years, pleading. Begging. This time he didn't bend to your will.

Your poor little body absorbed alcohol and cigarettes for the next few years. At age 15, you were binging every weekend. It's insane to think that such a young child could get their hands on booze and smokes and get away with it, but clearly, the adults in your life were consumed with other things.

And they remained consumed. Until one day they took your childhood away from you forever. From that day, your pushbike- the symbol for your freedom and innocence, gathered dust. You only dared ride it when absolutely necessary, and never ever leaving Mum alone.

Because one night, you woke to his yelling, as you opened your closed bedroom door to see them standing at opposite ends of the hallway. It feels so long, but also not long enough. He's standing at one end with a gun in his hand. She's at the other, shaking and sobbing in fear.

"Shoot me if you are going to shoot her," you told him. How brave you were for standing up for you and your Mum. It must have been terrifying and powerful all at once.

You must have called his bluff because night after night, you continued to stand up to him. Your confidence and strength increasing each time. Most people, let alone children, would not have had the guts. And fair enough! It was dangerous! Of course, no one was looking out for you, but you did what you had to do, and this should make you proud, even though it saddens me you had to experience it.

But you couldn't possibly protect your Mum always. Like the time you were 15, on a Mountain hike and your appendix burst.

The scars will remain on your body but they will remind you, not of the hiking or the surgery, but of your Mother when she came to visit you in the hospital.

You had to stay in the hospital overnight. At that time, Mums or Dads weren't allowed to stay with you. After spending a night alone, your Mother was a welcome sight the next day. Except that she had a scarf on, and it wasn't cold. You reached out to pull the scarf down and saw bruises on her neck. The doctors wanted you to stay another day, but you insisted on going home.

Do I need to remind you that you were only 15 years old? A teenager who lost their childhood and Father figure at such a young age. You didn't understand what was happening around you, but when tested, you survived with strength. The drinking and smoking were simply you acting out. Numbing. If not those things, it would have been something else, and it could have been worse. Anyone with a young brain would probably cope the same way. None of that defines you. You define yourself by your strength. Just look at the rest of your story.

At 16, your grandparents on your Father's side came for a visit. It was around the time of your parent's wedding anniversary and they insisted you wish them a happy one, even if you all knew things were 'off.'

I know how angry that made you. How your body stiffened when you tried to explain. How devastated you were when your Grandparents blamed your Mother for antagonising your Father. Telling you, and themselves, that it must at least be partly her fault for not being a good wife. I see how you wanted to cut them out of your life for good, then. But I also see how you were gracious and willing to give them another chance.

When you are older, you will move to Sydney and try to connect with them again. You will sit on their balcony together overlooking the nanny-goat hill as they, once again, explain how your Mother was at least partially to blame for your Father's behaviour.

It will infuriate you again that your Grandparents don't believe your perspective and are insistent on victim-blaming. You will want nothing to do with them after that. But you'll eventually learn there is much more to their story and history.

As a young boy, your Father often had to drag his own Father off of barstools and out of pubs. After getting your Grandfather home he would abuse your Grandmother over and over again. That's how your Father grew up; it's all he knew.

You didn't lose your Father, dear one. You thought you had and lost him, but no one ever really had him. Not you, not your Mother. He's lost, somewhere in that mind of his, somewhere in that pattern.

If you aren't ready to hear anything I've told you until now, please know this. And only this. One day you will make the decision to stop that cycle of family violence against women. You. This is your destiny. All the suffering you witnesses, all the pain you feel, the self-destruction, the fear and worry. It ends with you.

Life will still be difficult for a while, but things will improve.

One crisp sunny afternoon, you and your Mum will catch him red-handed. He will 'hide' his latest girlfriend's car in plain sight so he can take her to the footy game in a neighbouring town. You and your Mum will stand near a set of abandoned train tracks and seeing clearly. No more midnight express.

Even though you have exams the following day, instead of studying, you will choose to sit on the train tracks and help your Mum gather the strength to gain her freedom, kick him out for good this time. She tried many times before, but this time, it will feel different. You will tell her you believe in her, and she will believe you this time.

You will walk toward that car with your Mother and as she hesitates, you will gently push her, or maybe-not-so gently.

"You tell him it's over, or I will," you'll say, sounding more like a friend, or superhero, than a daughter.

In their passion, your Dad and his fling will be oblivious to your approach. You will stand back a little and allow your Mum to take over. You know deep down that this has to come from her own source of power. You watch her in that second, seeing this as a defining moment in her life- it will forever be 'before and after the confrontation.' You watch her soak-in the knowledge that everything will work out somehow. And soon. And you will be so proud of her.

You will spend the next few nights at your grandparent's place. Your Dad will stall, not wanting to leave the family home, so your Mum and her Sister will head over and throw his belongings into plastic bags, suitcases and pile them on the porch. This time he will be the one begging.

The abuse was never going to stop if you did not help stop it; you did the right thing. You did the right thing.

At age 11 you became your Mother's protector and at 17-years-old you will watch her break free.

You'll finish your exams and you do really well despite never talking to anyone about the abuse happening at home. Being such a small town, no doubt most of them knew. How could your teachers and friends not know? But you won't blame them because your circumstances will turn you into a leader and an advocate.

I'm sorry you will have to give up a childhood in exchange for being a leader. Standing up to the man who should have been your protector and role model will give you the armour to be the resilient woman you are growing into. Even the rebellion and acting out will be your teachers; those mistakes will allow you to reconnect with yourself later in life.

Even though the people meant to care for you couldn't, or didn't, you are still allowed to trust again. There is such strength in vulnerability, and you are one of the strongest. When you become an adult woman (in age, because you've actually been an adult before you were a teenager), know that you are allowed to feel loss and grieve for all of it.

Please remember that being a product of domestic violence may have shaped you, but it does not define you. Your life taught you more lessons than business school; your accounting degree or coaching certification will. You became a leader at 11 years old by circumstance. And sharing your experience will be one of the things that helps you heal. You are worthy of that.

One more thing. You will become a Mother yourself one day, and you'll be great at it. For now, you are still that little girl, brave enough to step onto the tracks and stop that speeding train. And once you disrupt your familial cycle of violence, you will be able to discover your true purpose. After all, it's why you are here, dear Brigid, to allow women's voices to be heard, to help stop patterns of abuse, to give Women a platform for expression.

So chin up, young woman. You have a lot of work ahead. But it's all going to be worth it.

I am so proud of you.

ABOUT THE AUTHOR

Brigid Holder is the founder and CEO if The Art of Grace Publishing House, on a mission to share the stories of women internationally to allow others the permission to change their circumstances.

During her successful senior management roles in the corporate world, Brigid and her husband launched their own traditional business that is today a thriving 17 year-old organisation where she holds the role of Company Director.

As an international best-selling author Brigid found the power of storytelling and is passionate to share and showcase this for other women.

Brigid operates both businesses alongside her husband and their two teenage boys from a small rural town in Australia.

"Through writing we are creatively releasing past trauma and in doing so, we allow others the permission to do the same." - Brigid Holder

Website: www.brigidholder.com

CHAPTER 20

COLLEEN REAGAN NOON

ear younger self,

Let go and let God

Your life plan will not go as you thought it would. Trying to hold on and control everything will not make any of it come back. The sooner you let go of these gripped reins, and the sooner you leave those big worries, the better you will be. But the question is: how? How can you face the biggest challenge of your life and just surrender your control? God's imagination is far greater than yours. Your thoughts for your life are limited compared to God who knows all paths that exist in the universe. I know you had that desire for the quiet life in the countryside with kids, the house, and the barn. And I know how much it filled your heart to have achieved that goal. But did you really want to achieve your life's goal at 30? You were built for more. You tackled that first life goal so quickly that it's actually the beginning of your next level, not the unraveling of everything you worked for.

Move past the guilt

You will have to work. Raising children is no longer your only task now. Not only do you have to work, but you need to figure out a way to fully provide for your children. You will have help from your parents, but that won't last forever and you have so much potential to tap into. Spending all of your time feeling guilty is not the way to do this. It's easy to get sucked into the pattern of guilt when you are building your business because you aren't spending quality time with your kids, then feeling guilty about not working on your business when you are caring for them. Dwelling on this will only put you in the victim mentality. You need the thoughts of a victor. My next two points are going to guide you from feeling like a failure as a parent because you can't devote all of your attention to your children.

Intuitive business hours

You are going to start your business as a nap and nighttime warrior. The adrenaline of pursuing a passion will briefly outweigh the exhaustion. You will join the ranks of so many women before you who started six or even seven-figure businesses with just a dream, a laptop, and a baby at their breast. Ignore all advice to wake up before your children to get work done. Leave this one to the morning people, and that is not you, hunny! When the time comes when you need more time than nap and night to get work done, the next logical step is to set some conventional work hours. These would be set times during the week when you devote only to work and then be fully present for your family outside of your working hours. I am going to tell you right now that you are never going to master this. You have never been one for convention and you need to lean into your intuition. Intuition; you know, that gut instinct or that first thought that flows through your mind. Listen to that. When you finally start letting go of that full-time stay-at-home mom role and the guilt of struggling to do that, your intuition is going to kick in and tell you exactly how to run that business. Surprisingly, Covid-19 is going to be just the push you needed to work from home, while your kids are home without the guilt. Each day is going to look different and you are going to embrace them each as they come. Remember all of that control I implored you to give up? This is where you reap that reward. Listen to your body, your kids, and your business needs. They all ebb and flow during the day and you are going to find your grove when you can catch the wave as it flows between them all. For this to go well, you are going to need to learn to work smarter, not harder. When you find yourself working too many hours for not enough money, this is the time to level up and find a business that works for you, not the other way around.

Get your astrological chart done

The biggest thing that will help you overcome the 'mom guilt' is to get your astrological chart done. This is probably going to come as a shock to you. Just trust me on this one. You will find out that while your soul is attracted to nurturing and building a family, that it is not your soul's purpose. Your soul chose to come to this earth to find itself. Where you are right now feels so painful and life-ending, but it is necessary to help you step into finding your purpose. Let go of those thoughts that you are just a mom and step into your full potential.

Give yourself grace

It's ok to be overwhelmed in an overwhelming situation. You are about to embark on a journey of being the sole care provider for two young boys for the next few years. Fully rising to this occasion will require you to let go of the idea that you can do it all and be all to everyone. This will be a tough challenge for you as a people pleaser. Take it day by day and tune into your body. Your body will tell you what you need and where your priorities should be. It doesn't matter if you couldn't get it all done today; as long as you stayed true to your intuition, you will know you are doing well.

Addiction is a Disease, and You Have it Too

I know what you are thinking. Why would he choose to do this to us? A thought that would invade your every thought until three weeks from now when you receive a call that changes the direction of your life in so many ways. A friend's friend will call and lay the groundwork for your husband to go to a long-term psychiatric and addiction facility in Florida. It is far from your beautiful home in Massachusetts and he won't return in three months like you have been told. Another life-changing transaction will happen on the call. This is the first time you will hear information that will cause you to think differently about addiction. She is going to tell you that he didn't make a choice. That his brain has rewired to protect his addiction, much like a mother protects her child. As a mother to a two-year-old and a six-month-old, this will resonate so hard that it helps you see that addiction is not a choice; it's a disease.

Research addiction

You are already finding out that the stereotypes of who substance abuse affects are false. There are far more families struggling from the effects of addiction and alcoholism in middle-class and upper middle-class suburban neighborhoods than anyone would ever guess. This is a co-occurring disorder; there is usually an underlying condition—mental health, trauma, or generational dysfunction. The biggest shift you will make in understanding this is that substance abuse is a symptom of the disease, not the disease itself. Remember when he went to a 30-day rehab last year and you thought it would be the golden ticket to his improvement? You were patient and supportive, but had no idea that the withdrawal from the substance was only the very tip of the iceberg for someone to be in recovery. He didn't go back to the substance because he wanted the substance. He went back to it because the pain and dysfunction that led him to the substance in the first place was still inside him and this was the only way he knew to fix it.

Find others who have been there

That deep pain inside you filled with anger, shame, and loneliness doesn't have to be the rest of your life. I challenge you to go out and connect with others who are in the same situation. You may have thought you are the only person in this position, but you're not. There are entire groups of people out there, both in-person and online, that have been exactly where you are. They won't give you advice or tell you what you should do, but you will hear their stories and relate to their struggles and triumphs, and your entire outlook will not only change but also open a window to an entirely new way to see the world and yourself in a way you never even knew existed.

Tame your own disease

You don't need to drink to be an alcoholic—or at least to exhibit similar patterns of distorted thinking and dysfunctional behaviors which, at first you, will be positive you don't have. You don't abuse substances and you are a nice person who has navigated life pretty well so far; how could you have this disease? It can look different in different people and even nice people who lead seemingly normal lives can have it. Remember that people-pleasing problem we talked about you having? That is part of it. Your disease manifests in worrying about what people think of you, trying to help or fix people, controlling your environment, and striving for perfection. These symptoms are very similar to people who identify as being an Adult Child Of an Alcoholic (ACOA). This is a term you are currently unfamiliar with, as is most of the world, but you will soon learn how widespread this is and that much like you don't need to abuse a substance to have the disease, your parent doesn't have to have been an alcoholic to identify with these symptoms. I know you don't see those traits as a bad thing, or anything resembling a disease. You aren't hurting people and you see yourself as helping people. But living by those thoughts and behaviors is damaging *you*. You have also now been exposed to someone with active addiction. This exposure is going to make your symptoms, these seemingly innocent thoughts and behaviors, much more pronounced and much more destructive to your personal sanity. You will not be able to move to your next level until you see this and work on yourself. The people you meet who have been there before themselves can guide you through this process of self-evaluation and transformation. It will take carefully examining your motives, which will challenge your worldview and your view on reality. It can seem like an impossibly hard task to take on, but it ultimately comes down to these three steps:

1. Pause - before you react or before your thoughts run away with themselves, take a deep breath and pause.
2. Turn it over to a higher power - you don't have to take everything on. Let go and let God.
3. Choose a new way to think - your thoughts are your choice. You have been conditioned to think a certain way for your entire life. Not that it was a right or wrong way to think, but those patterns of thinking are no longer serving you. You can choose a new way to look at any situation, no matter how devastating or frustrating.

Share your journey with others

One of the biggest gifts you are receiving right now, that I know you can't see, is that you will share your story with audiences of very small to large and create ripples that will become waves in other people's lives. All of that shame and embarrassment you feel right now that makes you just want to curl up in the corner and disappear because you would just die if someone found out what was going on with your family will not last forever. You will find empowerment in sharing your story.

Unapologetically You

There is a smallness you feel right now. As well as the all-encompassing feeling of failure. You feel like a fool for not having caught on sooner and for thinking that you were lucky enough for life to work out exactly as you had planned it to. The confidence and swagger that has accompanied you your whole life is sucked out of you, leaving you breathless. You have gone straight past being humbled to losing every bit of self-worth.

Invest in yourself

As someone who never used to think twice about spending money on yourself, you have done a complete 180. That urge to martyr yourself, which is also diseased thinking, by going without is a slippery slope that will drag you down. Financially, things have changed drastically and you will be much more restricted than you have ever been and you will have to make choices. But your mental health has to come first, even if it requires time and money that you think you don't have. I know you no longer feel worth anything nice. You will overcome impossibly difficult things over the next few years and handle them with an impeccable amount of grace and forgiveness. When your eyes are open to these shining gifts, your brilliance of you can be celebrated.

Invest in your business

Investing in your business is a form of investing in yourself. I found out the hard way that low-level investing in a business leads to low-level outcomes. Low self-worth can make you question yourself and your abilities and will lead to small goals that you often won't even make in a self-fulfilling prophecy that you aren't good enough. Build up your self-worth, then invest in your business in a high-level way and what once were your goals will look like ants from way up in your hot-air balloon.

Fail

Fear of failure can hold you back in every area of your life. Two years from now, your childhood friend will impart a perspective on you that is going to be the beginning of an entirely new view of yourself. Both of you joined many activities when you were young and you both quit most of them soon after. You have carried this feeling of perpetual failure with you through your life and have continued to collect anything that you tried and set back down as further evidence that you are a failure who never finishes anything. Your friend is going to say to you, "isn't it great that we weren't afraid to try so many new things as kids," and the black and white of your disordered thinking will shift to the color of a better, brighter way. You are not afraid to try new things and you never have been. Some of the many things you have tried have been great successes and others have not worked out, or not been for you, and that's ok. You never would have achieved those great successes without that passion for trying. Your passion for trying and innovating will produce many ideas and you need to go out there and unapologetically chase them.

Defy convention

From here on out, your life is about to look different from that picket-fenced suburban life that you had no doubts you would be living. While that life may be the norm for what you grew up with and for all the people you associate with, it does not mean it is the only way. You are creative and an innovator. You will not be afraid to reconstruct your family structure and be ok with things look different. You won't get a job, instead, you will follow your passions and establish a business that works for you. The now sober husband that everyone told you to leave will be a significant part in you and your children's lives, in a non-traditional way, because you were willing to look at reality differently. You were never meant to live in the box or color in the lines. This darkest day of your life is the beginning of an uncomfortable labor that will birth a version of you that shines brighter than your wildest dreams.

Dawn of a New Day

We have to survive the night to see the dawn of a new day. No matter how dark it gets in the middle of the night, there is always the promise of the sun's rays breaking through to bring beauty and light to the world. This is your night. But just you wait and see the day waiting for you on the other side.

Love,
The Colleen who is three years out from where you are now.

ABOUT THE AUTHOR

Colleen Reagan Noon is the founder of Wise Women Book Collective. She empowers women to share their wisdom and expand their impact by becoming bestselling authors. Colleen publishes multi-author books and offers publishing services to other female-owned publishers and authors.

Colleen is an international bestselling author five times over and has helped nearly 75 women become bestselling authors. Before founding her company, she was an educator working with young children and their parents. She focused on teaching parents about birth, trauma recovery, and parenting while in substance abuse recovery. She continues to be an advocate for parents in substance abuse recovery and their spouses.

Colleen is a mother of two and considers New York, Massachusetts, and Florida all home. She received her B.A. at Rollins College in Winter Park, FL, and her M. Ed at Lesley University in Cambridge, MA.

Website: www.wisewomenbookco.com
Email: Colleen@WiseWomenBookCo.com
Facebook: www.facebook.com/groups/wisewomenbookcollective

CHAPTER 21

GABRIEL FARAGO

 ear younger self,

There are journey people, and there are destination people. I'm a journeyman who listens to the lessons of the past, keeps a firm eye on the destination, but enjoys the journey. The past is just a memory, the future but an expectation; the only thing real is the present.

You can't put an old, experienced head on young shoulders, but you can delve into your memory-castle and remember ... What links us to our past is memory, and what allows us to progress is learning. Success in any field or endeavour is the sum of our experiences and that learning, and I know all of us can remember watershed moments in our lives that had a profound influence on who we are, what we have achieved, and the struggles involved in getting there.

If I could travel back in time and have a conversation with my younger self, what guidance and advice, what *little gems of wisdom* would I offer now, with the benefit of hindsight? This is a fascinating question. To answer it clearly, I decided to focus on my journey as a writer and the two most important things I learned along the way that shaped my writing career: *inspiration and motivation.*

Writing is all about inspiration, and to keep doing it is all about motivation. Becoming a writer doesn't happen in a vacuum. It is a journey in itself, part of which I would now like to revisit with my younger self.

I became a thriller writer later in life after a colorful and, dare I say, successful legal career spanning several decades and continents, which allowed me to become multilingual and multicultural. I feel 'at home' in many diverse countries. The storylines of my books and especially the characters, which are the lifeblood of any page-turning thriller, reflect this and are all anchored in real life.

Experiences that leave a mark and have a profound influence on our character, who we are, and what we are destined to become, often happen early in life when we are least equipped to realise what is happening to us and why, and it is only the passage of time and the benefit of hindsight that put everything into context.

I would like to share some of those watershed moments, which, looking back, have shown me the way to become a successful writer. The first such watershed happened a long time ago, on a bleak winter's morning in Austria.

I'm a storyteller, so let me tell you a story:

Coming home for Christmas: 24 December 1956

Winter came early to Austria in 1956. The mountains were hiding in dense fog, and a thick blanket of snow covered the countryside. Russian tanks rolling through Budapest had crushed the Hungarian Revolution that had erupted in October. The streets were littered with the bodies of freedom fighters who had sacrificed their lives for a dream.

The little boy shoveling snow in his grandparents' garden was one of the lucky ones. He and his mother had escaped the bloodbath by crossing the border into Austria before the iron curtain had descended with brutal efficiency, sealing off the troubled country. However, the boy's father—a freedom fighter—had remained behind, helping to hide and care for the wounded.

'You must leave now before it's too late!' he had told his young wife. 'Your parents are in Austria waiting for you. You have a home to go to in the West. There is nothing left for us here. I will join you later, I promise. Go!'

That had happened in early November.

This will be a sad Christmas, thought the young woman, watching her son play in the snow outside. *At least he's safe.* She hadn't heard from her husband, nor did she know if he was still alive. The horror stories that had leaked out through the Red Cross spoke of summary executions, chaos, hunger, and despair; the wages of defeat of a humbled nation that had dared to demand freedom and had lost.

The little boy was pushing the wooden shovel along the path at the bottom of the garden when something caught his eye: a dark shape at the gate, motionless and silent. Squinting through the snow falling all around him like sparkling tufts of cotton wool, he could see a man wearing a slouch hat and a long coat, watching him. The boy dropped the shovel and strolled towards the gate. With each step came recognition, hesitantly at first, but growing stronger and more certain.

'Daddy?' whispered the boy, his eyes wide with disbelief and wonder. The man put down his little brown suitcase and took off his hat. 'Daddy!' shrieked the boy as he flew into his father's outstretched arms. It was an embrace neither of them would forget.

Of course, the little boy in the story was my younger self. It had taken my father three weeks to walk from the smoking ruins of Budapest to my grandparents' home in Austria. Hiding in abandoned stables and chicken coops along the way, and living off the kindness of farmers prepared to risk all to help a fugitive, he finally crossed the border into Austria at night during a snowstorm. I remember his swollen feet looked terrible, and he was frightfully thin and very weak. But none of that mattered: he had come home for Christmas.

A few years later I was in high school, and we were asked to write a short story about an event that changed our lives. This was my story. The teacher entered it in a little competition run by the local paper and it won a prize. It was my first step towards becoming a writer, and the first time I had tasted success. It was a feeling I have never forgotten, and it still motivates me today.

Little gem: Never try to hide or suppress your emotions. They are the building blocks of your character that will shape your life.

The Key to the Attic

I can still vividly remember my tenth birthday. It was the day I was given the key to my grandfather's attic, which opened the door to a magic world.

The attic in my grandfather's hunting lodge in Austria was a wonderland, especially for a young boy. Just to get to it was an adventure. You could only reach it through a narrow set of winding stairs that always creaked.

Once you made it to the top, you entered a small room where a maze of massive wooden beams held up a steep roof. This wonderful room became my secret world. It was a place where I could dream and let my imagination run free. And there was plenty to stimulate my imagination —books mainly, hundreds of them—and a few fascinating objects to enchant a curious boy.

There were no shelves or bookcases; the books were all in old, cobweb-covered trunks. As a career soldier—a high-ranking officer in the Austro-Hungarian Army—my grandfather travelled a lot. He was stationed in various parts of the Empire, often for years, and his most treasured possessions travelled with him in those trunks.

A leather chair, armrests worn and faded, faced a dormer window with a splendid view down into the garden. Next to it was a wooden table with intricately carved legs. On its polished top lived two very special objects: my grandfather's old typewriter, and a gramophone.

Sadly, I never met my grandfather—he died many years before I was born—but in that attic, I believe I got to know him through his books and his music. I became a voracious reader. After school, I headed straight to the attic. Not to do homework, but to read. It was my introduction to the wonderful world of books, a passion that has never left me and which today, more than ever, guides my life. I believe this was my grandfather's legacy, a gift to the grandson he never met: literature and music.

I still have that typewriter and that gramophone, and I still have the key to my grandfather's attic.

Memory links us to the past. Without memory, we are rudderless, adrift in the turbulent sea of life without compass or anchor. Special objects are little memory-triggers that can conjure up thoughts and ideas hidden in the recesses of our minds. They are little souvenirs of life's stops along the journey.

Little gem: Inspiration is the cradle of creativity, and curiosity the key to progress. Trust your instincts and follow your heart. This will show you the way.

The Major and the Photograph in the Window

Ask any serious storyteller if they can remember the first story they told in public. I'm sure they can, most vividly. I certainly remember mine.

It happened at school in Austria many years ago. I must have been around 10 or 11. Before sending us home for the day, our teacher told us we would all have to tell a brief story to the class the next day.

Instead of being intimidated by this, I felt excited. I had been telling stories to my grandmother for years. I remember when she tired of listening to me, I would tell stories to Lumpi, our little dog, who was usually asleep by the fire. So, the most difficult thing for me was not to think of a story I could tell in class, but which one to choose. I settled on the one about the major and the photograph, one of my favorites.

When the teacher called us one by one to stand in front of the blackboard the next day, I could hardly wait for my turn. This was my story:

It happened in Prague on a warm Sunday morning in the spring of 1904. The dashing young officer—a major in the Austro-Hungarian Army—had just arrived by train from Budapest. Looking very dapper in his uniform as he crossed the Charles Bridge, he was on his way up to the castle to meet a friend.

When he left the bridge and entered the Little Quarter, something caught his eye in the shop window of a well-known photographer. The major stopped, lit a cigarette, and looked at the photograph displayed on an easel in the window. It was a portrait of a young woman sitting on a chaise longue. *She looks like a Greek goddess*, he thought, fascinated by the striking woman in the photograph. The officer stood there for a long while, oblivious of the throng of the passers-by giving him curious looks.

The major returned to the studio on Monday morning and asked to speak to the photographer who had taken the picture he had so admired the day before.

'Can you tell me who that young woman is in the photograph over there?' he asked, pointing to the picture in the window. At first, the photographer was evasive and didn't want to provide any information. The major insisted.

In those days, one didn't refuse a request made by a senior officer in the Austro-Hungarian Army. Rolling his eyes, the photographer relented with a shrug, reached under the counter, and opened his appointment book.

'The young lady is the daughter of a prominent doctor,' he said. 'The photograph was taken in the family home here in Prague a month ago.'

'May I have a name and an address, please?' asked the officer.

'The family lives near Bertramka—'

'The villa where Mozart composed the overture to Don Giovanni a few hours before its premiere?' interrupted the major.

'That's the one. The doctor lives next door.'

'I know where it is.'

The major called on the doctor the next day, introduced himself and described the curious incident with the photograph in the window.

'I can't quite explain it, but something about the young lady has affected me deeply,' he told the doctor. 'Is she here? Would it be possible to meet her?'

'Yes,' said the doctor, smiling. 'Come.'

He took the major to an open window overlooking a beautiful garden at the back of the house, and pointed to a young woman of about eighteen, sitting on a bench with a book in her lap. Looking up, she waved to her father. When her eyes turned to the handsome stranger in the uniform standing next to him, her heart missed a beat.

Three months later, the major and the young woman were married. That's how my grandfather met my grandmother.

Little gem: Make sure that your storylines and characters are always anchored in real life. Authenticity demands that, and authenticity is the hallmark of a successful work of fiction.

My Little Book of Inspiration

My Little Book of Inspiration has been with me for a long time. I bought it at the Grand Bazaar in Istanbul many years ago. What is it? Well, it's a little leather-bound notebook with replaceable pages. It's a cross between a diary, notepad, and sketchbook, I suppose. But it's a lot more than that: it's a companion, a trusted friend that guards valuable information for me. I use it to jot down ideas, impressions, names, and places, even words or phrases I come across in the most unexpected ways.

Early in my career as a young lawyer, my mentor—an eminent judge —taught me something important I've never forgotten: 'If you want to remember things later, write them down straight away.' I can still hear him lecture me: 'Because your memory will play tricks on you. And when that happens, it's gone forever.' For an inquisitive author like me who relies on interesting little snippets, that would be tragic.

I've lost the little book several times, but somehow, it found its way back to me on each occasion. I remember once leaving it in a felucca after sailing down the Nile. I was in Egypt researching for *The Empress Holds the Key*. I thought it had gone for good that time, but a young deckhand tracked me down, brought it to our camp the next day, and returned it to me with great flourish.

And then there was an unforgettable occasion in the Kimberley, Western Australia. I was writing *The Disappearance of Anna Popov*. My Aboriginal guide took me to a remote cave to look at some ancient rock art when the little book slipped out of my backpack and fell straight down a deep gorge below. Fortunately, it didn't fall into the water, but it had landed on a sandbank full of crocodiles sunning themselves. My guide had to retrieve the little book with a long stick while I distracted the curious reptiles by throwing pebbles at them from above.

Over the years, the little book has been soaked countless times, spat on by a camel, chewed by a donkey, singed around the edges in a campfire, and run over by a bus. But somehow, it seems indestructible and doesn't want to leave me. We've become inseparable, and now I couldn't be without it.

Little gem: Ideas are the spark that ignites curiosity. They are little treasures that must be preserved, and to do that, you must record them straight away, or they may be lost forever.

It was all Dan Brown's fault...

The Empress Holds the Key, book one in the *Jack Rogan Mysteries series*, took over ten years to write. The ideas that inspired the book reach way back to my childhood days and an early fascination with the Templars, the Vatican, and Egypt. I was still practicing law at the time and writing was strictly confined to the midnight hour. Not an easy task when you must be in court in the morning, arguing complex cases and addressing juries. However, I managed to travel to Egypt, studied Egyptology, and learned to read the hieroglyphs.

After finally completing the manuscript, it was submitted to a high-profile publishing house, and, to my great delight, the publisher expressed serious interest in the book. Rigorous editing followed, and I thought naively that publication was just around the corner. I was wrong. Editing and negotiating dragged on for months, and when I finally decided to bring matters to a head, I was told that the publisher had changed his mind and no longer wanted to proceed! Why? Blame it on Dan Brown and the *Da Vinci Code*, I was told.

Not only was I terribly disappointed, but I was perplexed; I didn't understand! After many phone calls, the editor I had worked with for months took pity on me and, over a cup of coffee, explained the situation: Dan Brown's phenomenal success with the *Da Vinci Code*—which had just been released at the time—had made the publication of my book too risky.

'How so?' I asked.

'Because *The Empress Holds the Key* also touches on some of the big questions Dan Brown has addressed in his book,' explained the editor.

Simply put, *Empress* was in the wrong place at the wrong time.

So, my book was put back on the shelf for several years, and would have languished there had I allowed this crushing experience to stop me. But adversity can be an excellent teacher!

Instead of throwing in the towel, I took control and became an '*authorpreneur.*' I set up my own publishing company, Bear & King Publishing, and from then on, no longer had to rely on others to publish my work. The door to success had been opened!

Little gem: Never let disappointments and setbacks discourage you or stop you. They strengthen you and can open doors to success you could not have imagined in your wildest dreams.

Inspiration and motivation are still at the center of everything I do. The joy of learning and pursuit of excellence are the main reasons I keep doing what I love most: writing. Literary awards and the hundreds of top reviews my books have received over the years are the public recognition and reward that really count, and what every writer strives for.

So, looking back at my long career in both law and literature, what are the little experience-gems I would share with my younger self?

Never stop striving and never give up. Believe in yourself and don't expect to succeed with your first attempt. Don't be discouraged by failure; it's part of the journey and only makes you stronger. Only write about subjects you are passionate about and never forget the importance of meticulous research. And most important of all, don't be afraid to follow your instincts and your heart.

And yes, there is one more thing I would tell my younger self: remember, the best is yet to come, and *fear nothing, but fear itself!* (Franklin D. Roosevelt). If you really believe this and put in the hard work, *you will succeed.*

ABOUT THE AUTHOR

Gabriel Farago is an international bestselling and multi-award-winning author, lawyer, and publisher of thrillers for the thinking reader—The *Jack Rogan Mysteries series.*

Gabriel is the CEO and founder of *Bear & King Publishing* and has written 11 bestselling books. His *Personal Guide to Self-publishing* helps authors to write and independently publish their work.

Website: www.gabrielfarago.com.au
Amazon: www.amazon.com/Gabriel-Farago/e/B00GUVY2UW
Goodreads: www.goodreads.com/author/show/
    7435911.Gabriel_Farago
Facebook: www.facebook.com/gabrielfarago.com.au and
www.facebook.com/gabrielfaragoauthor
LinkedIn: www.linkedin.com/in/gabriel-farago-36a85a71
YouTube: www.youtube.com/
    channel/UCLnLzyWEV6XBy40PhDmoQsg

CHAPTER 22

JESSICA VERRILL

ear younger self,

Sweet Jess, I see you in this pivotal moment of your life. I hold you. I love you.

It's a hot, humid day in June—the 27th to be exact. It was your 34th birthday yesterday and all you wished for was rest, sleep, and strength. For the past two weeks, you have had broken sleep; in each period of nighttime rest, you are jostled awake with intense pains in your lower abdomen and uterus. You roll out of bed to move and allow the soon-to-be daddy to rest. As soon as daylight comes and he is off to work, the contractions stop. Each night has been the same. The days had melted into weeks and you are grateful your obligations of school and work have ended.

Today is different. After a brief reprieve, the waves of intense contractions return, fierce and piercing, like an earthquake rippling through the earth, shaking your foundation, leaving you exhausted, sleep-deprived and anxious. I recall these moments; the long and uncomfortable ride to the birthing center, the smell of the greasy pizza your husband had stopped for, the countless hours between the birthing tub and walking, the intense nausea and the level of exhaustion you could not even imagine.

At some point after midnight, your midwife tried to break your membranes to help your birth proceed. In each moment, you feel a plethora of emotions; anxiousness for the world you are bringing this child into (including the personal relationships laced with conflict), strength when connecting into your ancestors, the wisdom of the mothers who came before you, excitement about motherhood and irritation at yourself and your support team for not knowing how best to ask for or give support.

There is barely any sense of comfort or familiarity in your experience. You had fantasized that in these moments something would be activated in your body and your soul, that the support of your guides and spirit helpers would rush through you and activate some primal aspect that intuitively knew how and what to do. It did not.

In the decision to transfer to the hospital, the disappointment and shame you felt in yourself, your body and its inability to proceed the way you had wished for came rearing out. You held strong to have as little assistance as possible, but once the Pitocin was rushing through your body, the depth and intensity of your contractions felt like your uterus was being squeezed in a vice grip through each and every wave.

As your body slipped between conscious and unconscious states, the decision was made for additional intervention. The first mild intervention had absolutely no impact, and the anesthesiologist was called in for an epidural. I know that you felt defeated in this moment. This is not the birth or the start you wanted for your child and your relationship with her. Yet your body needed support and we must have compassion for ourselves when our best laid-out plans and intentions do not work in the ways we had wished.

Once your body was able to have some much-needed rest, you did it! You birthed a gorgeous baby girl, while still experiencing the sensations and feelings to fully connect into your baby's entrance. It felt like the entire world stopped and everything got quiet when she came out—she was silent. While you lie there completely depleted and in shock, the team swooped in and supported her in putting the precious air she needed into her lungs. When she was laid on your chest, it felt like a dream, a hazy dream. What you had always dreamed of—motherhood, a child—had come to be. At the same time, all the dangers, challenges, and imbalances in the world felt overwhelming.

How would you protect her from all of the physical, emotional, and spiritual challenges? How could you allow her the innocence of a child, keep her spirit strong, and keep her safe? How would you respect her as an individual while still teaching and supporting her as a new member of this societal agreement?

I know it feels overwhelming. And I also know this will be a passion-laden and inspiring catalyst for you to be all you can be and to do all you can for her.

That is, once you work through the isolation, anxiety, lack of support and challenges of being a new mother in a very busy and separated society, it will be. In these moments, and coming months and years, the intensity of not having the support you needed and wanted from a community you so desperately wished for burned through you. It felt so dark. You yearned for someone to bring you a meal, offer to help you with housework or hold the baby so you could nap, shower, or eat.

Your husband would leave for work and you would spend hour after hour trapped in a house with a very fussy baby who hated the car seat, couldn't be put down, wouldn't take a bottle. All the baby gadgets, gizmos, and toys would only appease her for maybe 2-3 minutes. You learned how to shower with her, get bits of exercise in, nap with her and adapt.

You became resilient.

You always have been.

As you think back to the times as a child when your father was so sick and how he wished to hang onto his life, you will remember him standing in the living room of your childhood home, a modified saltbox style with a cathedral ceiling, skylights, sliding glass doors and a huge picture window. You remember him gazing into the clear night sky and wishing, praying, asking for a being of higher intelligence and alternate planets to come and heal him.

218 I THE YOUNGER SELF LETTERS

How could he wish for his life with every cell of his being and you wished so much to be free of yours?

On that Easter morning, many years ago, you were sitting at your Uncle Gary's house, playing with a blue pencil topped with a yellow ducky eraser you had been gifted. His home was closer to the hospital, so you would frequently go there before or after visits, and being a holiday, your aunt and uncle gave you and your little brother some festive items. You heard the phone ring from the other room and you instantly knew they were calling to say your dad had lost his fight for his life. At 8 years old, you learned how to depend on you and your knowing.

When your mother's boyfriend moved in soon after your father's death and was emotionally and sometimes physically abusive during a time you need compassion, support and understanding. You learned to depend on you.

At 14 years old, when your boyfriend pushes his way on and into you because it was what HE wants for his birthday, your tears engulf you, and blood begins to emerge from your most sacred container, you are forever changed. You asked him to stop, while Mick Jagger belted out Honkey Tonk Women, and the last piece of your self-worth was gone. Taken. You learned how to depend on you.

Through the years of abusive relationships, sexual assaults, manipulations and trials, you learned to depend on you.

The years of intense rage that feels like acid pouring through your veins, eating away anything left of your hopes and dreams derails you. In the rare moments it subsides, pain and emptiness take hold like a fog so thick you can't see your hand in front of your face. In an effort to cope, you indulge in drugs, alcohol, sex and anything else that might give you a brief feeling of either numbness or a welcome reprieve from feeling as if your whole being could completely collapse inside of you from the deep hole that was lurking within.

You learned to depend on you. You learned how to escape from your pain and push it deeper and deeper. You learned to walk through life almost as a ghost, the depth of pain and sorrow of what could have been vibrating through you—going through the motions and trying to fulfill expectations while failing intensely.

You have come so far in your healing journey and yet, here you are. Alone, fearful, and angry.

Now, I'm asking you to reach deep within and see how well that is serving you. How can you open up your life more to the support and community you so deeply crave and need?

You have to become vulnerable.

You have to ask.

You have to keep asking.

You have to create it.

Since this time in our life, I have grown. Through the resilience and coping skills I have gone deeper. I have let go of expectations of others; I have begun to ask and create what I wanted and needed. Not only for myself but for others.

I wanted a community where I could share my thoughts, knowledge, experience, and support with others during challenging times. I have connected deeply to my spiritual team, my power, my soul, and my mission, and am guided by these things. I help others do the same.

I wanted to be around others who were on the same mission as me, who understood the same universal truths that I do, had a passion for health and wellness as I do, so I found them.

I needed to know there were many others who saw and knew of the depths of the pains and injustice in the world. I need to surround myself with the people who were also driven to the depths of their souls to create change on this earth.

I needed to support these change makers, visionaries, paradigm shifters, consciousness-accelerating people in their work in every way that I could.

My heart, my mind, and especially my soul ached for these things. Just as yours does. Through my resilience, I rose up again and again. I overcame obstacles, pivoted, adapted, changed course, rested, nurtured my wounds, stood back up again and didn't give up.

Why?

It's bigger than me. It's bigger than you—or us.

The reason you feel the ache and pull so intensely, like a child crying for its mother, is because that is what you are here to do, what you are here to create, whom you are here to help.

You are not simply here to live the life of a wife and mother. You know this. You have always known this.

You were a child that was often called sensitive because you felt everything in such a way that you were overcome with your feelings and emotions bubbled up, burst out or exploded. Since then, you have known you weren't like others.

Since you were a child, you were misunderstood. The one who loved being by herself, with animals, in the woods, writing or reading a book. You knew.

When your father would gaze through those sliding glass doors, you were intrigued. You felt connected to something bigger, and you knew there was so much to this universe than most people understood or spoke of.

As a teenager, when you were raising money and creating school clubs to save the rainforests, you knew you were here to create change.

All the times you were called opinionated; that you questioned everything, resisted systems and deeply felt there was a better way—a better system, a better world, a higher consciousness, you knew.

You knew, but didn't know like I know now. You felt it pulling you forward. You felt it in the rage, sadness and angst. It was there, but until you were brave enough to look at these pieces of you, you didn't really understand. All of the aspects of you called 'too much', 'difficult', 'pain in the ass', or the myriad of other phrases uttered by people you were both close and acquainted with are all the best parts of you.

I will say it again.

The parts of you that were too uncomfortable, too weird, and too deep for other people. These are your genius parts. This is what you needed to accept and welcome. For too long, you pushed them away to fit in and to be comfortable.

Sweet love, you will never be comfortable with the masks and disguises of normalcy.

That is not what you are here for.

You are here to create change. To activate people. To get them to think differently. To show them how to own their power, so they can step into their mission on this earth.

Your opinions, rage, and unwillingness to accept the status quo is what makes you beautiful and they are your strengths.

Yes, the very things that make other people uncomfortable with you and around you are your magic. It's not you, it's them. Unhealed people cannot accept other people's strengths and raw energy. They feel triggered; they feel attacked and threatened.

It's not about you. It's about their own wounding from pushing away their own aspects of themselves. Their own pieces of power, strength, and genius. When they see someone owning theirs fully, it is both scary and painful for them. They aren't conscious of it, but it is driving the train.

Most people won't be brave enough to answer the calls of their soul. I hope they learn to, and I will be here to support them when they do, but releasing the programming that isn't serving them, connecting into who they are and trusting themselves can be very scary. It can upset or throw off the balance of their entire lives and that is overwhelming.

The programming is really strong and is embedded in us since infancy. So often, we are not aware of the implications in it, let alone question it. Yet it impacts our career, relationships, friendships, self-esteem and every single aspect of our lives. It helps us fit in. It helps us be "comfortable." What are we sacrificing for this supposed comfort?

Not us. You are a warrior. You were born with gifts specific to your mission here in this lifetime. If you ever question that, go deep inside. Feel into your heart center, connect with your soul, your higher self or your guides. Feel that flame burning within until it encompasses everything else.

Follow the suggestions, the ideas, and the whispers. Let it guide you. Trust. Surrender. Continue checking in and form a community with others who do the same. Find your people.

Your life and being here now is a gift. The moments of despair and struggle are what create the ridges for us to peer into. It creates the opportunity and availability for us to access the depths of our souls like no other. These times are gifted to us to allow us to transform ourselves, developing into something and someone our minds could not bring us to alone. It is all within us, yet, the experiences polish and shine our brilliance. You have the choice of perspective—how you wish to perceive your life's challenges. You may see the gifts in them, or you may simply look at the thorns.

Question your beliefs. Release what isn't serving you. Heal your traumas. Follow your truth. Keep tuning into you. It is the best way to help others and create the change you are here to bring.

Your story isn't unique. Many experience sexual assault, the loss of a parent, and sometimes much worse. Children around the world are subject to human trafficking, hunger, and homelessness. They endure in a day what most cannot fathom. Knowing this doesn't minimize your pain; it gives you the strength you need to overcome your demons, to look them in the eye, send them love, and integrate them into you. At first, it may not feel as if you're doing this for you, and you're doing it so you can give voice to the voiceless, that's okay. We need to support ourselves so we can fully support others, and if this is the way you need to start, it is still bringing you into yourself, which is where you need to be.

Even with the pain and trials you and I have experienced, we have so much privilege. There are many that would trade places in a moment, to have these events to be some of the worst they have experienced. It doesn't change the pain, but invites us to dig deeper and rise up to become a voice for others, to stand up against injustices and use what privilege we have to make an impact of change. It is not only our calling but also our duty. It starts with us.

The truth is, every pain, wound, trauma, and experience we work through releases power and energy that we can integrate back into ourselves. Strengthening yourself, you transcend more into your power. Your voice becomes stronger. You know that what hurt you before only has the power that you allow it. You choose to reclaim your life in each and every moment. Integrate your shadows, work through triggers, and delve deeper into your spirituality every day. You have this power within you. It is a choice to access it.

When it feels like it's all too much, reconnect to what is most important to you. Your family, helping others, using your privilege, and strength to be a light to and for others. It is bigger than you; it always has been and always will be. You are one soul here on a mission to create impact, and your mission is incredibly important. Without you in your power, there is a deficit of the exact gifts and genius you came into this world to be.

Life is but a series of choices. We make our way based on where we choose to put our energy.

Choose love. Choose yourself. Choose community and support. Over and over again.

With so much love,
Jess (the happier, healthier, more supported version)

ABOUT THE AUTHOR

Jessica Verrill is the founder of House of Indigo, a multimedia publishing company that supports spiritual leaders in sharing their unique gifts and teachings. She is also an international best-selling author.

Her skills as an intuitive coach and energetic alchemist supports high levels of growth and alignment, while working directly as a channel to her personal guides. As a life-long learner, she is often immersed in books and classes, including all aspects of herbalism and flower essences, health, wellness and personal development, spirituality, and enhanced psychic development.

Jessica lives in Maine with her husband, daughter, and black lab. She loves gardening, communing with nature spirits, hiking, exploring nature, being around water, and traveling.

Email: publishing@jessverrill.com
Website: www.jessverrill.com and
www.house-indigo.com
Facebook: www.facebook.com/HouseOfIndigoPublishing
Instagram: www.instagram.com/Jess.Verrill
Clubhouse: www.clubhousedb.com/user/JessVerrill

CHAPTER 23

KAYLEIGH O'KEEFE

ear younger self,

I see you; sitting by yourself at the poorly lit kitchen table of your first San Francisco apartment. I see you scraping the last bit of Trader Joe's Cookie Butter from the jar, a meal that you've had alone every night this summer. I see the tears forming in the corners of your eyes as you lick the last bite from the spoon, knowing full well this is not really you.

You had moved to San Francisco for your career - and for a chance to see and be a part of an iconic city as its star was on the rise! And in less than a year, your initial enthusiasm for the romantic fog and steep hills had mutated into a profound sense of confusion and loss.

You thought you were depressed simply because you were overwhelmed. You had a lot on your plate as a full-time consultant racking up the frequent flier miles every week and as an executive MBA student with a never-ending to-do list of papers, projects, and presentations.

That wasn't it, though. You isolated yourself every evening after work that cool summer at age 28 because you were not expressing yourself authentically.

Your Soul Medicine is Expression

I know; I can see your eyes rolling. Authenticity? They laugh. What does it even really mean? Isn't that what I am doing anyhow? Allow me to say it another way.

Expression is your soul medicine. It is your gift to the world.

Don't believe me?

Remember that photo of you as a little girl? The one your grandmother sent you as part of her Christmas gift tradition? There you are, standing on the rocky shores of Maine as a six-year-old. Your brown eyes are sparkling with the reflection of the sea and your smile shines from ear-to-ear. You're wearing a white sweatshirt you and your grandma had decorated together. There's a pair of pink ballet slippers ironed on it, outlined in sparkly pink puff paint. Sticking out of your right short pocket is a tuft of blue hair. The head of a troll doll is there, a companion on your excursion for the day. And then there is your stance. You have your hands on your waist and your chest puffed out slightly.

You are so proud to be uniquely *you* in this moment. The creativity and beauty of ballet on your clothes. The mischievousness of the troll in your pocket. The confidence and belief in self in your stance. The trust, faith, and love in your smile. This even-younger-Kayleigh knew exactly what her mission was: to live as she so desired.

That younger version of Kayleigh seems like a long-lost child as I watch you.

The cookie butter didn't suppress your negative emotions enough, and I wish I could cry out and hold you in my arms before you pick up your phone to order that pizza. I wish I could embrace you and take away all the pain. I wish I could help you release the deep resistance to your unique purpose.

You see, in this moment, you believe your purpose is first and foremost to achieve—specifically, to continue seeking approval by winning at the things the world seems to respect. But, my dear Kayleigh, you were never meant to excel within the confines of existing structures and institutions. Oh, yes, you *can* do it! You *have* done it! But it is not your ultimate path, as you will soon find out.

You Desire to Live an Authentic Life

Kayleigh, you have made yourself feel wrong for so many things over the years. You've blamed yourself for being raped in Madrid just days into your study abroad program. You felt your innocence slip away, and you hid your shame by playing small. Wrong again when you didn't want to stay in a role that you felt you had outgrown. You had felt trapped and misunderstood by your boss. Wrong again when you felt and acted on an attraction to women. "Well, this certainly won't help me earn acceptance and make it easy to have children," you thought. Wrong for wanting to align a team around shared meaning instead of operations. "I guess business is just about getting stuff done," you resigned.

Kayleigh, don't you see the truth though? You *have* lived your life in a way that actually *is* more in alignment with who you are and who God made you to be than you think, and yet you cannot see it in this moment, because you believe, deep down, that living an accomplished life is more impressive than living an authentic one.

There, I said it. I've cut at one of your core beliefs at age 28. Achievement is more important than authenticity. Kayleigh, you *can* have it all, but it must start with being authentic.

It's funny. Yes, you attended Duke University because you wanted to attend a top-tier university since you were a top-tier academic. But remember what you did there? You selected the most open-ended liberal arts major you could—International Comparative Studies. Remember pouring through the telephone-book-like course program the summer before your freshmen year and specifically deciding "Oh! I like that one. I can take a course in any subject that I like and it will count toward my major!"

Or that time when you celebrated your first year of sobriety at age 25 by traveling back to Spain, a place that you had left as a shame-filled shell of yourself. You wanted to reclaim Spain as a place for deep spiritual connection and rebirth, and you did. You walked over 200 kilometers on the northern route of the Camino de Santiago pilgrimage, enjoying the moments of deep prayer and solitude along with ones of instant camaraderie with your fellow *peregrinos*. When you hobbled the last steps on a

228 | THE YOUNGER SELF LETTERS

sprained ankle into the cathedral to mark the end of your pilgrimage and watched the incense fly overhead in the *botafumeiro*, you had integrated a piece of you that had been forsaken.

You see? You put yourself in positions you thought were advantageous based on a set of standards that you thought you valued and you *also* made your experiences a true-expression of yourself. You are incredible.

Oh, Kayleigh! I wish I could help you see this as you open the door to accept the large mushroom and onion pizza for one at your doorstep and open up the computer to numb your mind with episodes of *Orange is The New Black*.

Because here is the thing, Kayleigh: your path to becoming an entrepreneur—and expressing yourself fully—first requires you to recognize and accept all parts of yourself. How free does this idea make you feel in this moment? OK, OK, I see you don't *feel* free, but I *do* see that tiny side smirk that you do on the left side of your mouth when something strikes you as true, and you know you will come to accept it in due time.

You Will Create Platforms for Self-Expression & Wisdom

Kayleigh, my dear, you are one of a kind. You will soon discover that your mission—and later that of both Soul Excellence Publishing and Soul Excellence Leadership—is to be a source of inspiration for all people to allow more in their lives.

You're not going to believe this, but you're actually going to start your own company. Who, you? Yes, you! What your MBA-educated mind won't fathom either is that you will voluntarily leave a $250,000 a year job to launch a business whose future you don't even know yet! Yes! You will do what your friends and family will tell you is crazy, irresponsible, and too risky. You will give yourself permission to just be and then sense what you are really here to do and create in this world. Oh, and there's more! You'll do all of this in the year 2020 when a global pandemic hits and government-mandated lockdowns throw a wrench in everyone's plans.

Do I have your attention yet?

Do I see you putting pieces of pizza in tin foil to save for later? This would be a first this summer of isolation where you've stuffed down the whole thing in disgust. This must mean that I've piqued your interest; that you are starting to believe you are on the right path! I wish I could tell you that upon receiving this letter, you'll snap out of it instantly. You'll stop the anti-depressants you recently started that made things worse, take up a yoga practice, recognize the power of your voice, and start this business in just a few months.

That's not how this will work, though. You'll need to experience this lesson more than a few times until you move from logical understanding into embodiment. I know it sounds frustrating, but I promise there are more trials to turn into triumphs, more experiences for you to have to tease out your personal preferences, and things you must do to accept that you have been put on this planet to reflect the God-given human desire to express and live authentically.

You won't believe this, but two summers from now, at age 30, you *will* quit your job after eight years and take a three-month position as a fellow for a non-profit working in Bolivia and Argentina. You will celebrate your 30th birthday surrounded by your "Bolivian family," the beautiful parents and daughters who have taken you in for the summer. You'll embrace the tradition of eating birthday cake in the morning—by biting into it directly—before enjoying a local soccer match. You'll be reminded that you have an innate ability to connect with people from the heart, when you can no longer rely on your vocabulary to connect to the head.

What's more is that when you return from South America, you'll join an early stage real estate technology start-up, Snapdocs. There, you will learn how to hold to a clear vision and take daily action toward it and learn how to hire for character and build a team. It will be at this special place where you will come to believe that being a CEO is a mindset and a set of behaviors that anyone can embrace, though few will be brave enough to try. You will be brave enough, Kayleigh!

So, you see, from this dark moment in that dark kitchen, you will gather the experiences and learn the lessons that will empower you to break free from your own set of limiting beliefs and start your entrepreneurship journey.

You Will Learn These Important Lessons

Kayleigh, I love you so much. I want to seed these lessons in your soul at age 28 so that when your future self reads this letter in six years, it will resonate deep within her bones and remind her of her divine purpose.

Pay attention to, yet do not identify with, your emotions

This will come as a shock to you, but even more powerful than that big brain of yours is your heart. And yet you will eschew emotion for most of your life. You will view emotions as barriers to progress and achievement. You've just misunderstood what emotions truly are. They are points on a compass, signals of whether or not you are in resistance or allowance to what you desire. Happiness, peace, joy; these feelings will spur you along on the right path. Guilt, frustration, and the shame that you've carried on your heart signal resistance to your true nature. The secret you will learn soon enough is that your simple task in life is to face resistance head-on and release it.

Drop into your heart to express

This is not to be confused with the lesson above. Your heart space is not an emotion, it is an actual place where you can communicate most effectively. Kayleigh, you are brilliant. What makes you brilliant is not your IQ. Your brilliance comes from your enthusiasm. Your enthusiasm comes from loving something and taking an interest in it. You shine brighter than a round, brilliant cut diamond when you engage with people and share your ideas from your heart space. Doing this will be simple, though not easy. It requires focusing on what is occurring in the present and releasing the mind from thinking too far ahead or accessing an old playbook in order to respond.

Focus on solutions and possibilities to align with the highest expression of your message

OK, I realize this one sounds like a mouthful, so let me give you an example from a recent epiphany I had. The world I live in claims to want to fight racism using the term and framework of "anti-racism." What these individuals do not understand is that these two concepts are the same low-vibrational energy, just as the notions of war and anti-war are. Why? Because pushing *against* a problem instead of focusing on the solution will only magnify the problem. It's why society has never succeeded in a war on drugs or war on terrorism. You will come to believe this as universal law.

And here's what this seed I am planting in you now will mean when you read this in the future. You will begin to focus only on solutions so you can align to the higher vibration of that positive, exciting energy and become more magnetic in your expression of what you desire for yourself and everyone. To come back to the example I've given, the solutions to focus on are tolerance, family unity, and wisdom. Trust your voice to speak out on these solutions when the time is right.

Share a message of expansion for all and create the "new elites"

Remember how you started only reading the *New York Times* and listening to NPR religiously on your long Sunday strolls through the National Mall when you graduated college and moved to Washington, DC? Oh yes, you had begun to adopt the behaviors of the coastal elites of your new "elite university credentialed class."

What you and I failed to realize then, but know now is that the values this particular class advocates for are misaligned to yours. In 2021 when J.D. Vance, author of *Hillbilly Elegy,* calls upon college-educated elites to "become a traitor" to your class, you will smile and say, "I already have." You will commit to seeing individuals through "God Goggles" and share the message of individual freedom and responsibility as solutions to the problems of expanded state control and corporate censorship. You will become a leader among the "new elites" that travel the spiritual path of individual expansion.

Hold high to your personal standards

Kayleigh, you have so much to learn about boundaries, and when you do, you will realize you have a great capacity to love and to serve. Right now, however, you allow any comment from anyone to enter your mind and live in your consciousness for too long. You came here to express, and by giving weight to what other people think, especially the critical ones, you disconnect from yourself and withdraw. You will feel responsible for other's success. Once you fully embody that you are the CEO of you and you alone and seek to live in alignment with your personal standards, you will feel that you can take significant risks and accomplish things you had only just started dreaming of.

Your voice is your superpower

I can read the thoughts you have in this moment. You wonder, "What is my purpose? What am I here to do? What gifts do I have to offer? Ugh, I don't know and nothing!" you protest, as you decline a phone call from your best friend.

Kayleigh, your voice is your greatest gift.

You have come into the world to be a messenger, and your voice has the power to heal. It's never been about what you've said, it has always been, and always will be, how you say it. You have a unique ability to soak up life's experiences, translate them through a prism of joy and wonderment, and relay timeless wisdom to other people.

I know that this awareness does not give you much relief in this moment. I ask that you trust that one day, when you feel called to create your own company aligned with this purpose, you will feel this to be true. And then you will proclaim, "Well, of course! I've used my voice as a broadcaster in the middle school morning announcements. Later, I used it to write a thesis in college about professional soccer and inspire fellow graduates at commencement. And my career has been teaching, facilitating, and sharing ideas. This all makes perfect sense." You'll laugh.

Your Awakening Has Begun

Kayleigh, I know that things this summer of 2014 will get worse before they get better. You'll make a fool of yourself by starting up an old, long-distance relationship. You'll break down in uncontrollable sobs in front of your family on a vacation. And you'll make a slight improvement from a Speculoos spread at dinner to just a few small bags of chocolate-covered almonds.

But one day, you will look back on this period as the start of your awakening, an ever-building awareness from within that you came into this world to experience it all so that you could live authentically.

You will soon see that you are here to reflect light back out into the world.

Your life, as expressed through your business, will reflect the universal virtues that you embody and will activate those within every single person in the world. You will give others permission to live authentically.

Your voice is your gift. Step onto the stage.

ABOUT THE AUTHOR

Kayleigh Marie O'Keefe is the founder of Soul Excellence Publishing. She works with leaders who desire to shape the culture, amplify their impact, and leave a legacy by sharing their stories in bestselling books. She has published the international bestsellers *Leading Through the Pandemic: Unconventional Wisdom from Heartfelt Leaders* and *Significant Women: Leaders Reveal What Matters Most*, featuring fifty exceptional leaders.

Before founding the company, Kayleigh spent over a decade as an advisor to Fortune 500 executives with CEB (now Gartner) and as a commercial leader at Snapdocs, a Series-C real estate technology company. She received her B.A. from Duke University and her M.B.A. from the University of San Francisco.

Kayleigh also runs Soul Excellence Leadership where she helps rising leaders to clarify their mission and activate their purpose through selective masterminds and retreats. She has walked over four hundred miles across two different routes of The Way of St. James pilgrimage through Spain and Portugal. After spending most of her career in Washington, D.C. and San Francisco, she now lives and creates by the beach in Ft. Lauderdale, FL.

> *Website: www.kayleighokeefe.com and*
> *www.soulexcellencepublishing.com*
> *Email: kayleigh@kayleighokeefe.com*
> *LinkedIn: www.linkedin.com/in/kayleighokeefe*
> *Podcast: www.apple.co/3rn4lyV*

CHAPTER 24
LISA I. PEREZ

ear younger self,

I am going to give you a roadmap for resilience because you will need it.

Remember when you were only eight, and you dreamed of being a business owner, sitting in your dad's glass shop. This has been your fondest childhood memory when you were in second or third grade. You came home from school and the bus let you off right in front of your dad's shop. You will forever remember the day he let you answer the phones. "Brown's Glass Shop, can I help you?" he'd told you to answer. That was the day you knew you were destined to be a business owner one day. But you are now 17, and those dreams now seem so far away and unachievable to you. You want to be shopping at the mall with friends, playing handball in the park or at the corner store with those last few quarters in your pocket, trying to beat your big brother's score at the arcade games. You yearn to be back in high school instead of studying for your GED and you're sad that you won't finish high school with your friends, or go to prom or your graduation ceremony, your school wouldn't let you return, because of your "condition." Yet, you are determined not to be seen as another ill-fated teen pregnancy statistic, like the girls that are whispered about in the housing projects of Brooklyn, New York—of that, you are certain.

You need to know that everything your mom did that took you away from high school in that final year was because she loved you and she was trying to give you and your siblings a better life. A better life that you will want to give to your own children—like the little one growing in your womb right now. And a better life you will give them after all. The decisions you make intending to give them a better life might hurt them too, but when it's all said and done, they will always know it was because you loved them.

While you certainly are intent on not becoming another teenage statistic, the life journey to your future will be filled with many amazing triumphs, yet wrought with just as many, if not more, disappointments, setbacks, frustrations, hinderances; but you will overcome them all, emerging as a Phoenix rising from the ashes on the other side, VICTORIOUS, again and again. So read these words carefully, purposefully, discerningly and apply them as needed when you encounter such circumstances. They will help you navigate the life journey ahead, providing sound guidance and instruction to help you achieve the resilience you will need for these times, but also give you the ability to summon that resilience with a little less trial and error. This letter is not meant to be a crystal ball that will show your future, what decisions you are to make, or which way to turn—those decisions must be your own. This letter is meant to give you fundamental philosophies that will encourage you, focus you and equip you to overcome what lies ahead.

When overcoming your adversities on that road less travelled, the key will simply be F.A.I.T.H. I want you to write F.A.I.T.H. vertically on a piece of paper. Go ahead... do it, trust me, actually trust yourself. When you have it ready, keep reading, we'll get started with the meaning of F.

F's fundamental philosophy is First Things First

As you navigate life, remain focused on your main life priorities. People tend to have several main life priorities that might include things like family, spirituality, vocation, developing mind and body, financial stability, socialization, leisure activities and/or community responsibility. You can imagine the number of things that will require your time, attention and devotion. You'll be inundated with the many things you'll have on this to-do list of life and others will be more than happy to help your list grow or derail it entirely. When this happens, remember *First Things First* in all things. This means you must remain focused on your goals, and since there will be no way you can accomplish them all, choose the top three things that are the most important in each main life priority. What are the non-negotiables that must be accomplished and pursued? What are your "I absolutely must accomplish"? Then do the work that is required to achieve those dreams by making those priorities evident in your life through action. This will be reinforced later on as you begin your purpose-driven career when you will be introduced to an author by the name of Steven Covey, but the sooner you can put that one principle to work, the better. Keep in mind that your main life priorities are just as important as anyone else's. Your strategy should be to determine whether the requests, priorities and needs of others somehow align with your own, creating a win/win opportunity for both. When you have this alignment, it makes the decision to do or not to do that much easier. When you don't, you must have the courage to gracefully decline the request. Not that you shouldn't support someone else's needs, dreams and requests, each decision—large and small—must be taken on its own merit but think them through lest you find yourself completely misaligned from your own path by even the most seemingly insignificant decision.

Right now, I recommend you read books from **Napoleon Hill and Dale Carnegie** but keep an eye out for many great books to come by authors like **Steven R. Covey and Sharon Lechter.** I can't stress enough that you NEED to read both business and personal development books to expand your mind and allow your brain to create ideas that help you expand your resilience and ability to brainstorm solutions to life's trials for yourself and others. You will be induced to enroll in college—an opportunity that you must not miss as it may not come again—so when it does, humility and courage will be required, but seize that opportunity.

Opportunities are laid before people in various ways so when an opportunity presents itself, remember, First Things First. Distinguishing whether or not the opportunity is aligned with your main life priorities will help you decide whether to take them, leave them or consider them in the future. However, some opportunities must be considered swiftly, as they will not always be accessible. Recognize when to seize an opportunity that may not present itself again, but always remember alignment with your main life goals and your core values.

When your main life priorities suddenly shift and force you to focus on the shaken foundation of your financial security, continue to restore that stability through humbly seeking out every financial resource available to you. Hold your head high in that humility. There is nothing you should be ashamed of; you are just passing through those seasons where you need to ask for help. Keep your eyes focused on your end goal and someday you will have the means to pay it forward. Look to books regarding financial education to obtain increasing levels of financial acumen, building continuously toward the next level of knowledge. Remember, "An investment in knowledge pays the best interest." - Benjamin Franklin.

Maintain your commitment to the spiritual journey you began a year ago. This journey will continue to mold you, like clay on the potter's wheel. You will commit and recommit to your Faith which will allow you to one day hear and experience God in a way that will strengthen your relationship and trust in Him to guide your every step. He will bring healing to your pain and shame, soften your heart to find reconciliation and forgiveness for those who have hurt you. Allow that transformation and release to occur, because only then will you begin to experience true joy.

Your journey will bring you to your predestined vocation and life purpose. You will know it immediately. Listen to that inner spirit telling you so. When it is strong, it is true. Trust the processes and decisions that will take you there, keeping a focus on First things First. Which leads me to the next letter in F.A.I.T.H.

A's fundamental philosophy is Awareness & Action

Along your life journey, *Awareness* will be required when you are struggling, but it will be *Action* that will help you endure them. Awareness comes as self-discovery. Aristotle says, "Knowing oneself is the beginning of all Wisdom." Do not wait to begin the process of knowing yourself. There is pain inside you because of your childhood sexual abuse. This trauma must be confronted head on and dealt with—it is the only way to heal from it. Life can and may spin out of control due to some different choices you could make. Notice I didn't say wrong choices, because, while some decisions may cause more pain and turmoil, they will produce introspective experiences and profound change within you. Once you are aware of the root causes of your choices, take Action on what you've discovered. Heal from the hurts, clear your mind and do the tough work it takes to overcome those early adversities. While I said this letter would not be a crystal ball, I will tell you that the sooner you face this hurt and pain, shame and blame, the less it will control your life journey. It will be hard work but can be accomplished through therapy, mental health counseling, emotional intelligence awareness or self-discovery assessments—I highly recommend D.I.S.C. Assessments. Stephen Covey says, "Self-awareness involves deep personal honesty. It comes from asking and answering hard questions." I am going to tell you why I think Self-Assessments are so important. Throughout your life journey, you will encounter times when you are going to clash with other people for several reasons. Have you ever heard someone say, "that guy rubs me the wrong way"? That's what I'm talking about. Others may not like you, you may think you don't like others, but you must find a way to build rapport with anyone, to work or live together and find connection. When someone *RUBs* you the wrong way, it really means you have *Really Unbalanced Behaviors*. When your behavior style differs from another's, it causes the reaction of dislike when in reality, it is only just a difference. When this happens, and it will, you will have one choice to make and that is what ATTITUDE you will have about what you've just experienced. You have an opportunity to create a better connection by changing only one person: YOU. That's being resilient. Resilience is 99% attitude. You can choose pain plasticity by allowing the painful truth about what RUBs people the wrong way about you to inspire you to Action and mold you or pain avoidance by denying you are part of the problem and refusing to make the tough internal changes necessary to achieve better rapport with others. It will be your choice, but people who can get along with anyone tend to have more joy and success than those who don't, and that success is not monetary. Self-Awareness will allow you to see the value of your own personality and communication style but also see your blind spots. Self-awareness will help you modify your behavior and communication style to meet the needs of others, both personally and professionally, while navigating challenges more effectively and resiliently. That's the Action part! You may have heard knowledge is power, but in reality, knowledge in ACTION is power. You must take action once you are aware of what you can do differently to create the best version of you, but heed this word of caution. As you embark on the road of Awareness and Action, you may be tempted to compare yourself to others. Don't. You are beautifully and wonderfully made to be uniquely YOU and whatever actions you take must be grounded in what the next letter of F.A.I.T.H stands for...

I's fundamental philosophy is Integrity

You will exemplify Integrity in many ways, yet you will encounter individuals who do not understand its significance and consequence. It is at these moments when you will demonstrate it to others. You will exemplify it when:

- you insist on doing the right thing especially when no one is watching or while being encouraged to do otherwise, because YOU will know;
- you have high expectations of others yet hold yourself to a higher standard of performance, because YOU strive for excellence;
- you are tempted to cut corners to accomplish goals but avoid it

and take the long road, because this builds your determination;

- you refuse to shift responsibility even when fear of admitting a mistake overwhelms you, for it will produce courage;
- you admit mistakes and apologize when you are wrong, for it will cultivate humility;
- instead of comparing yourself to others, you stand on your own merit, for it will build character, strength, and self-confidence.

So, never relinquish your integrity and while it will not always be easy, you will sleep a lot better at night. Holding steadfast to your Integrity will result in continuous...

T's fundamental philosophy is Transformation

This is the opportunity to look in the mirror and continue to transform into the best possible version of yourself. There will be times in your life when you won't like what you see in the mirror. Sometimes it will be due to what has been done to you, but other times something you caused yourself. This is when you must do what needs to be done to reconcile yourself to either yourself or someone else. *Transformation* will be a constant process of hard work to heal and overcome the adversity that will exist from your formidable years, your teen years, and throughout your adult years. There will be tears, remorse, regret, but then... resurrection. Do the hard work it takes to recover from the hurt so that you can continue transforming and emerging as a Phoenix rising from the ashes on the other side, VICTORIOUS, again and again.

That brings me to **H.**

H's fundamental philosophy is How

Asking *How* means seeking sources that provide the way for you to accomplish your next step or goal. It is the:

242 | THE YOUNGER SELF LETTERS

- How will you overcome the adversity you face?
- How will you get the information or education you need to make it to the next level?
- How will you pay for that college course?
- How will you get that next promotion?
- How will you finish your degree?
- How will you launch your business?
- How... fill in your own blank

How, How, How and strategize on it—brainstorm about it. Research all the ways that How can be answered and don't forget to ask for help, ask those around you, don't be afraid to tell people your wishes, hopes and dreams because they may be just the perfect person to show you the HOW. You don't ask; you don't get. Don't let anything stand in the way of securing the means for HOW you will overcome that next hurdle to take you to that next level. Don't be afraid to take a step back if those steps will give you a better running start to push you further forward in the long run. Steps back are not defeat; they are lessons in patience and provide wisdom to take that step forward again, this time with new insight. Your entrepreneurial journey will have twists and turns, trials and errors, starts and stops, but stay the course. Seek the answer to HOW and never lose hope, never stop answering and taking action on the answers to the HOW questions. This will ensure you continue to overcome the adversities you will face.

This is your roadmap for resilience. As you forge ahead, put First Things First as you consider the right balance of your life priorities with the Awareness to take Action where and when it will be required, having the courage to live with Integrity as you Transform yourself into the best version of who you are meant to be while always asking, How you will overcome the next hurdle that life will throw your way. And overcome you will, despite the adversities you will face, with the one thing you must always remember: you gotta have F.A.I.T.H.

ABOUT THE AUTHOR

Lisa I. Perez shows managers, leaders and entrepreneurs human resource compliance and effective employee relations soft skills to ensure, "no matter how tough the conversation, every employee walks out of their manager's office with their dignity intact", so that they reduce liability, increase employee retention, and improve business performance.

Lisa I. Perez is the CEO and founder of HBL Resources, Inc., The Complete Manager Makeover, and National Management Training Week. She is on the mission of *Transforming the Human in Human Resources®* to reduce the statistics which reveal that, employees say managers are the reason they left their company.

Originally, from Brooklyn, NY, she is a wife, mom, grandma and considers herself a craft geek.

You can connect with Lisa at:

> *Website: www.lisaiperez.com and*
> *www.thecompletemanagermakeover.com*
> *Facebook: www.facebook.com/LisaIPerezTheCMMi and*
> *www.facebook.com/groups/thecmmpublic*
> *LinkedIn: www.linkedin.com/in/lisaiperezsphr*
> *Twitter: www.twitter.com/completemanager*
> *Instagram: instagram.com/thecompletemanagermakeover*

CHAPTER 25

MARISSA SASAK

ear younger self,

It is difficult to have confidence in this now, but every desire and knowing that you have regarding your divine path will someday blossom and become reality. Your environment and experiences will provide you with many periods of adversity and suffering, yet it is these moments that will catapult you into your fullest potential.

You knew since you were a young child that you were meant for greatness and that you would one day be working for yourself and helping people in a very profound way. Have peace, my dear, in the fact that you will one day arrive and that there is so much more to come!

In fact, there are an infinite number of destinations along the way; it is not the arrival that is important; it is the journey. One of the grandest lessons you will learn is how to live in the present. This is the key to moving beyond fear and living a life of conscious creation and pure joy.

As the years go on, you will feel pressure and confusion about what you are meant to do with your life. You will be told to get very specific about your career at a very young age. This will create a separation from your soul because you are not just a lover of one thing in this lifetime, you are passionate about many things. At heart, you are a martial artist, engineer, singer, musician, writer, artist, entrepreneur, psychic, healer, dancer, traveler, athlete, yogi, coach, and above all, a teacher.

You will feel afraid of following your intuition and your soul's path, so you will do what society expects of you instead in order to feel safe and validated. You will get your degrees in engineering, ignore many of your other passions, and become disconnected from your soul self in the process. Because of this separation, your belief in yourself will dwindle and you will spend many years trying to find your confidence.

However, my love, it has always been your motto to have no regrets. Every path you choose has its purpose, and this path will prove to be a safe foundation for you as a period of transformation begins in your life.

It has always excited you to face your fears and move out of your comfort zone. At one point, you will begin your journey of travel. You will live in three different countries: Japan, Germany, and England. During this time, your world will expand, yet you will experience heart break like you have never felt before. You will lose who you think is the love of your life and true friends in the process. This experience will crack you open and force you to finally face yourself.

As you become aware of depression in your being for the first time, you will no longer be able to hide from yourself. Your journey of seeking happiness in your life has begun and there will be no turning back at this point.

You will always know exactly what you need in order to come out of this darkness. However, you will be faced will challenges in finding this support in the beginning. Please trust that your soul will always guide you when the time is right. As humans, we must face the darkest parts of ourselves before we experience the light.

You will begin to manifest teachers in your life that will take you to the next level in your growth. Surrender to the guidance that these soul mentors have to offer you, as they are simply a reflection of everything that is within you already. You may feel as if it is them doing the work and that you couldn't possibly have the inspiration without them, but they are in actuality an extension of your own soul.

You will reach a point where you find yourself back in your home-town after your travels. You'll have had an incredibly full life up to this point, opening up your eyes to different cultures and developing lifelong friendships, all while attaining your master's degree. Yet you will experi-ence an extreme sense of disconnection and loss once again.

Everything in life until this point always felt like it flowed well, even in the midst of depression. Yet, you will struggle to find a job in engi-neering for two years and will find yourself completely alone and without purpose. You will begin to question everything about yourself and your career.

In order to fill the void, you find yourself in a toxic, addictive relation-ship. You will begin smoking marijuana to cope with the emptiness and start working at a job out of desperation instead of passion.

You will find yourself stuck in a vicious, seemingly endless cycle of low self-worth, depression, anxiety, and suicidal thoughts. However, you will never lose hope and you will continue to surrender to the healers and teachers that you have invited into your life.

You will eventually stumble upon the practice of yoga, meditation, and healing medicine, such as acupuncture. Have faith that you will continue to be given tools and knowledge that will propel your growth forward.

Your entire world will start to expand, and you will gradually begin to feel a connection with your soul and divine purpose. Be patient though, as it takes time and experience to unfold the layers of your human self and the lessons that you are meant to learn here in this lifetime.

As you continue to awaken, you realize what circumstances led you to attracting such codependent and addictive relationships in your life. You were raised to see and experience relationships in an unhealthy way. These unhealthy patterns of relating have been passed down the genera-tions and you will begin to see clearly that it is part of your destiny to change these patterns.

After experiencing the mind-calming and confidence growing effects of yoga and meditation, you will immediately begin your journey in yoga teacher training. You know deep within your soul that this is your calling and it will help you heal many aspects of your life, as well as help heal others.

This experience will not only help you bring more peace and harmony into your life, it will reunite you with one of your first loves: music. You have a divine gift for healing and inspiring yourself and others through the sound of your voice and music that you create. You are meant for this, my dear!

Although you still struggle for some time with codependency and addiction, you will welcome light into your life more and more. Your corporate engineering job will give you the stability you need to explore and grow your higher self and purpose.

You will come to a point in which your life is so at ease. You will experience a calm that feels as if it will never disappear. You will have committed yourself to a daily practice that fuels your entire being. Your depression and addictions will have disappeared and you will be passionately teaching yoga, helping others to ease their pain as well.

The more you express yourself with teaching yoga and playing music, the more you will begin to realize that you cannot stay at your corporate job forever. Something about that career path has never felt quite right for you, even though you will feel very skilled at what you do. You won't feel fulfilled in this career because you won't feel recognized for all of your gifts or feel that you have the ability to offer all of your gifts. You will feel trapped if you stay here, but just know you are never trapped!

You begin to dream of opening up your own yoga and wellness studio. Again, you remember that even as a little girl, you dreamt of having your own business and doing something great in this lifetime. The moment you decide to make this dream a reality; your whole life will begin to transform.

The path toward your dream is not an easy one. It will start to become clear to you that in order to open your own business and share your music with the world, you will need to be okay with being seen.

You will ask yourself, "How do I share myself with the world without facing the risk of rejection and failure?"

The disconnection with your soul that started as a child forced you to hide your true self with the world as you grew older. You never really felt safe being you. It seemed that you received more love and attention when you met society's expectations instead.

Every failure or heart break that comes your way will fill you with shame and anxiety. You will feel so afraid to do something wrong or to lose love that you will strive to please everyone and be perfect in all that you do. You will have trouble standing up for yourself and will avoid conflict. You will obey and respect authority, never questioning it.

For many years, you will live in disconnect and in fear of rejection for you who truly are, and this is what will ultimately lead to your depression, and most importantly, to your awakening.

As you can see, there are many more things you will need to heal within yourself before your dream becomes a reality. It's important to know that the nature of your dream will shift and grow as you do. Please trust that this is all part of the process and have patience, my love.

When you begin to learn to release attachment and be at peace with letting things go, things will begin to manifest in your life that are not only in line with your soul's purpose but also beyond your wildest dreams. You will learn that your patterns of attachment were just a construct you built in order to keep yourself safe and loved.

Your decision to make your dream a reality will unexpectedly bring you into another growth period. You will have no choice but to face the fear within you of sharing your authentic self to the world. You will experience even more significant loss and death in your life. You will also experience great anxiety and insecurity when you begin to share your music with the world.

The culmination of this fear and pain will drive you back into your codependency and addiction coping habits, anything to escape from the pain and avoid the fear. The tools you learned to feel peace and joy in your life will feel like they are no longer working. In a way, this will feel like the most painful and hopeless period of your life. It will feel like there is no way out. You will keep looking outside of yourself for love and recognition.

What you don't realize now is that your reaction to this culmination of events is actually a healthy response. Any symptoms you will feel like depression, anxiety, chronic pain, gut issues, etc. are your soul's innate ability to warn you when you have drifted away from your truth.

You will learn that it is your negative perception of reality that is causing pain in your life. You will also learn that the feeling of peace and resilience you felt in your life previously was not entirely bulletproof. You had learned to spiritually bypass your emotions and force positive thinking in order to distract the more challenging emotions from surfacing.

You will feel like a failure and imposter because of your inability to cope healthily with the gloom that has entered your life again. You will feel you have no right to start a business that helps other people when you cannot even help yourself. You will feel that you have no right sharing your music with the world, when you are merely just a beginner. Please allow this to motivate you to heal on an even deeper level, because you are ready!

Take time to notice how it feels when you are disconnected and how it feels when you are connected to your soul's purpose. During this time, you will become more aware of your thoughts and how they are attracting your present reality. The more you focus on things that you don't want, things that you dislike, or things that you are lacking, the more you will attract that into your life. You will learn that you can consciously create your reality by focusing your energy and thoughts on what you want instead.

You will learn how to become intimate with the interconnections between your mind, body, and soul and how to master the presence and fluctuation of your energy and emotions.

When you are ready to arise out of that darkness, you will. Your relationships will become healthier and more loving. You will start to see them in a completely different light.

An opportunity will present itself that will lunge you forward into being closer to your dream career. You'll realize that taking baby steps is okay, and working just for yourself at first is a lot more manageable than opening a wellness studio. You will get guidance on creating a business that allows you to teach and coach people virtually. This model will align so well with your soul in that moment because it will allow you to choose your own hours and spend time on your many other passions. This path will feel a lot more achievable, because you can nurture it while feeling financially supported at your corporate job.

This shift in your dream helps you become aligned again with your purpose. You will begin to heal and make changes in your life to release addiction for good. The relationship that you manifested in your life at the beginning of this period of loss seemed confusing and painful at first, but you will realize it has been one of your greatest teachers. You will break the chains of codependency, and this relationship will be the healthiest and most fulfilling that you have ever experienced.

Even your corporate job becomes more manageable. You struggled for a long time there, feeling that you were being held back and not recognized. Yet you will finally manifest an environment in which you get to work from home, enabling you to manage your own time and work on your business and music whenever you like. You will have a change in manager, one that finally believes in you and sees your value.

Overall, you will experience less resistance in moving toward your soul-aligned purpose in life. Everything will begin to fall into place as you become more of a conscious creator in your own life and learn how to move through pain with compassion and resilience.

You will finally gain the courage to begin sharing yourself with the world.

You will have an instinctual feeling that you are the bridge between the overworked corporate world and the spiritual, energetic, creative realm. You will begin to realize that your struggles and experience in the corporate world have given you the ability to speak their language. Your growth and experience in the energetic realm have taught you how to heal the many struggles that are common for those in the corporate world. You will attract many clients from this world and realize it is your passion to coach them into a different way of living, one that aligns more with their own truth and brings more harmony into their lives.

What you might have thought of as failures and imposter syndrome were actually experiences that have given you the compassion and ability to empathize and understand those that are going through similar experiences. You will become an expert at helping people move through their own dark night of the soul, and every ailment that might come with it such as depression, anxiety, stress, overwhelm, insecurity, addiction, chronic pain, perfectionism, negative thinking, and so much more.

You will eventually have learned many life lessons and tools that have helped to propel you forward into the courageous and wise entrepreneur you are today. You will grow your business and take on clients that you need just as much as they need you.

Keep in mind the following as you navigate the ups and downs of this wonderful life:

- Depression is the catalyst to enlightenment and transformation.
- Embrace and have gratitude for any guidance that comes your way.
- Don't take life too seriously; be playful and curious—that's why you're here!
- Allow yourself to feel *everything* and then allow yourself to let it go.
- Notice when your thoughts are taking you out of the present moment and come back in.
- Just because society is saying something is the right thing to do, doesn't mean it's right for you. Listen to your higher self and don't be afraid to break the mold!
- There is no such thing as perfection, so never let that to be your end goal. Allow yourself to do things badly; mess up, fall, and *have fun* in the process.
- You are *never alone.*
- Greatness isn't something that you need to achieve or attain, it is who you are.
- Addiction and codependency are merely coping mechanisms you will no longer need once you become your own best friend.
- Your business is an extension of your soul.

- Fear only exists in your mind. Your ability to trust and surrender will manifest your goals in a much more effortless and painless way.
- Competition and comparison don't need to exist in your reality. You are beautiful and unique just the way you are!
- Don't waste another precious moment hiding yourself from the world, because it so desperately needs your healing presence.

Last but not least, never stop growing, creating, and embracing life to the fullest as your brave and authentic self!

Love,
Your more evolved self
Marissa Sasak

ABOUT THE AUTHOR

Marissa Sasak helps people struggling with perfectionism, imposter syndrome, anxiety, negative thinking, and addiction uncover the root of their suffering so that they can experience a more soul-aligned, peaceful, and joyful life of their dreams.

She is the owner and founder of Dharma Dojo, where she has programs and services that enable her to intuitively coach and guide people into attracting more fulfilling relationships, careers, and most importantly a deeper connection with themselves. In her spare time, she passionately creates and shares healing, inspirational music with her clients and friends around the world.

You can connect with Marissa here:

Website: www.thedharmadojo.com
Email: marissa@thedharmadojo.com
Facebook: www.facebook.com/MarissaSasak
Instagram: www.instragram.com/thedharmadojo

CHAPTER 26

MATTHEW DAVID HURTADO

 ear younger self,

One thing is sure in this human experience: you will find yourself in times of adversity and you will have to face your fear. What I will tell you, I want you to hold dear in your heart; for my message will lead you to safety.

It is with love and gentleness that I come to you with an offering on this beautiful occasion. My arms reach far and wide in search of your affection, for we are the same. I have battled a few fiery dragons along my journey and faced what seemed like impossible odds on many fronts.

The most significant discovery I have made in this world happens to be the one thing this world knows nothing about: **Perfect Love**. You see, a famous book called The Bible refers to *perfect love* as the thing that casts out fear.

Let me share a synopsis of what Perfect Love has helped me achieve and overcome:

- At age 13, I transformed from being unable to look at myself in the mirror due to facial acne and social ridicule to become sought after by the most popular girls in high school.
- At age 19, an eating disorder called bulimia devastated my life for five years until, in just one night, the power of God's grace set me free.
- At age 28, I became bedridden and bankrupt with Lyme disease—by far the worst physical trouble yet. Turning to the *First-Principle Idea* and Perfect Love (as I will describe below) gave me freedom and a vast fortune; manifesting millions of dollars in the process.
- At age 43, I saved my marriage and gained mastery over the impulses to be anything other than an honorable husband.
- At age 44, doctors said I suffered a heart condition and should refrain from all physical activity. In two days, I was back doing what I love and expressing my joy in working out, lifting weights, and running!
- I could share many more examples. Although the challenges may be different, what has helped me overcome them has always been the same.

As a side note: we often get so distracted by what's happening in our outer world that we fall asleep in a "material dream" of existence. Each time, in all the examples above, I used the same process described below (First-Principle-Idea based prayer) to gain victory. You can, too!

Back to the story...

But, oh, how I struggled to win the hearts of many and tasted the bitterness of betrayal in the process. At death's door, as I faced an incurable illness in my late twenties, I caught another glimpse of Perfect Love. My human strength had failed me, and the whole world seemed too overwhelming to carry on.

I saw myself as less-than-loveable, defeated, and broken. Pain and suffering were all I knew during those long, scary days. Nothing worked in terms of helping myself get well and feel good again. All my friends were distant in my memory, and I barely left my room, confined to a bed for most of my days.

After digging on the internet to find others who had overcome impossible odds, I discovered all roads led to a Divine Principle. You must comprehend the words "Divine Principle" relating to *an origin from and belonging to God.*

In that first moment that I saw the truth, *I was shocked.* Here's the thing: in our brief communication here, I can't share the whole story. However, in a nutshell, my inspiration came directly from God. The world is not too keen on God because God disrupts virtually everything about the world outside of you.

The world argues that our bodies consist of flesh, bones, blood, and that we need to obey material laws that govern physical bodies. Academics and scholars, doctors, clergy, and even our loved ones profess that we arrived on this planet in little physical bodies and will die one day. In the middle, between birth and death, we are supposed to make the best of our lives.

What I profess is that the opposite is true on both fronts. First, I believe our bodies are of Spirit, not anything material at all. Yes, it feels like we are solid creatures, and I'll address this in a few moments. Second, **I believe that we never left heaven!** In other words, we are in a state of "dreaming" where we occupy physical bodies and appear to have landed on a planet foreign to whatever they call "God."

As a young boy, I would always daydream and invest plenty of time in my imagination. Strangely, those vivid experiences I lived out in my mind often came to pass after some time had progressed. The irony I ask you to consider is: if the image (visualized in my mind) was present multiple times, both while daydreaming and while occupying the so-called *physical* reality days, weeks, or even years down the road...

How could my imagination cross over into the realm of physical life and my physical body lack the ability to do the same? In other words, I cannot take my physical body into my dreams at night, nor can I take it into my imagination. Yet I can carry my vision with me at all times and even live in it—the same way that little children play—to construct a better world than what my physical eyes see?

For example, you can hold a stick in your hand and visualize it as a sword or even a magic wand. But can you take the same stick in your hand and make that interfere with the action or activity of your imagining a magic wand right now? Can the physical stick in your hand prevent me from visualizing a hockey stick in my hand?

I can clone the thing you hold in your hand and carry it in my imagination. What I can't do is bring that physical "thing" into the realm of non-physical thought and give it life; it **remains bound to a single place of time and space.**

According to how we live as human beings, we sleep about a third of our lives away. We have thoughts carrying us away from what is right in front of us. We think about our past or future for much of the remaining two thirds of our lives. Most of our thinking is worrying over what could happen or regretting what we did or didn't do.

I am saying that we invest our attention and focus in our minds for most of the time we are in existence. Wouldn't you agree? Last, since our minds can travel to the past and future, clone objects we see, and even change them into something more desirable, doesn't that seem creative?

After all, the world agrees from all perspectives that whatever this "God" is, it is a creator. Interestingly enough, some people don't believe in a creator, and yet they are standing in creation—for if they weren't part of creation, they couldn't exist. Your ability to create in your mind is the same as the Creator's ability to create in (Father-Mother God's) Mind.

This fact is, what I am explaining to you is Divine Principle: *an origin from and belonging to God.* For instance, if you can clone an object, make a replica of the stick someone else is holding in your mind, it means that the **Divine Principle** *is an **Idea** held in* **Mind.**

Alas, we have a marvelous story about a man named Jesus who walked the earth, healed the sick, raised the dead, and laid down his physical body to give all who believe eternal life. Have you heard that story?

Of course, the tale goes on about how awfully the world treated him, and yet, he only knew Love. The same type of Love I was healed by on countless occasions: Perfect Love. The skinny on that story is that you can do all that Jesus accomplished and more!

Would you like to find out how?

I'll clue you in on a secret that I've been getting prepared to reveal to you this entire time: **Perfect Love IS God.** Yet, you won't perform miracles and find the answer by just agreeing with me on this big idea. For my next installment, I must convince you to find out for yourself that what I'm saying is true.

To get you into the proper position to claim your inheritance from God, as a beloved child, given dominion over the whole "material realm" (the world outside of you), let's examine Perfect Love.

Since we can understand that you create thoughts in your mind the same way God creates thoughts in His Mind, **Perfect Love is a Principle Idea of God's thought towards you, His child.** The same way that no material stick in your hand could enter your imagination and disrupt the perfect image of thought you hold of something you love, God allows no harm to come near you.

Nothing material, *including your belief in a physical body*, can enter God's thought of Perfect Love towards you. Here's why: the physical realm is an idea that God didn't create. Therefore, you've never lived in that realm, nor could anything from that realm ever interfere with the expression of God's creation. You live, move, and have your being in His creation. Life, all Life, exists in God's Mind and is forever held in its proper place by His Idea of Perfect Love.

God imagines you into existence! Anything that is not bringing forth joy, peace, love, kindness, gentleness, goodness, humility, moderation, patience, and harmonious living is not God's creation. If you are observant and get quiet so you can let it sink in, you'll see that all strife, sickness, poverty, and evil are illusions we perceive from a "material world" out there. Guess what? That material world "out there" is just like that physical stick that cannot interfere with God's Divine Idea, His Perfect Love for you as His beloved child of fortune.

It is as unreal as the boogie man in the dark that you used to fear when you were young. You see, the same interaction is the source of all of our suffering: ignorance of The Father, God. The antidote to all our human despair is to bring our creative mind back home, to its root: the idea that **God is All-In-All**, and there is no other power, presence, cause, or activity.

What gets us in trouble is when we see, hear, taste, smell, or touch something through our physical senses. Like when I was a little boy, and my grandma appeared to suffer from a heart attack—I was terrified. Grandma, in her physical body (as my human eyes perceived her), was no different from the stick you could hold in your hand. Her physical bones and fleshly heart are supposed to have caused her death, as she passed from cancer shortly after a heart attack.

When we observe our world in this way, we make assumptions that form beliefs in our minds. Unfortunately, these beliefs are foreign to God. Being only the source of goodness and Divine Love, God never imagines anything He created as anything less than His reflection!

If you were standing in front of a mirror and saw something other than your reflection, would you be pleased? You wouldn't identify with it, would you? In how the world perceives God, because it knows nothing of Him, *human belief argues that the image and likeness of God can stray from the Divine Principle Idea* that God reflects of Himself. After all, God created all, and He declared it was good.

What I uncovered is the mystery within the riddle of the question, "Who Am I?" You are God's child. His reflection. Made in His Image, meaning, you reflect His Imagination! You are held forever in place as a Divine Principle Idea that Perfect Love holds together in a Spiritual-substance of thought that the world has mistakenly called "your imagina-tion." How could the world know God if it didn't know that you exist from a Divine Imagination and, therefore, they see only the stick-figure that human eyes perceive as flesh and bone?

Now, to make your way back home and return to the place of safety and rest from your worries and concerns, recognize that anything "out there" is void of Divine Principle, since it cannot enter those realms of Spiritual-substance. Yet, since we know God exists in and of everything, everywhere at the same time, now, in what I call now-space, can you see how God's Spiritual-substance (your imagination) is this very Divine Principle of Perfect Love? It is the ONLY THING that can be everywhere and in all space at the exact moment of now-space wherever you happen to find yourself in the "material dream" of living.

You're doing great; focus along these lines with me for a few more moments. I aim to get you home and show you the path to return at any time. Knowing that your actual life is in Spiritual-substance, what the world calls your imagination, clears up half of the confusion. When you ponder, "Who am I?" You are a child of God, living in His heaven, what is known as "child's play" or merely daydreaming far too often. You can't die, you are set apart from the world, you're not from it, and yet you're dreaming in the material world, all at the same time.

You see, it's the exact opposite of what they told you. You are dreaming in the physical, and you are alive in Spiritual-substance. The final frontier we must embark upon is to root ourselves in our thought back to Divine Principle Idea and allow for Perfect Love to "cast out our fears," as it is written in 1 John 4:18[1]:

> There is no fear in love; but perfect love casteth out fear: because fear hath torment. He that feareth is not made perfect in love.

It is fear that causes us to suffer, whether it is sickness, a lack of money, or lack of any good thing. When we identify as a physical "thing" —a body, living in a material world with all its seeming troubles—we experience the torment described in the above passage from 1 John.

The escape is always the same. Your road home is to spiritualize your thinking and enter the realm of Imagination and purify your *personal* thought. Not to convince the people out there, or try to manipulate the circumstances around us, or attempt to heal a sick body. We recognize that everything is first a thought; nothing material has any ability to occupy or enter that realm where everything exists—material "things" are void of causation. They cannot enter the kingdom of thought unless we clone them in our Imagination and bring them in!

Do you see what I just said? If you see evil, you saw nothing, because God is All-In-All, and only goodness exists in Him. Evil has no resting place and can only tempt you to believe in it by bringing it into your mind and giving it a home. It is an illusion, and the material world is also an illusion. It is no different from watching a scary movie and then being afraid of the monster you saw. The monster in the film was unreal, as was the clone of it in your mind that you imagined, giving "evil" a place to torment you.

A maxim in law states that how you bind something must be reversed in the exact opposite way in order to be unbound. Law means that which is set or established. So, if by placing an inharmonious picture-image or thought-idea in your Imagination is how you became bound by fear, you reverse the process. You begin this by starting from the *First-Principle-Idea*, the root where all begins: God is All-In-All.

If God came first, and established Himself forever as supreme and ruling over all creation, forming all He made within Himself and declaring it as good, there is no room left for anything else. Turning away from the physical body, we argue for our existence as a Spiritual-Idea in the Mind of God, forever held in place by Perfect Love!

As we insist on this right to bear our privilege of being given dominion over every creature and "thing" on the Earth, we see that it is God that exists, and we are alive in His reflection of His perfection. This control of our mind is the battle you must fight, my dear one.

In closing, I will submit to you that as you *draw nigh unto God* by persisting in this way of thinking and contemplating your Spiritual-Life as the only Life that exists; every idea of "life in a physical realm" must be negated and cast down. Physical existence is not the image and likeness of God, and all the ideas that are not full of peace, love, goodness, kindness, gentleness, joy, and patience are not God's thoughts. You will measure your success in the end as these qualities, and in how well you expressed them into the empty-world of physical reality.

When you align with these thoughts and attitudes as reflecting from God, you will be set free from the bondage of the world of material form. Divine Love will always meet your human needs. You will remain as safe as God, for you are only known by God when you identify as His offspring, meaning you observe only His Image and likeness in your *personal* thought, attitude, and behavior.

After all, you came here for a purpose. You are the Light of the world!

Selah.
Matthew David Hurtado

---

1. King James Bible: https://biblehub.com/kjv/1_john/4.htm

ABOUT THE AUTHOR

Matthew David Hurtado is the lead minister at Allow Ministries, #1 international bestselling author, and hedge fund manager. After being bedridden and bankrupt in 2009, then overcoming late-stage Lyme disease in 2015 while building a seven-figure online company, Matthew shifted his life's work to teaching the same spirituality that prospered his family. Developing specific techniques to harness the full potential of Biblical wisdom, tens of thousands of students have benefited worldwide from Matthew and Sabrina Hurtado's workshops, books, and live streams.

You can get more information at his website below, or pick up a copy of his latest bestseller, *Trust - The Most Powerful Force in The Universe!* Get the book on Amazon and a FREE video training course, teaching you all Matthew's techniques to enrich your life immediately!

Website: www.MatthewDavidHurtado.com

CHAPTER 27

RAIMONDA JANKUNAITE

ear younger self,

There will be a time in your life where you will lose your voice, your power and your sense of your true self, but this experience will make you stronger and the most authentic you have ever known.

Sometimes you have to lose everything to build yourself back up and find your path again, and this is the part of your journey that will, in turn, inspire others to find their own deep sense of self-worth and self awareness.

I see you, 24 years old, striving, going through life and chasing your dreams. You are the kind of girl who has big dreams and doesn't give up easily—in fact, you know exactly what you want and you are determined to get it. But life isn't always going to lend its hand to you, and you will sometimes face defeat. Only in those moments of defeat will you grow stronger and find new wisdom that will carry you through life with more hunger and determination.

One of those defeats will happen in your mid-20s when you will be forced to give up on your dream. At the age of 21 you will have a big entrepreneurial dream; a mission to build a business with purpose to fight the battle of reducing plastic waste caused by single-use plastic bottles. This will be your first big idea that you will find a true purpose in and want to pursue with all you you've got. You will put up a good fight, but it will not be the success you envision. After many years of trying, you will face a decision to give up on your dream. Not only because you will hit roadblocks you cannot conquer, but it will drain your finances and you will have no choice but to move on. Moving on from your first defeat will be harder than you thought and it will leave you crushed for few years to come. It will take time for you to come to terms with 'being a failure' and even though you will be told to stop dreaming and get yourself a real job, of course you will rebel and continue to strive for your entrepreneurial dream. In the end only you know the vision that no one else can see and it is part of who you are, anything else would be compromising yourself to please others.

Remember that 'God doesn't give the hardest battles to his toughest soldiers, he created the toughest soldiers out of life's hardest battles'.

Searching for Your Life's Purpose

No matter what, just remember that all those years of working on your vision and bringing your first business idea to life at such a young age will not go to waste. From this 'failure' you will learn how to bounce back even higher, and although it will break you down and bring you to your knees for a while, you will find a way through it and come out stronger. So trust the process, as it is here to teach you lessons that will carry you through life.

After this soul-crushing defeat, you will search for a solid ground and a new purpose in life. You will desire feeling accepted and validated, but unless you validate yourself, you will fall into the trap of seeking validation.

One day, you will meet a man who will make you feel as if you have found something special: a partner you can build a life with. He will invite you to fly across the sea from London to his home in NYC and paint a vision of how you will fit into his life plans. He will convince you that you are meant to be together, propose his love to you and pressure you to move in with him within hours of meeting him. When you meet this man, you will quickly realise that you are not in the right place and something inside just doesn't feel right. On another hand, you will wonder if this is part of God's plan for you, because you will know there is a reason you are there. Even if it means learning a valuable lesson.

Despite love praises, your first trip won't even last 24 hours due to your first fall out. But few months later you will travel to meet him again because he won't give up on pursuing you so easily. You will be lost, trying to figure out if this indeed is part of your life's plan or you are simply being trapped into something that you should walk away from. At the age of 23 you won't yet have the depth of self awareness, so it will be easy for this man to persuade you to give it a try again. Things will not be rosy, and in fact, the promised romance will soon turn into a toxic and unstable long-distance relationship.

Over the next few trips, you will realise that this man is a narcissist who only sees you as a trophy wife; a great addition to his perfectly built life. He will hope to mould you into the perfect wife and children bearer, but you will know that this is not your path. You value freedom and true and honest union between two people out of love, and this will feel like something out of a movie scene. Your relationship will be rocky and fuelled with drama, which is the opposite of who you are.

The last straw will come almost a year later when he will invite you to fly out to yet another destination to simply get back at you for all the times you have turned him down and fought for your freedom. During this trip he will be on a mission to humiliate you and take advantage of your body and your naive but kind soul. He will intentionally make you miss your flight home and leave you stranded at the airport. After this trip, you will not be the same. You will come home full of fear and shame knowing he took advantage of you and deceived you. Standing at the airport hall all on your own trying to figure out a way to fly home you will swear to yourself that this will never happen to you.

Right after this incident, you will travel with your mum to your home country for a short vacation to see your family friends. Usually a trip to Lithuania would be filled with laughter, celebrations and great memories.

But the only thing you can remember from this trip is being silent, feeling hurt and fear of speaking up. People will look at you strangely, of why you would not say a word, but you would rather hide inside to hide your pain and fears.

Only late at night you will be able to speak to your mum, who will know something is not right. You will start to experience hyping jerks in your sleep, your body experiencing shock from the trauma you have encountered. At the time you won't be able to process what has really happened to you yet nor be able to speak about it. So you will retreat, feel small and insignificant, humiliated and ashamed. So you stay silent. Like the many women who have been silenced by their experiences like this.

You will look into your eyes and you will not see yourself.

After this incident, you will feel deep shame—the shame that only another human being can rip you off of your dignity. You will feel anger towards yourself and the person who hurt you. You will feel fear of judgement and that feeling will make you shrink and question your existence. You will want to run and hide, cry and scream, but you will not be able to speak up or ask for help.

Some days your mind will scream from the inside, "Rai, SPEAK! Just say something, anything. Just let one word out. Please, I am begging you, find yourself again. This silence is killing me." But every time you speak, it will feel like it is the voice of a stranger. You won't recognise it and you will be afraid to use it.

Remember that no matter what, you have a pure heart—a heart of gold—and those who attempt to rip it off will only have their own dark shadows that they are scared to face. No one's behaviour reflects you, so when you look into the mirror and hardly recognise yourself, look deeper into your heart and soul and know that you are loved by those around you.

In the middle of all of this, you will be pursuing a business and you will cry to yourself to write something on social media, but even a short post will feel so frightening. You will hide for a long time. You won't ask for help or tell your friends or family of what you are going through. You will go through days and weeks of being self-isolated. Some days you will feel so exhausted from your own thoughts and stay in bed all day in a dark room to avoid facing the world.

Right now you may be facing your darkest moments in your life, but only these moments of darkness has the power to shape you, creating more meaning in your life. Sometimes you have to stay silent in order to learn the power of voice, and magic of listening. During this time, you will start to hear your heart and listen to your soul.

The One who saved you

Over the months to come, you will battle with depression and lack of self worth. You will go out regularly and consume too much alcohol to just to numb the pain you're in. You will start to slip into a place of self destruction and you won't know how to pick yourself out of it all on your own.

On May bank holiday weekends, somewhat still hangover from the night before you will walk into your local pizza shop and meet a man. Confident, funny and full of charm, dark brown eyes and black shiny hair like his brand new black Bentley parked outside his shop. He will make you laugh and find the perfect excuse to get your number. You see he has already had an eye on you for several weeks and he's been waiting for his chance to make his move. As the owner of the shop, he would check the cameras or ask the staff, of when I do come in so he could meet you.

Over the coming days and weeks, he will be relentless in delivering food to your door looking for excuses to spend time with you. You won't be ready to meet a man yet, but with every meal together he would grow on you. He would sit with you for hours talking. Pouring his heart out, sharing his life stories, his deepest secrets and regrets with you. You see, this man has never truly shared his life story or who he really is, walking through life trying to live up to people's perceptions of him. Through the many hours of talking he will find his healing in you, and you will find your healing in him and eventually you will both fall in love with each other.

He will not be part of your plan or you of his. But over time, you will both get more and more invested in each other.

He would sit with you for hours, asking you to share your life stories. He would watch you so intensely and study your every move, every smile and every expression of you. You will not know how to cope as no man has ever looked at you so deeply and intensely, with so much admiration and love. Like he is trying to graduate from a university of you. He will travel to your mum's wedding to Lithuania and treat your mum and stepdad to a lush honey moon, and that will seal the deal for your love story to come.

This is the beginning of your love story that will last 6 years to the day of this book. As I write this very letter, I reflect on just how far I and we have come. From being silenced due to trauma, to finding real love in the most unexpected ways. From flying the world to date a man, to finding love on my doorstep. Growing through pains and challenges of life and becoming a better better along the way. Although the road together was not always easy, it was life changing in so many beautiful way. You truly both learned to embrace your true authentic selves, live together for the right reasons, learned to fight battles together as well as your own.

As I write this letter to my younger self, your now fiancé is diagnosed with yet another cancer in his lower back. A condition you both battled with since the very start of your relationship. Many sleepless nights, weekends in hospital treatment rooms, days of recovery post chemo. The emotional rollercoaster, trials and tribulations of the harsh reality. This condition may prevent you both from living life to the full, but his condition is what will make you proud of the man you have. Strong, resilient, eternally positive, still charming and someone who never gives up on life or you. He will fight battles for you and always be your hero and your no 1 fan. Respect him for who he is, as it is you who built him up and made him who he is today, authentically himself, for the first time in his life.

You never knew how long you'd have him from the start, but however many days, weeks or years you spend with this man, named Valentino, it is a precious day for both. Yes, people may not alway agree with your love story but only you two know what your love is pure and how it truly feels like to have a home within the person you love. Live life fully and love deeply, because tomorrow is never guaranteed.

From this experience I want you to remember to also love and accept yourself just as you are—with scars and wounds, with pains and shames. You are not perfect, but imperfections make you beautiful. So be proud of your journey and all the battles you have fought as this is what made you who you are.

Self Mastery is a journey

This will be a gradual process of finding your voice again and rediscovering who you really are. The journey of pain will become your mastery, your wounds will become your strength, and in the years to come, you will find your authentic self, more than you have ever thought possible. You will care more deeply, feel more passionately, live with more purpose and speak your truth from new found wisdom.

You will master the power of listening that will build your wisdom. You will start to hear the unspoken and observe and listen to your intuition. You will build up new values that will shape the next decades of your life. Over time, your quietness will become your greatness, because you will never take your voice for granted again, and when you speak, you will make every word count. The power in your voice will become even deeper, it will have more meaning and conviction.

In the years to come, you will begin sharing your story. You will host events and host hundreds and thousands of speakers on your stage. You will find your purpose and your mission. You will draw inspiration from the times when you didn't have support when you were isolated and hurt. This will be your drive to support and empower other women to become successful, independent and confident leaders and entrepreneurs.

There will be thousands of women attending your events; hundreds of women attending your talks and being inspired by your journey. Don't shy away from your story, your pains and your struggles, as these were the defining moments that made you who you are.

This is the reason you become one of the most respected and inspirational women in business, because you feel deeply, show up authentically, and serve from the heart. No matter where someone is coming from, you will always have time for another woman because you hate to see other women being torn down, broken, and stripped of her confidence.

Your beauty will shine from within, so embrace your power, your uniqueness. You don't need to impress anyone, compete with anyone, or make yourself stand out. Over time, you will simply start to shine and flourish again. Like a beautiful peacock who opens her feathers, as you grow in confidence your beauty will grow with it.

Pouring into others

As you become well known in your work and in all your beautiful endeavours, remember to follow your heart and listen to your intuition as this will never fail you. Choose the people you let into your life carefully, because not everyone will have the right intentions. Some will come to take, others will come to give, but with every person who comes into your life, you will learn.

Continue pouring into people because what you give out into the world will keep coming back to you ten times more. This is the law of reciprocity. You will make an impact beyond your imagination. There will be thousands of women reading your daily posts, your stories and every time you choose to speak you have the power to transform lives. So never lose sight of how powerful your words can be. Use it wisely, use it intentionally, and you will make an impact in this world.

Stand for what you believe and dare to speak the truth because your mind will reject all else.

Using my voice as a tool to inspire others

You may not be able to fathom this today, but your voice will become your secret weapon to inspire others. The more you speak, the more lives you will touch.

Ghandi said: "Be the change that you wish to see in the world." Follow the wisdom of great leaders and they will become your mentors. You will draw inspiration and power from ancient wisdom that will give you depth and insight. Keep learning, because you have your whole life ahead of you to share your story, to impact others and make a difference in this world.

"Let your wounds be your inspiration, your story your motivation, and your voice your secret weapon to inspire others."
- Raimonda Jankunaite

ABOUT THE AUTHOR

Raimonda Jankunaite is the founder of the Women in Business Club, an international community for female entrepreneurs with an expanding global audience of over 300k. After losing her voice due to trauma, Raimonda found her power in her voice again that propelled her to become an international event host, powerful motivational speaker, and cheerleader for other women.

Raimonda now helps entrepreneurial women to be seen in the media and heard on global stages, to share their message with confidence and become the go-to authority in their field. She helps women unlock the power of their gifts so they can succeed and thrive in business and life.

Connect with Raimonda at:

Website: www.raimondajankunaite.com
Instagram: www.instagram.com/RaimondaJankunaite
Twitter: www.twitter.com/RaimondaJan
Facebook: www.facebook.com/RaimondaJankunaite

CHAPTER 28

RAYSON CHOO

ear younger self,

Here's a quote for you: "Aspire to inspire before you expire." This quote means a lot to me because it keeps me going. This is the divine power that allowed me to stay driven and make a difference in many people's lives, including mine. Look, life is not as easy as it seems. It's not always rainbows and sunshine. I get it. Life is always filled with ups and downs. You have to be strong and never give up.

You may be wondering why I would share such a motivational message with you? Well, my friend, I've been through a lot in my personal and professional life. These experiences have turned me into who I am today—that's why I am writing this to you so that you can strive to be the best you possibly can.

I have this very fond memory when Mummy left home for work when I was seven years old. On that fateful night, she didn't come back after her work. She ran away from home, not because of Dad's incompetence or the fact that he had another lady, but because of her condition of

Schizophrenia. The delusions that she had from this mental condition had caused her to believe that he was performing black magic on her.

Because of this, Dad and I had to spend weeks scouring the island to find her. Then a month later came the tragic news and that was she wanted a divorce. That was the first time I saw Dad cry miserably. I still vividly remember what happened after the divorce. I recall the times when I was teased and heavily bullied by some of my primary school mates. They would do nasty things like hiding my bag inside the rubbish bin and hurl vulgarities at me, and one of them even called me "motherless".

There were times when I would go crying and ask Dad, "Why is my surname Choo and not any other Chinese surname?" I cried because of the name-callings on the school bus or assembly area and how I wished that would stop. But it didn't. There were even times when I felt helpless because some of the taller or chubbier boys in the school bus would attack me for being weak.

I want you to remember this: Being weak is a choice. Same goes with being strong. Instead of asking 'Why me?' why not say 'Try me'? You never know how strong you are until being strong is your only choice. Like the great Bruce Lee said: "Do not pray for an easy life, pray for the strength to endure a difficult one".

This reminds me of another story from the year 2014 I want to share with you. The first half of the year was pretty disastrous. I was hired as a Japanese Clinic Nurse right after I graduated from the army. At that point, I was pretty naïve. I was thinking to myself: "Hey, I have this diploma in nursing," so I thought I could go anywhere I wanted in terms of nursing. But it wasn't the most ideal situation after all. I was beaten down by this big ego of mine and my low self-esteem at that point of time. I managed to work in the Japanese Clinic for a couple of months. However, due to my poor concentration and performance, I was laid off. It's like as if Murphy's Laws were acting upon me because after I've been laid off, two weeks later, my ex-girlfriend and I broke up. I lost my love, job, income and everything in an instance.

Instead of being caught in a pity party to myself, I decided to be better than who I was at that time. I then gave myself a timeline. I told myself that within the next three to five years, I'd be way more successful than I was then. That's where my personal development journey started. I started to read books and to watch YouTube videos by Gary Vaynerchuck, Grant Cardone, Tai Lopez and many more. I also started to have affirmations every single day.

Affirmations such as:

1. I am completely confident!
2. I love myself!
3. I am a winner!

You might wonder why I have to say such things to myself. Well, it is quite interesting how we can be so kind and understanding to other people and yet be so hard on ourselves. Too often, we speak to ourselves from a place of anger, frustration, and resentment. If you are going to accomplish your goals and create a life that's focused on happiness and success, you have to realize that the things we say to ourselves affect what we do. These affirmations act as positive reminders that I have been repeating to myself over and over and have helped to instil confidence, belief and positivity in me.

If you have to repeatedly go through setbacks until a point when you feel like life happens *to you* and not *for you*, you need to start thinking positively. Remember: "Everything starts from within." Every legacy starts from within. Every positivity starts from within. Every negativity too starts from within. Therefore, you need to change that mindset early. Remind yourself that every setback is a set-up for you to become successful.

This reminds me of a phrase that goes like this: "Tough times don't last but tough people do." It's not always about how hard you can hit but how hard you can get hit and keep moving forward. That's how successful people do it. Remember: pain is inevitable. Suffering is optional. Don't let pain harden your heart. Instead, use your pain for good. All these experiences serve a great purpose. Learn from the difficult times in your life. Like the great Dalai Lama said: "Pain can change you, but that doesn't mean it has to be a bad change. Take that pain and turn it into wisdom." When you go through difficult times, don't hide your pain and isolate from others. Learn to share your truth and use your story to help others to feel less alone in theirs. If you do this, you will never waste your pain.

After that very experience of losing everything, I realized a very important fact that life is going to be like a rollercoaster ride. It'll not be ascending every day. Sometimes, it will be stagnated. It will be stagnant and then after that, it'll plummet. It will be stagnant again and then it'll rise.

It'll never be fun if it's always in the down side or if it just keeps moving slowly. Sometimes we love it fast, especially when it's going down and then it slows down for a while before it goes up and fast again.

Life's just like this. When you reach success, you may reach a plateau and remain there for a while or you might even hit rock bottom before you can push yourself up and reach your goal again. Nothing is easy in life. Giving birth is tough. Pushing the baby out will be incredibly tough and painful. Earning the first million dollars will be tough. You'll face countless of rejections, obstacles, naysayers, and what not.

Life is never a one-way street. It's never a one-way ticket to success. This is what I've always truly believed in. Nothing worth having comes easy. It took me at least seven years to be where I am today. Many people would think that success comes in an instant but, boy, how wrong could they be. What they don't know is the effort and process it took me to be where I am today. In fact, it took me loads of reading, searching for mentors, overcoming trials and errors, seminars, grit, guts, faith, confidence, and even failures to reach where I am today.

Trust me, it's not going to be easy, but I believe in YOU. I believe you can and will succeed as long as you are willing to open up your mind and change your mindset about life and success. The choice is yours to make. But here's the catch: "Are you willing to go for it?"

If your answer is *yes*, what should you do?

First, you've got to have a vision of what you truly want. A vision is about what you're going to create—a vision that really works and that excites you. It has to have the power to pull you from your bed every morning that you'll want to go and accomplish it.

Second, if you've got a dream, you've got to work hard on it and protect it. No matter what, there should never be a plan B. Just like Chris Gardner said: "Plan B sucks." Always. Literally. Why is it not ideal to have a Plan B? Well, if your Plan A is to be financially free in 5 years but Plan B is just to be comfortable and work, then it is not aligned with your goal. You can have different strategies to achieve Plan A but not Plan B to Z. With that said, if you want the lifestyle of your dreams, then you have to work on it. If you want to be an author, learn and then do it. As famously said by Anastasia Soare: "It was my intention, my commitment, that even if a door was closed, I would bang on it, I would break the door, or I would get in through the window. There was no way that I would not make that happen."

Third, once you have decided on doing something, just do it! But here's a word of caution: for certain things that you are going to do, remember to strategize before you have to bear the consequences. What do I mean by this? Well, after reading and learning from so many gurus, I thought I could build a profitable business by joining a business course. However, that's not the case. Instead of earning money or even breaking even from the course, I spent thousands of dollars on knowledge that I couldn't fully utilize. In the end, not only did I waste my money, I also wasted my time and effort because I was still confused after that. There were days when I only had a few hundred dollars to survive because of the payment plans. Therefore, it is important to know who can guide and help you as well.

Last but not least, when you give your best and it doesn't work, don't get upset. Evaluate, practice, and try again harder. Once you expand your limits, you can't go back to how they were before. As famously said by T. Harv Eker: "How you do anything is how you do everything." If you don't give your best in life, life will not give you its best. Hence, I would implore you to focus on enjoying the process.

People tend to focus on the final result, not what it took to get there. They see the glory, not the heartache. The time freedom, not the sleepless nights. Struggle and make sacrifices for a few years to get a lifetime of freedom. When it hurts, just keep fighting like your life depends on it. Keep moving forward. No matter what it takes, keep moving forward!

Sometimes, people may try to shut you down, but they have no idea who they are messing with! Keep moving! Life will test you to see how serious and determined you are. Do not take it personally. It comes with the territory. No test, no testimony. Keep Moving!

Sometimes your funds are low and your bills are high. You have to fake a smile when you want to cry, but keep moving forward! When your back is up against the wall, lean onto it and stand tall. Keep moving, even if you fall. Crawl if you must and look up, but keep moving forward! Every dream comes with a test and demands your best. You must have faith. Take massive actions. Prove to yourself and the rest of the world that you can do it! Remember, it will never rain forever. After the rain, the dark clouds will pass and the sun will shine again.

Never give up because you'll never know what will happen if you push ahead towards your goal. You are just one step or few steps away from it. If you give up, you'll definitely regret not getting what you could have gotten or achieve. Stay on and stay strong. Preserve and persist until you get the results you want. Trust me, it's painful but, hey, it's definitely worth it. You only fail when you stop trying.

Quick question: Do you want to know what happened after I took action and learnt from my mistakes in 2014? Here's what happened: within two to three months, I found myself a full-time job as a psychiatric nurse and, on top of that, I was motivating many secondary school students accompanied by my mentor. My story was then featured on the popular local newspaper, hospital's magazine and I was even invited on stage as a guest speaker. Seven years later, I have built a very successful podcast called The Raygacy Show which has featured the best entrepreneurs around the world such as Gary Vaynerchuck, Grant Cardone and many more.

Here's the thing: without a certain great virtue, all those things that I have mentioned earlier wouldn't have materialized. The virtue that has served me well is none other than gratitude. When I started adopting gratitude in my life, the more beauty I see in this world. As the saying goes: "A grateful heart is a magnet for miracles." With an attitude of gratitude, you will habitually focus on expressing thankfulness and appreciation for the limitless opportunities available in your business and life.

When you have an attitude of gratitude, you will start to feel more abundant, grateful, productive and happier. So how can you cultivate gratitude? You can start by focusing on appreciation, surround yourself with grateful people and be intentional in the present.

Speaking of people; have you ever heard of this quote, "Your network equals to your net-worth?" Well, it's true! Who you choose to surround yourself with rubs off on you. Take a look at where you are today. Are you on the path you want to be? If not, you might want to look at who you spend the most time with. Are your friends pushing you forward toward your dreams and goals or are they keeping you idle?

Take a good look at who you talk to, text, and interact with on social media daily. Are these people pushing you higher or holding you back? If you aren't where you want to be in life, you might need to surround yourself with other people. Remember, if you want to be a lion, you must surround yourself with lions and train with them. Period.

Therefore, harness the power of networking. Know that it is not just about trading information between two people or even in groups. Understand that it serves as an avenue to create long-term relationships with mutual benefits. The ability to network is the most important skillset anyone needs in order to survive and thrive during this era. This reminds me of how I managed to collaborate with many different entrepreneurs to co-author books like this or even speak at their summits. Thus, treat others how you want to be treated.

With that said, there's one last principle that I would like to impart to you and believe will serve you well too is filial piety. According to Confucius, there are three degrees of filial piety. He said that the highest is being a credit to our parents. The second is not disgracing them and the lowest is being able simply to support them.

Hence, I would implore you to care for and be good to them. Show them respect, love, courtesy and support despite any misunderstandings. Soak up every little moment you have with them. Call them and let them know how loved and treasured they are because their time on Earth is limited. Let them know how much you love them, not only in your words but also in your deeds. Make the most of your time together. It's not about your presents but your presence when you are with them. Be grateful for all the sacrifices they've made for you because they love you more than you know.

As we have come to the end of this letter, here's my final message to you:

> *Ignore the haters, work your hardest and be the best that you can be. Sooner or later, success will come your way. Be patient and grateful for whatever you have in life. Don't stay in your comfort zone and rot there. Go and find your why. Once you know what you want, the things that you yearn for will come to you. Trust me, they will, as long as you have faith. Don't let your fear hold you back.*

That's all for now. With that, I wish you all the best in your future endeavors! Remember: you have greatness within you!

Love,
Your future self

ABOUT THE AUTHOR

Rayson is dubbed as The Celebrity Whisperer. Through his podcast, The Raygacy Show, he picks the brains of the best entrepreneurs in this world, such as Gary Vee, Grant Cardone, and more, to learn some of the simple and effective steps millennials can take to experience success most swiftly and effectively.

The millennials who have listened to his podcast have experienced personal transformation after learning the tips they need to move forward.

His mission is to inspire people around the world and create a bigger impact, legacy, and joy with his unique experience and knowledge in personal mastery, personal branding, and professional networking.

He is a well-respected authority in personal branding and professional networking fields. He has featured on numerous local and international media such as The Straits Times, 938. Live, Lian He Zao Bao, and Brainz Magazine, to name a few.

He lives by the belief that if we all knew how much we've missed out on by being uneducated, disconnected, and broke, we'd be working a lot harder towards our goals. The person you will be in a year from now is based on the content you study, who you are mentored by, and the people you surround yourself with today.

Facebook: www.facebook.com/raysonc
LinkedIn: www.linkedin.com/in/hireraysonchoo
Instagram: www.instagram.com/raygacy
The Tribe of Raygacy: www.t.me/theraygacyshowfamily

CHAPTER 29

RYANE BROUSSARD

 ear younger self,

I've had the privilege of having a front-row seat in your life's rises and falls over the past 36 years and counting. You've grown into a successful entrepreneur, married the love of your life, and have four amazing children that have changed your life. I want to fill you in on some lessons I have learned that will help you grow into the woman and entrepreneur I am today.

Let's face it, not everyone supports you. As sad as that is and as awful as that may make you feel at times—it doesn't mean that you aren't qualified or able. As a matter of fact, over the next few years and into decades, you will face many obstacles and challenges, but don't let that cause you to give up. You may be tired, lonely, bruised, and battered, but you must keep going. You got this. What matters more than anything is that you believe in yourself and your dream, whether anyone else does or not. And, from my perspective now, hindsight, you have more in your corner than you know.

Along your journey, you will have to pursue and surround yourself with relationships that elevate you and launch you into the person you know you can be. Who you surround yourself with is a major key to your promotion as an individual and a leader.

Thinking back now, do you remember when your college coach said to you, "You won't get much playing time because your body fat is too high this week."? Those words crushed you and caused you to play them over and over like a resounding record for years, leading to substance abuse and disordered eating. What you really heard when he said that to you was, "You aren't good enough. Your striving, proving and achieving aren't good enough. You are only as good as the percentage of fat on your body and it must be low in order to be worth playing. Your value and worth are in what your body looks like, your ability and the measure in which we critique both."

Those words couldn't be any farther from the truth. And trust me, you will hear voices like this for years to come—even in your career, your marriage, and as a parent. Here's my advice to you the next time that happens: Get dressed, lace up your cleats, and go out there and give it all you have—leaving everything on that field.

Fight the thoughts that are trying to creep in that are telling you to quit. Fight the voice that will try to become familiar telling you: "It's not worth it, YOU are not worthy of playing time. What you are doing is not enough and will never be enough."

Expectations. That is what it comes down to. What others expect from us become the rules and beliefs we adapt and, if not careful, our identity.

You are no stranger to striving and preforming to meet others perceived expectations; this dance started at a very young age with you. Being the product of a father who held collegiate athletic records and a mother who grew up in a military home, you felt early on to perform athletically and measure up in discipline. I want to give you some advice that will change your perspective and life when you apply it. We've all heard the phrase, "If only I knew then what I know now." Well, let's have that conversation.

First, let me take this opportunity to interrupt the pattern and cycle that will try to engrain itself in your mindset by first telling you, it's going to be ok. YOU are going to be ok. Use everything that you encounter as fuel to move forward. Just because you fail at something doesn't make you a failure. Your struggle is a part of your story. Never be ashamed of the hardships you face that you can learn from. Failure is one of your best teachers. Let it teach you so that you will not have to repeat the same grade/test again because you chose not to pay attention.

There is power in your testimony. There are lessons and opportunity in what seems like failure. Success isn't only in the victory; it's found in the overcoming of obstacles and challenges that you face as well. Do not let someone's words or expectations dictate your success or failures in life.

Listen close, you will need what I am about to tell you in the future. There are five lessons that I learned over the years that have helped build and shape me into a better person, friend, wife, mother and entrepreneur that I am today.

1. You have the dream; but you need a vision.

Vision without action is merely a dream. Action without vision just passes the time. Vision with action can change the world. - Joel A. Barker

Being an entrepreneur is exhilarating! Ask anyone you know who is one and they will smile from ear to ear as they tell you their business' origin story. Yet great things are commonly birthed from tragedy, hard times, and failure. The birthing of the dream is one of the greatest stories you'll tell, yet without a vision for the dream, it will never be birthed.

No one sees the grit and the grind behind the success. They don't see what it takes to get to what is seen. The fruit of success and the lifestyle portrayed are often romanticized. However, there are often multiple challenges and obstacles that you must overcome to get to the success and lifestyle part. It's part of the journey. It's the process of the vision to the dream. A dream without vision remains just that—a dream.

My dream of playing sports professionally started with making a team. The vision was simple to start: make the team, become the best and repeat until the collegiate level. There was a flaw in my vision, and it included health. Had I known then that the healthiest version of myself would never demand unhealthy habits in order to reach a goal, that time in my life would have looked extremely different. With any dream, you have to have a vision of how to get there, and in most cases, how to get there in the healthiest way possible; whether physically, financially, spiritually or mentally.

2. Be intentional with the voices you allow to speak into you.

You can be whoever you want to be. Don't let those voices or noises, whether they're inside or outside, distract you. - Ally Brooke

The voices that we listen to from the moment we are born are the ones that help shape us and, if not careful, define us. We have to be intentional with both who we surround ourselves with and whose words we allow to guide us, shape us and often dictate us.

I'm a mother of four children. From as little as in my womb, my husband and I would talk to our children and pray over them. We were told they could hear us and be able to recognize our voices over anyone else's, even at birth, if we did this. So, being young and impressionable, we partook in talking to my belly. Honestly, I do think there is something in this theory because I can remember our babies being hours old and turning to my husband's voice as I nursed them. As they grew into toddlers, we would often be places and sometimes we would become separated by people or distance. I would call to them whether to warn them of something, call for them to come near or to correct them.

Do you remember when you were a little a child and you did something you were not supposed to be doing and you heard your mother's or father's voice call you? You knew their voices over anyone else's around. My children know my husband's voice and they know mine as well. So much that we could whisper their name in a crowd, and they would turn to see. It's the same with any voice that we allow around us. You become familiar enough with it, even a whisper of a lie can enter.

Remember what my college coach said to me that day about my body? Of course, I respected and honored my coach—I was taught to do so—but his voice was one that I allowed to pervert my perspective of myself. In all honesty, he wasn't against me; he was against losing. Where I went wrong was allowing that voice to do more than guide and train me. I allowed his words to define me. His beliefs, whether based in wisdom or on false belief, I adapted as my own. Both the fat on my body, or lack of, and my athletic performance defined who I was. Speak to yourself the words you desire to see outlived in your life.

3. Find mentors and be a mentor.

All of us are mentors. You're mentors right here and now. And one of the things I've always done throughout my life, I have always found that person, that group of people that I was going to reach my hand out and help bring them along with me. - Michelle Obama

As an entrepreneur, you can often easily fall into the same cycle. It is said that entrepreneurship and leadership are both lonely journeys to travel. It is your dream, your vision, so no one will work as hard as you to fulfil it. This is true. It's a sacrifice but one that is worth it when you see the fruit.

Your attention, time, and efforts are all focused on birthing and growing your business. Sure, you may hire people to share in your dream and vision, but at the end of the day, it is your name and your grit tied to the businesses' success. This is where the third tool comes in: mentorship.

It was said to me once that you need three different types of mentorship in your life.

- One mentor who is far beyond you and has walked the journey and made it to share wisdom of both success and failure.
- One mentor just ahead of you 3-5 years who can also share

wisdom of success and failure but relative to the current time and industry.

- One you can mentor who you are just ahead of to pour your wisdom into.

These people are entrepreneurs; they relate to you. You are able to have the access to their journey and their mistakes, and they are able to do the same with yours. It makes sense to learn from someone else who has been there then to continually all make similar mistakes.

It is also important to become a mentor to other entrepreneurs coming up. This goes beyond a typical "pay it forward" mentality. This is an intentional relationship in order to grow those around you because of the growth that has taken place within yourself. A full circle approach. Let's be honest, getting to the top is fun, but it's not meant to be a solo experience. We thrive best with a team and with others along the way.

4. Get a coach. Yes, even coaches have coaches.

Behind every great athlete is a masterful coach that inspires the athlete to evolve into the strongest performer they can become. - Cathy Engelbert

In my years of sports, I've had my share of coaches—both good and bad.

Coaching is defined as: *The belief that the individual has the answers to their own problems within them. The coach is not a subject expert, but rather is focused on helping the individual to unlock their own potential.*

This definition is the exact measure, whether a coach is a good one or not. As a player, I had all the ability I was going to have. Could I work harder to enhance and elevate this ability? Yes. But it is the belief in myself that was going to make the difference in the game. If my coach could call that out of me, then there would be success. He wasn't calling out anything that wasn't already there.

Having a financial, life, business, health and fitness coach is a game changer in life. You have what it takes to get you to a certain level in areas, but it will take someone else to take you even further than what you could do on your own.

I possess a greater than normal amount of self-discipline. I race marathons and training to that capacity takes extreme discipline. I can remember when each race I would PR, (personal record, for those outside of the racing terminology) then suddenly it was as if I had hit a wall. Marathon after marathon, I was hitting within a minute of the same time. What was it going to take to reach my goal of qualifying to run the Boston Marathon? A coach.

You might think that's odd because not only am I a runner but also, among my qualifications, I am a run coach. But any good coach also needs a coach! It took someone else calling greater out of me in order for me to reach my highest potential. The work I did for myself prior did not go to waste. It best prepared me for being coached and reaching my highest potential.

5. Utilize your network.

"The ability to ask the right question is more than half the battle of finding the answer." - Thomas J. Watson

It was told one time by my business coach that 'we already have within our network everything we need.' This was a foreign thought to me prior to his explanation. You see, we will have—or begin to have— access to everything we need by asking the right questions of those we are already in relationship with. This opens us up to what they have access to in their network.

Whether in my career as a fundraiser or just in my connection within my community, it was my job to know anyone and everyone. They could either give of their time, money and resources, or they knew of someone who could give of their time, money and resources. I would often sit with business executives in our community and ask questions. The answer to these questions is how I would best assist them in finding the right place for their resources. One day, I was with a very wealthy man and he gave

292 | THE YOUNGER SELF LETTERS

me the best advice. After he wrote me a check that was going to change many lives in our community, he asked me if I was going to ask him who he knew. Being green to the non-profit realm at the time, he was giving me the best tool that I adopted as a staple for years to come in all areas. He was teaching me that his resources were great and could do a lot of good, however I was leaving some resources untapped by not asking him who he knew that I should know and approach.

So, before closing this letter, I want to help you peek into the future for a moment. You are now the CEO of PACE Fitness—a fitness company that exists to help women from all walks of life achieve their fitness and health goals and change their families' lives in health. Yes, you took the years of torment from collegiate sports and used them as fuel to pursue bigger and better. You took failure and positioned it as a teacher, enabling you to far surpass your small-minded adolescent goals. You are a wife, mother, active member in your community, and you thrive on helping others achieve success through coaching. That's right, you are a coach now. It has been your privilege to speak words of truth and life into your clients so they can live a life of freedom in their health and fitness.

These tools that I mentioned above are simple, and perhaps easily learned through trial and error. But it was through life experiences that these tools were given to me and served me well once I applied them. Your future is bright and your success is generational. You wouldn't believe me now if I told you that you will LOVE the future you...but you do!

ABOUT THE AUTHOR

Ryane Broussard is a third-generation entrepreneur. Her grandmother was a pioneer for both her time and gender, and it was her grit that she admired and became an accelerator behind birthing her own dreams and ambitions.

Ryane has had a passion for sports and fitness since a young age, manifesting in becoming a collegiate athlete. It was through that time she developed many of the hidden characteristics of an entrepreneur.

Pushing through limitations has been her mantra, as she has accomplished much outside of her career. She has raised multi millions of dollars for nonprofits around the world, has obtained her pilot's license, she has devoted her life to training and competing in marathons, ultra-marathons and various endurance races. One of her most valued accomplishments is founding an international organization that rescues women out of prostitution and provides them a dignified way of providing for their family.

She now devotes her time to coaching people in health and fitness around the globe. Helping others establish an identity of health that they envision for themselves, reach and maintain their goals.

Ryane is married to the love of her life Blake, and is a mother of four beautiful children. She's a Texas girl at heart, but now calls Louisiana home.

Website: www.pacemyfitness.com
Email: info@pacemyfitness.com
Facebook: www.facebook.com/pacemyfitness
Instagram: www.instagram.com/pacemyfitness

CHAPTER 30

TARRYN REEVES

 ear younger self,

Your life thus far has been a series of challenges that seem to roll in like the never ending waves against the shore. Each time a big one comes and the sea of life seems angry and intent on crushing you, beating against you as you try to resist the change and control the elements and you feel like you are alone and drowning, stop resisting, allow and trust the natural flow of things. When you remember this (and you always eventually get the message! The waiting times are shortening so *yay* for progress!), you always navigate the waves like a skilled sailor in your trusty boat—at home, on the raging seas of life.

Life is like a river we are all floating on. On the 'good' days, you lie dreamily on your back, floating through the calm water and listening to the sounds of birds and absorbing the sense of peace around us. Inevitably, you are going to hit turbulent waters and the journey becomes a little less peaceful. And then there are the rapids; the periods in life when it seems like you are being hit from every angle. The weight of the water slamming against you feels bone crushing. Your resolve can erode like a weather-beaten rock on the stormy shoreline. You kick madly and struggle to keep your head above water, gasping for air, grasping for anything to pull you out, always missing and flying headlong downstream. You tend to find a big rock and hold on to it for dear life. Resting for a while whilst the chaos around you rages. Resisting the natural flow of water downstream. Grounding yourself in the turbulent waters.

Do not ground yourself in turbulent waters. Let go of the big rock that is your comfort zone, trust that all is happening for you, lie on your back and allow yourself to be carried to calmer waters. Soak in the lessons from your journey like water to a sponge and embody the next bolder, brighter version of you. Will turbulent waters keep on coming? Absolutely! Will they break you? Absolutely not! You were born to navigate uncharted waters and to light the way for others.

Now that I have shared that bit of philosophical magic with you, I want to give you the heads-up; another period of turbulent waters is lapping at your feet. I know you feel it. Leap and let me be the voice in your ear as you step into the unknown.

It's the end of December 2020 and you are, once again, considering adding another dimension to your business.

Being in the back end of different businesses and having a natural gift for seeing big picture ideas and breaking them down into smaller puzzle pieces, knowing exactly what goes where and what system or person is needed to make it all work means that you aren't scared of big ideas. What you have also come to realise is that there are some clueless people doing really well in business and making large amounts of money with apparent ease. Now, I know you don't want to be like those people. Your values of transparency, honesty and integrity are too ingrained to lead anyone up the proverbial garden path. But you want to make loads more money with ease (sales with soul is what you like to say). And when you want something, there is no stopping you.

You have just 'finished' splitting your business into four branches—I have no idea why you thought that would be a good idea, by the way! Too many balls to keep in the air and loads of work to do. Four websites plus four socials and multiple procedures for the team equal a time-consuming *suckhole* unnecessary for your success; but you needed to do it as your next step on the path to seeing your vision and purpose more clearly.

Congratulations on buying your new house and good luck putting your new one on the market come the new year. I know how much you love your home and how hard it will be to leave, but know that you will receive more money for it than you even thought possible. You will move into your parents' whilst your house is on the market and it won't be as bad as you think.

You have been working in the back end of a few publishing houses now through your virtual assistance and web development agency and watching the rise in popularity of female-owned publishing houses with some interest. Heading this movement is a woman you have had little to do with and have never even spoken to but is about to challenge you in ways you never thought you needed.

An increase in profit margins and a closer relationship, working with your lifelong love affair with stories, feels like an easy decision and she did say that the business model she teaches would fit seamlessly into your current business structure, so you book the call to speak with her. You liked what she had to say, and she made it sound easy, but the investment in her services shocked you. Knowing yourself, the group program was never an option for you. When you commit, you commit hard, and you want 1:1 attention to do things once and do them right. This is by far the biggest investment in your business to date and it scared the pants off you.

Despite your fear, you trust your intuition and jump into the experience with no backup plan after two weeks of agonising over your decision. Your motto for this type of decision is always "If you break it, you can always fix it."

After only two sessions, it becomes apparent that you and your new mentor are on different pages, possibly different books entirely! A huge and uncomfortable series of conversations arises. You can't understand why she is getting annoyed at working through the issues with your current business structure and she can't understand why you would even want to keep the current business structure. You are upset because you have invested a large amount of money and she wants you to 'burn your current business to the ground.' She tells you that you are not seeing the bigger picture and that you are playing too small. Deep down you know she is right, but this sets off a 10-day period of intense anxiety, your first panic attack in over 17 years, sleepless nights, vicious self-talk and mountains of self-doubt. On the surface, you are angry. *How dare this woman come in here and tell me how shit I am? Who the hell does she think she is? I paid her, for fuck's sake!* On the inside, you are scared witless. Your higher self knows that this is the painful birthing process of the next version of you, but you are scared, anxious, and alone. She tells you she is considering terminating your contract and even though you are hating on her right now, you don't want it to end this way. A part of you knows that this is exactly the shake up you needed to get you to move outside your comfort zone and become the person you are here to be and to do the work you are here for.

Here are some feelings and experiences you will find yourself seemingly drowning in over the next few weeks:

Anxiety: Yes, your anxiety is back, and it seems intent on cutting you off at the knees and driving your face into the dirt this time. One moment you think you are fine and the next your heart rate rapidly increases, your mind races, your stomach clenches and you feel sick. You are robbed of your usual sharp thinking, your quick wit and left shaken and scared.

A panic attack: Thought you had left these back in your early 20s? Unfortunately not. They are back for a one night sold out show! The venue? Your body and mind. You are in the middle of a meeting with your team and you suddenly can't breathe, you can't speak properly and you feel the need to curl up into a ball and disappear for a bit. You leap up from the desk, mumble something about needing a minute, run outside and crouch down on the floor, rubbing your legs, hyperventilating and murmuring "You're ok" over and over to yourself. It only lasts for two minutes.

Sleepless nights: You are the type of person who can only function when you have slept well and the bad news is you are barely going to get any sleep over the next few weeks. The constant narration from your mind, combined with the physical effects of the anxiety, are keeping you wide awake.

The inner critic: You have always held yourself to impossibly high standards and your inner critic is a vicious banshee who, once let out, will tear around your heart and mind, screaming obscenities and causing harm. This period in your life releases her in all her glory.

Self-doubt: You put up a brave face and confident can-do-anything attitude to the world, but some days the quicksand of your own self-doubt tries to suck you under and suffocate you.

And just in case you will try to bury your head in the sand, ride out the wave and return to your old habits, the universe sends you one last kick up the bum. Just to make sure you get the message.

Your most regular client in the virtual assistance agency has outgrown the style of service you are offering. She doesn't realise it yet and as a result is getting more and more frustrated and making incessant demands on the team. The team is under pressure, walking on eggshells and making silly mistakes as a result. To put a cherry on top, it turns out your happiness coordinator isn't actually that happy and informs you she is 'in the middle of a breakdown' and is giving two weeks' notice to quit. You had planned to take a week off to move into your new home and you were really looking forward to having the space to be with your family during the change.

Sitting there at 10pm on a Wednesday night, you decide to stop being the victim and step up. Time to straighten your crown and put this runaway train firmly back on the tracks!

As hard a decision as it is, you immediately terminate your happiness coordinator. You are worried about her and want her to take care of herself and you need to take care of your business, your team and your clients. CEO decisions are often hard to make but they need to be made.

You immediately start interviewing for a replacement team member.

You give yourself a good pep talk and ground into what needs to be done. You are always good in a crisis and can take control of resources and people to get the job done.

You have an honest and frank conversation with your mentor and you both realise what occurred and what needed to be done to move forward into a harmonious partnership.

You advise your client that you will be terminating the contract and will no longer be working together.

These decisions were hard for you to make, but you made them, anyway.

The most important thing you did was to DECIDE.

You decided to no longer be available to work with people who demanded a lot and paid little.

You decided to be the person who sits on the throne of her life and commands from a space of aligned intention.

You decided that the level of abundance you were used to accepting was no longer aligned and that you demand to be paid well for your gifts.

You decided to step up and do the big things that you are here to do. Hiding in the shadows was no longer an option.

You decided and recognised that you are an amazing human being who is extraordinarily good at what you do and that people need what you offer, so why not yell it from the rooftops?

You decided that taking risks is worth it every time and recognised that you were butting up against the edge of your comfort zone. You had a choice to lean right in or to shy away and stay put. Like I said before, you don't do things by halves so you jumped all in with no backup plan.

The birthing process to expand to the next level is never easy. It is downright painful and ugly. There is no 'personal growth epidural' but you can assemble a support team and ask for help.

You know you need to support your struggling nervous system. You can't do what you need to do when your fight-or-flight response is constantly being triggered. You see your naturopath and inform her that you need all the support she can give. She arms you to the hilt with herbs and tinctures which do the trick.

You are on the lookout for any negative self-talk that could trip you up and make it your mission to reframe any setbacks instantly.

You surround yourself with inspiring entrepreneurs who have achieved what you are aiming for.

You put strict rules around your social media use and closely monitor what you allow into your mind.

And you take a step. And then another. Then another. You climb that mountain, one step at a time, and enjoy the journey. You know nothing is impossible and the only way to get where you want to go is by putting one foot in front of the other.

You are making progress but still have that annoying syndrome that so many high achievers suffer from: imposter syndrome. Your mentor is recommending you to everyone she knows and you are making sales in your new business model, but you still feel like a fraud. Like you aren't good enough to be operating at this level. Then suddenly it hits you! You put your mentor (and those seven figure entrepreneurs you are targeting) on a pedestal; thinking that they somehow must be better than you or have something you don't. What a lie! What a misconception! What a disservice to self! What a joke!

When you realise this, you start to laugh. Your husband thinks you have finally cracked but you haven't; the delusion has cracked—wide open! And now you see clearly. You clearly see your purpose, your gifts, your light, and your absolute right to be successful and abundant beyond anything you actually thought would come to fruition. You see how unique your expertise is and how needed it is. You see that if you didn't show up and serve, others could not expand to their fullest potential. You see the beauty in collaboration and sisterhood. You finally feel aligned, impactful, and on purpose.

When you choose to live life this way, to make it non-negotiable, then you really come alive. Autumn loves *The Greatest Showman* and the words from *Come Alive* say it all:

> *'Cause you're just a dead man walking*
> *Thinking that's your only option*
> *But you can flip the switch and brighten up your darkest day*
> *Sun is up and the color's blinding*
> *Take the world and redefine it*
> *Leave behind your narrow mind*
> *You'll never be the same*
> *Come alive, come alive*
> *Go and ride your light*
> *Let it burn so bright*

Reaching up
To the sky
And it's open wide
You're electrified
When the world becomes a fantasy
And you're more than you could ever be
'Cause you're dreaming with your eyes wide open

Growth is painful and challenging. Pain is temporary. You've got this. Keep going. There is no mountain you cannot climb. I believe in you.

ABOUT THE AUTHOR

Tarryn Reeves is the CEO and founder of Four Eagles Publishing and The Publishing House Concierge.

She works with high-level coaches to create bestselling books that multiply their business on autopilot. Her specialty is creating an amazing reader experience that converts book sales into clients.

She is an international bestselling author and has a global client base. She resides in Australia with her husband and her daughter. When she isn't creating bestsellers, she is scouring the local book shares to add to her collection.

You can connect with Tarryn at:

> *Website:* www.tarrynreeves.com
> *Facebook:* www.facebook.com/tarryn.reeves
> *Instagram:* www.instagram.com/tarryn.reeves
> *LinkedIn:* www.au.linkedin.com/in/tarrynreeves

ABOUT THE YOUNGER SELF LETTERS

How this project came about

During meditation Adriana asked for guidance on how to create a Wall Street Journal bestseller. She was given a name and typed it into Google — Michelle Kulp. During their first call they instantly hit it off and over the next few weeks realized they could bring their experience together to create a multi-author book that could become a WSJ bestseller. During a casual chat the words, "what would you say to your younger self?" came up and—boom—they knew this was not only the title but the series they would trademark and create a brand around.

It is tempting to write books that show off an author's knowledge, but what readers are craving is to see the person behind the success. What the climb looked like and what lows lead to epic heights.

If you would like to participate in their next book or would like to become a brand ambassador, check out...

www.TheYoungerSelfLetters.com

Made in the USA
Monee, IL
17 June 2021